MW01627198

Dancing with Darwin

Challenge Therapies for Optimal Health

Steven J. Saltzman, M.D.

Cold Water Publishing
Annapolis, Maryland

Praise for Dancing with Darwin

What a great book! You feel like you personally know Dr. Saltzman and wish your doctor was like him. He has discovered the keys to having more energy for life, and he freely shares that wisdom without the need for a prescription. Whether young, old, extremely fit or struggling with a medical condition, this book will help every human being to have a higher quality of life by changing people at the cellular level. I believe Dancing with Darwin will change the world and how we think about health and wellness.

Phil Campbell, M.S., M.A., FACHE-R, ACSC-CPT
Fitness author and performance coach at the Riekes Center for Human Enhancement
Creator of the Sprint 8® Cardio Workout

Integrative medicine is the future. Dr. Steve Saltzman has done a great job by clearing the paradigm. Way to go!

Wim Hof, The Ice Man

Dr. Saltzman masterfully summarizes how we can improve our quality of life by introducing new tools and therapies that force us to adapt and respond to challenges of all kinds—from exercise, to fasting, to temperature extremes, and even appropriate doses of ozone. Dancing with Darwin showcases the power of hormesis. It offers us a road map we can all follow to overcome disease and function at our best using a non-invasive and natural approach.

Adriana Schwartz, M.D.
President, Spanish Association of Medical Professionals in Ozone Therapy
Director, Clínica Fiorela, Madrid.

Dancing with Darwin is a fast, easy read and well organized. I really like the way Dr. Saltzman's brain works and how he brings it all together! This book will be an invaluable tool, bringing it all together for someone brand new to these ideas and concepts.

Dr. Nasha Winters, ND, FABNO
International integrative oncology expert and author of The Metabolic Approach to Cancer

This book provides a proven blueprint to avoid age-associated disease and enhance how our bodies function! Leading with experience, Dr. Saltzman guides readers to take the optimal steps on the road to improved health and vitality.

Karlie Intlekofer, PhD
Neuroscientist and Exercise Physiologist
Global Wellness Researcher
Johnson Health & Wellness

STEVEN J. SALTZMAN, M.D.

For information contact:
www.vitalityhealthchallenge.com

Cover/Layout: www.thegetitfactory.com

ISBN - 978-1-7338227-0-1

This book is dedicated to my grandfather, Harry Jurman, who was forced to drop out of school in the second grade to help provide for his family. He lived the American dream and always valued education for his family. He was able to provide college educations for all five of his grandchildren as well as my medical school education.

Table of Contents

Top Ten Learning Points

1. Why a healthy diet and exercise are no longer enough to overcome disease, ensure longevity, and promote peak performance.

2. The crucial importance of the human body's innate resiliency—and why we should quit taking it for granted.

3. Why certain evolutionary adaptations in our bodies work against us in the presence of modern comforts—and how we can tap into those adaptations to heighten metabolism, build immunity, and increase cardio performance.

4. How cellular oxygen levels determine whether we are vibrant and healthy or whether we fail to thrive and become disease prone.

5. How our circadian rhythms control much more than just our sleep/wake cycle and the surprising implications for how and when you should exercise and eat.

6. A simple and scientifically proven method for weight management that radically transforms your body without counting calories.

7. Why there's some scientific truth to the saying, "What doesn't kill you makes you stronger" and how to harness your body's hard-wired adaptive processes to improve your health.

8. The biological differences between someone who takes a wintertime "Polar Plunge" and someone who benefits from intelligent, controlled cold exposure.

9. The scientifically researched protocols that allow us to consciously influence our own immune and hormonal systems.

10. How strategic combinations of natural therapies can create powerful whole-body synergies—and the health breakthrough you need to journey from Disease to Vitality.

Foreword

I've known Dr. Steven Saltzman as a colleague and friend for over twenty years. I have watched him live and breathe his wellness philosophy. As a physician who is so utterly dedicated to building health instead of treating disease, he has developed a vivid *healing confidence*. For most people, when a healing crisis hits—and it will hit everyone to some degree at some point in life—they simply allow themselves to be directed to the typical "sick care" strategies of drugs and surgery. Dr. Saltzman has a totally different approach, drawing from his well-founded healing confidence.

In the heat of a healing crisis, he knows and trusts that your body, when properly nurtured, can and will find a way to mend and heal. Most people in healing crises don't have that level of confidence. Instead doubt settles in. Doubt in the body's innate capability to do what it knows to do. This is when you must rely on someone who has accumulated the wisdom and experience to guide, teach, and motivate you through the steps required to truly recover. I had to do that for myself. After a major athletic injury, I asked Dr. Saltzman for help.

Dr. Saltzman's definition of recovery is not just the absence, or masking, of pain or symptoms. Drugs and surgery can often do that. Rather, true recovery is the absolute return to optimal function and, more importantly, a return to peak performance. This is what Dr. Saltzman did for me back in 2012.

At the age of 45, I was without question, over-training. I was exercising six to seven days a week, pushing my body to the limit. Just because I felt okay, I was quite proud of my level of performance. Unfortunately, my recovery was very limited. As a chiropractor and as a chiropractic patient, I was receiving regular adjustment. But I found out the hard way that this wasn't enough. While on the tennis court, very early in a match, I took off in a full sprint to retrieve a drop shot. I heard and felt a loud pop in my right groin—and then searing pain. I needed help off the court and to get home. I realized I had severely pulled my hip flexor and adductor muscles and, quite literally, could not lift my leg to walk. This was not a strain, but an actual tear.

Rest, ice, heat, laser, gentle range-of-motion, acupuncture, massage, chiropractic—all had their place and helped to a limited degree. But the deep hip flexors are very slow-healing tissues. I hit a plateau after eight weeks and was stuck for months. Stuck physically. Stuck emotionally. I was a proud physical athlete at a time in my life when I was still getting faster and stronger. As a chiropractor, I took care of many other people, and here I was at a point where I could no longer work. I couldn't even take care of myself. I became frustrated, depressed, and embarrassed.

It was at this point that I reached out to Dr. Saltzman. His analysis of my condition felt spot on. What he said made sense. Due to the poor blood supply to the hip flexors and groin, after injury, those tissues typically heal with tight, tense, and rigid scar fibers that can stay rigid forever. Scar tissues are adhesions. A crisscross network of gunky, gluey, collagen fibers that are inherently weak, rigid, and soon-to-be very sensitive. You've probably heard of someone with an old injury being able to tell if bad weather is coming because of an increase in pain. That's the sensitivity I am talking about, and that is where I was heading.

Dr. Saltzman shared with me that if we could get oxygen into those tissues, it would soften them, and then we could start to mobilize the area. That's exactly what we did. The specific rationale and treatments he used are described in a case story in Chapter 4 of this book. But for now, let it suffice to say that what I experienced was nothing short of transformational. In a matter of weeks, I began to see legitimate glimpses of the athlete I once was. In a matter of months, I was back to training the way that I wanted. I returned to competing on the tennis court at a 4.5 rating. More importantly, I was back to being physically able to care for patients as a chiropractor. My limitation, both physically and mentally, had been lifted. All without surgery or a single drug. Not one. I thank Dr. Saltzman for helping me get my life back.

All that he has shared with me is available to you. He has written a wonderful blueprint of ways to get healthy, so your body can heal and mend from whatever is limiting you. Whether you are facing a disease, seeking longevity, or interested in peak performance, his program and the powerful science behind it works. Along the way, he'll show you why mainstream "sick care" doesn't work. You'll learn about the role of oxygen and whether oxygen therapies are right for you. You'll discover the right way to exercise and why it's so crucial to vary your heart rate. You'll also learn how the autonomic nervous system impacts your healing. Perhaps the most important thing to take away is this: *Don't ever give up*. Don't blame your limitations on time or age and surrender to being less of who you are made to be. This book is your next step toward recovering your health and exceeding your goals. The pages abound with generous life-changing insights. Run with them.

On countless occasions, after working out together or after I've completed a Vitality Health Challenge therapy, I've heard Dr. Saltzman chant: "This is who we are! This is what we do!" The reality is, Dr. Saltzman walks his talk. Everything and anything he recommends to you, he has already tried and researched for himself. He lives the health and wellness lifestyle that he shares with his patients at Vitality Health Challenge and with you in this book. He leads by example, first and foremost. This is why I continue to follow his health and healing recommendations for myself, my loved ones, and anyone else I meet who is seeking a healing breakthrough.

Good luck, and enjoy your journey!

Dr. Jeff Muneses
Founder Muneses Chiropractic Center
Ellicott City, Maryland

Introduction

I was in the middle of a 24-hour shift during my final year of residency when I heard a dreaded anesthesia STAT call to Operating Room (OR) five. Something had gone incredibly wrong at the start of a surgery. Brain surgery. Only they hadn't even gotten to that part yet. Whatever was going on, I knew the patient's life hung in the balance. I raced down the hall and saw the neurosurgeon rush past me headed in the opposite direction, clearly no time to brief me. My mind was racing and my heart pounding. Even though it was not my case, I felt the weight of the life and death scene that was steps away.

When I entered room five, a quick look around immediately told me what was wrong. The sterile surgical instrument trays were open. The room was lined with more than twenty OR staff, all looking equally horrified. The patient lay in the middle of the room, turning blue. The anesthesia drugs had already taken effect. But there was no breathing tube. That meant the anesthesia team hadn't been able to intubate or breathe for him. It was every anesthesiologist's worst nightmare: The patient was in that deep anesthetized paralysis, unable to breathe on his own—with no breathing machine hooked up to him yet.

It was a surgical emergency. We needed to get a tracheostomy tube inserted immediately. Going by the book, either an Ear, Nose, and Throat surgeon (ENT) or a general surgeon was most qualified to do this. But the surgeons weren't here yet—*where were they?*—and this man would be dead in another minute or two.

It took me seconds to grasp the facts of the situation. The team present had done all they could and were now waiting for a surgeon to arrive and perform the emergency tracheostomy. No one else in the room was comfortable attempting that procedure. My choice didn't require deep thought. Making eye contact with the senior-most attending anesthesiologist, I picked up a scalpel. I mouthed the words, "May I begin?"

He didn't say yes. He stared at me, white as a sheet. He didn't say no, either.

I made an incision on the man's neck to begin the surgical airway. The bluest blood I'd ever seen rushed out of the wound. I continued working until the ENT surgeons blew in, took their rightful place, finished the procedure, and inserted the tracheostomy tube. The patient survived.

It wasn't a difficult surgery; I'd participated in far more complex procedures as an intern. But it was a major breach of protocol. I was pretty sure I'd pay for it as soon as the dust settled, and the patient was stable in the ICU. Instead, my Attending Physician took me aside and said, "What saved that man's life was *somebody doing something*." He left it at that. I felt like I'd dodged a bullet.

Still I felt uncomfortable about the whole situation. I knew I'd done the right thing. If I had a chance to live through that moment again, I'd make the same choice. It was bold, but boldness was needed to save that man's life. No, what nagged at me was a strange, new sense of disappointment in the medical system itself. Something was horribly wrong if it took a breach in protocol to save someone's life. Why had everyone else stood motionless on the sidelines? Normally, the incredible teamwork and trouble-shooting I witnessed every day in the operating rooms was seamless.

It was the first of many cracks in my pristine illusion of modern medicine. Until then, I was convinced physicians could handle almost anything that came our way. We were wonder workers. Given my training up to that point, I had no reason to think otherwise.

No Medical Pedigree, Just Hard Work and Dedication

I didn't come from a family of doctors. I had no parent or aunt or uncle telling me inspiring stories of their own bold decisions in surgery or the emergency room. But for some reason, I was always drawn to science and scientific knowledge. I always wanted to become a doctor. Since there were no relatives in my family who could answer my questions, I sought out work experience early on. During my freshman year in college in the mid 1980s, I visited several hospitals asking about summer job opportunities. No one seemed interested in hiring a part-time undergrad for anything. Finally, a small hospital in Greenwich, Connecticut responded kindly. They had an anesthesia aid who had family overseas. She left for two months every summer to visit them. If I wanted, I could fill in for her role.

That short-term job involved ordering and stocking anesthesia supplies in the operating rooms. It was simple work, but I was elated to see an OR for the first time and meet anesthesiologists and surgeons. I came back the following summer, a little less nervous, and much more familiar with my tasks.

The surgical staff had more confidence in me too. Sometimes when I was stocking supplies, I'd hear my name over the intercom, requesting that I transfer the new pulse oximeter machine from one OR to another. The pulse oximeter—that tiny device clipped to the patient's finger to measure pulse and oxygen levels—is now completely standard and built into every anesthesia monitor. But in the eighties it was a medical tech breakthrough. The OR suite had purchased only one, and I had unofficially become the staff person on call to cart the machine wherever it was needed. This task let me see the inner workings of the OR as surgical teams prepped for a procedure. It was exciting.

Little did I know, that formative experience drew me toward anesthesiology as a practice, and that choice would lay the groundwork for my later interest in innovative oxygen therapies. I found the anesthesia docs intriguing. No one else in the room had such a big picture understanding of the patient—not micro-focused on the incision site, but rather responsive to all of the patient's body functions throughout the surgery. Interestingly, they seemed like healthy people too. They had balanced lifestyles and interesting hobbies. It was almost like their big-picture sense of patient health affected how they lived their own lives outside the hospital. That summer job gave me my first workplace interactions with medical doctors. It left quite an impression.

I worked exceedingly hard to get into medical school. I had no one to give me tips on the application process. No family with *alma mater* ties. But I got in and was fascinated by the first two years of sheer book knowledge. I remember thinking, "In college, you can study for a test and have a sense that you'd learned everything. In medicine, you can learn and learn and *never* know it all!" It was a new feeling. That feeling increased exponentially when I began my internship at Harford Hospital and then completed a three-year residency at the world-renowned Johns Hopkins Hospital in Baltimore.

My medical training introduced me to the world of 28-hour shifts and constant learning in the face of massive human trauma. You might glance at your watch and wonder if it was two a.m. or two p.m.—during a shift like that you were never sure. The hours were unbelievable, but the work was entirely energizing. I felt like we really knew what we were doing. How could this much knowledge not translate into powerfully impacting people's lives?

I saw it happen weekly, if not daily. I remember one completely broken body brought in, a construction worker who'd survived a major fall. He had multiple bone fractures and soft tissue injuries throughout his body. His airway was unstable too; he was choking when he came in. Our response could've been chaos. But it wasn't. The injured man needed trauma surgeons, anesthesiologists, X-ray technicians, nurses, and blood bank personnel. Everyone was immediately present and knew their tasks. That was the beauty of trauma surgery and trauma ICU. I was struck by how well our teams ran, how smoothly severe crises were managed. Every specialist was in the room at the same time, all of the patient's body systems were cared for, all staff worked in concert to save a person's life. We always began with the trauma ABCs—secure the airway, establish breathing, maintain circulation. Every medical miracle began with those basics. And that's precisely what we did for that construction worker. He survived.

Trauma teams worked these miracles on a regular basis. I was proud of what we could do. But I hadn't even completed my first full year of residency when another crack appeared in my shining view of modern medicine.

Cracks in the System Come Closer to Home

One day, as a first-year Resident, I was called to the administrative offices to take an emergency phone call from a relative. It was my mother. She'd just been diagnosed with breast cancer. For the next several months, I balanced my 80-hour work weeks with calls and visits home to support her through surgery, reconstruction, and chemotherapy. She was only 55. Hard questions began to form in my mind. *Why did they have to weaken her to make her better? Were these invasive procedures and toxic drugs really the only answer?*

A childhood friend got cancer too. Metastatic melanoma. We were still in our twenties when he passed away. *How could the medical world completely fail him?*

Still, after my residency, I forged onward in my medical career and kept to a fairly conventional and successful course. I held multiple academic and teaching posts, and I advanced in both anesthesia practice and administrative roles. All the while, loved ones continued to struggle with increasingly complex health challenges. My stepfather died of heart failure, complicated from medication side effects. Friends developed multiple food allergies and chronic fatigue. As I got older, many of my peers took it for granted that they struggled with major weight gain, metabolic problems, and chronic pain. They all had general practitioners and growing lists of specialists. No one was able to actually help them get back to vibrant health.

My work in trauma and intensive care had accustomed me to viewing "full recovery" as the standard. It was our mission to address the initial emergency, stabilize, heal, and *restore*. You always hoped your patients left the hospital on their own feet, doing well. Recovered. We helped people get through and *get better*.

With cancer and chronic diseases, it seemed medicine had a totally different tack. As far as I could tell, it went like this: Throw pharmaceutical drugs and invasive procedures at the patient until something successfully covered up the primary symptoms. This was radically different from what I'd witnessed in trauma care. The reality was, trauma care was the only thing we could do well. With common chronic conditions—heart disease, diabetes, autoimmune disease, cancer, cognitive challenges, and the complications of aging—our results were abysmal. I was no longer frustrated. I was devastated. I faced the truth. Far too often, my beloved medical system took sick people and made them worse.

I finally recognized that most doctors failed to make the distinction between *surviving* and *thriving*. Most of the people I knew who had chronic diseases were purely surviving. Most had forgotten what it meant to thrive—to wake in the morning feeling well rested, to have energy, move freely, and heal injuries naturally. When treating these patients, most doctors failed to appreciate the concept of real health and how to fully restore it.

Having my illusions shattered was demoralizing. I wanted to be bold again. But there was no scalpel or quick fix for this situation.

I felt like I needed to complete a whole new residency in a different form of medicine. Only nothing like that existed. In the late 1990s and early 2000s, the only significant "alternative health" research I had access to were studies focused on nutrition. I pored over those. Medical school hadn't taught me about nutrition, so it was captivating to learn about the pioneering work of Dr. Weston A. Price. As early as the 1930s, Price had found that when healthy rural populations shifted from ancestral diets to high-starch and highly processed "western" foods, both their dental and metabolic health plummeted.[1] Reading Price's findings whetted my appetite to learn even more. I spent my off hours perusing medical journals and internet archives, and I used rare vacation time to explore the medical practices in other countries.

I wondered how I could apply what I was learning. It would take bravery to recommend such things in a clinical setting—an attitude that wasn't exactly encouraged in the conventional medical world. Medicine is well-regulated, and MDs are given narrow guidelines to perform within. Licensing boards immediately rein doctors in if they deviate from the norm. Anything "complementary" or "alternative" is often considered taboo or even dangerous. I realize regulation is necessary. But over the decades, layers upon layers of regulation have resulted in a medical system that is stagnant and unable to grow. Trying anything new can make you a target for investigations. Threatening the status quo can be incredibly costly.

Still, I hit a point where I couldn't remain silent. I remembered that case from my residency, the patient in the OR who was unable to breathe and turning blue while everyone looked on helplessly. Since that day, too many of my loved ones were failed by our medical system in scenarios that felt strangely similar. Initially I shared tips with family and friends only. Soon I branched out.

Venturing Into Integrative Practice

In addition to my anesthesia work, I branched out to serve as a medical director for a clinical psychology practice. One of the patients in that clinic was a 18-year-old girl who was developing renal failure from an autoimmune condition. She was almost forced to drop out of college because of her condition. Her conventional physicians had no further treatment options. I met with her and her family and encouraged a significant change in diet based on what I'd learned about foods that aggravated autoimmunity. I only hoped to mitigate some of her symptoms, but her autoimmune condition actually reversed. She experienced remission of her illness through dietary changes alone! That early success fueled my desire to learn more.

As I dug deeper into scientific literature and learned about more natural and non-invasive approaches to health, I simultaneously discovered a troubling trend in the medical community. Physicians often heard about leading edge discoveries in their fields and, even if the science was solid, they disregarded the findings. If a study's conclusion challenged their current medication protocols, they ignored the study. This tendency continues today. Even worse, there is significant manipulation of research data, which often leaves the American public confused and suspicious of the latest results.

One of the most powerful examples can be found in the 29 billion dollar statin drug industry.[2] Countless studies claim statin efficacy for lowering cholesterol, despite a concerning side effect profile. Yet other published research claim that the cholesterol-lowering benefit is deceptive, because the industry does not report the one-percent "absolute risk reduction" of these drugs. One-percent absolute risk reduction means you have to give statins to 100 patients before you'll see one less heart attack. Statins might lower cholesterol, but that "benefit" doesn't result in significantly fewer deaths from heart disease.[3,4]

Sadly, accurate medical knowledge was, and continues to be, hard to acquire. Why would we have a medical system that was not in our best interests? I had much more work to do.

During those years of research and learning, I remained in anesthesiology practice and served as director of a hospital-based anesthesiology department. My work in the world of critical care stood in stark contrast with what I continued to learn about general medicine and chronic illnesses. I still admired everything that was good and effective in trauma care: *The complete real-time teamwork between specialists and the rapid acceptance of new techniques that could improve survival rates.* Unfortunately, those gold standards were absent for patients journeying through the medical system with a chronic illness. If you weren't in a critical care unit, your care was mediocre at best. In the world of chronic disease, both doctors and researchers seemed siloed to the point of total disconnect. There was limited teamwork and communication between specialists. Treatment-changing research was ignored or regarded as suspect. The more I learned, the more frustrated I became.

If I'd had a personal motto in that time period it would have been: *When it comes to health, what you don't know, can hurt you!* I wanted everyone I knew to understand that heartfelt concern. But far too often, people didn't want to listen. On a whole, conventional MD colleagues didn't want to hear about my after-hours gleanings.

By 2008, I'd decided I needed to forge forward on my path regardless of the opinions of others. My initial curiosity about nutrition and supplements expanded to include detoxification therapies, natural hormone restoration, and much more. I learned about transformative new therapies supported by solid published research. I obtained board certifications in anti-aging, regenerative, and oxidative medicine. My vision for my own clinic, what would become the Vitality Health Challenge Clinic in Maryland, was beginning to take shape. The time for bold action was approaching.

state. What if there was an integrative medical clinic with primary practitioner oversight that also featured a teaching kitchen, a gym for both rehab and performance goals, chiropractic care and massage, and also oxygen, ozone, and IV therapies?

The more I studied, the more I realized that no matter how fit or how unhealthy, every human could experience powerful benefits from addressing these core issues. As friends and family accepted and implemented my tips, I saw that the principles that helped athletes reach their next personal best were the same core principles that helped someone in very poor health. The individual therapies would differ dramatically, but the principles did not. We all needed to address nutrition, toxin exposure, hormone balance, and stress management. From that foundation, everyone I worked with also benefited from analyzing their health through seven key lenses that I'll outline in Chapter 7.

Finally, with those basics addressed, I found that certain lesser-known therapies became tipping point treatments for many of my early clients. These whole-body therapies drastically heightened oxygenation in the body and measurably altered metabolism and immune function, among other impressive effects. These therapies reintroduced a sense of positive physical challenge into the client's life. They are the unique therapies that I will describe in depth throughout this book.

I've found that the secret is in the synergy generated by implementing multiple natural treatments and therapies at once. In essence, effective integrative treatment first addresses **modern day health threats**, and then re-introduces **healthier physical rhythms** and **positive physical challenges**. Whole-body treatment helps the body return to and restore its most basic and neglected evolutionary needs. Effective treatment doesn't treat disease. It restores health. That is both bold and true.

Building Health: Empowering the Awakening World of Functional Medicine

After over 20 years of research and pursing additional training and certifications, I am starting to see fruit from that work. My Vitality Health Challenge Clinic is here, and I am witnessing an awakening among medical doctors today. A new world of functional medicine has begun to take root and grow. This is medical care that looks for root causes, creates fully personalized treatment plans, and draws from the best of both conventional and complementary modalities. I prefer to use multiple, synergistic, natural therapies to reverse disease, promote longevity, and enhance athletic recovery. My personal goal is always *health restoration*, not symptom management. I hope that this book extends the reach of my Vitality Health Challenge Clinic and similar clinics worldwide. These pages serve up the knowledge, insight, and understanding that I gained from years of effort, research, travel, and personal struggle.

No physician or medical program will cure everyone. But I know this book contains game-changing therapies and knowledge that can provide crucial missing links in your own health program. Always keep in mind that your journey toward health will require a whole-body multiple-therapy approach. Be ready to shed the "magic bullet" mindset—it walks hand-in-hand with the single-pill pharmaceutical mindset. Wherever you're at, whether you struggle daily with a serious disease or you're an endurance athlete who feels plateaued, getting to your next level will involve multiple integrative modalities. You are where you're at right now because of multiple whole-body challenges. You will need wise diagnostics and a personalized holistic plan to move forward.

Remember how, as I completed my residency, I looked at my sick loved ones and faced the fact that conventional medicine was failing them? At that time, I felt like I needed to start another residency, one that taught me how to *restore health* for those with chronic illnesses.

We're well into the 21st century, and no physician has yet completed a formal Disease Reversal Residency. But I do hope for a future where that is commonplace! I hope this book is yet another step in a much healthier direction.

Chapter 1

Time for a Different Approach

It takes work, but you have the power and resiliency to change your health

When Chris came to me, he was in very poor health, coping with hypertension, obesity, and sleep apnea. He used to be active but had no idea how he could recover that quality of life. Similarly, Mary came to me frustrated with both weight gain and diabetes, as well as new arthritis pain that had forced her to cut back on the athletic activities she used to enjoy. Another client, a chiropractor, came to me after a major sports injury. He was in great shape before, but was limping badly at that point and was worried that conventional methods might not result in full restorative healing.

Throughout these pages, you'll get to meet these individuals and others and learn how their treatment progressed. I have worked with such diverse clients with wide ranging health challenges. At their first meetings with me, I told each one the same thing:

> *"You have hope. You have hope because your body is inherently resilient."*

Each of us is a scientific experiment in the works. We are our own laboratories. Each day our 40 trillion cells provide us an opportunity for study. We can try something new, change something, challenge ourselves, and observe the results. We get to do this because we are living organisms hard-wired to adapt to our surroundings. We are resilient. Sometimes we change for the better, sometimes not. But all of us have much more ability to tap into our resiliency than we may realize.

Our resiliency is part of the fabric of who we are. We can harness its power and use it to our advantage by making active positive choices about our health. Or we can take our resiliency for granted, forcing our bodies to tolerate our poor habits year after year. Our bodies will indeed respond to our chronic insults, our poor care, doing their best to maintain countless crucial functions. We can exist with disease states for decades and cope with limitations of all kinds. Our bodies find ways to survive, to deal, to get by. Many of us are walking wounded in some way.

These coping abilities stem from our resiliency. It is our greatest asset. It keeps us going. But in modern medicine we make a crucial mistake. We fail to appreciate this impressive gift. In fact, we attack it. What if we could target the human body's resiliency in a positive and productive way? What would that look like? How would we do it? Addressing those questions is my passion. No matter what your body has experienced in past years or decades, good treatment choices today can begin to yield real gains in a relatively short time. There is hope because of how resilient your body is!

I promise, this is not another book on a disease-reversing diet or a miracle supplement protocol. There are plenty of resources already that can help you with those foundational whole health principles. But what do you do when you've tried to eat gluten free and ketogenic, and you've already got over a dozen supplement bottles in your medicine cabinet… and you still feel stuck? If conventional medicine has failed you, if alternative health has left you frustrated too, or if your athletic performance has plateaued, this book is for you.

Working with everyone from diabetics to cancer patients to elite athletes with championship goals, I've traveled and researched globally to find over-looked breakthrough therapies that help everyone. I've discovered surprising common threads between people with serious disease states and those who simply want to reach a new personal best. These pages are the result of decades of reviewing research and implementing the most powerful functional medicine therapies. More importantly, it's about combining multiple therapies appropriately for each health goal. You'll get to explore the extensive, powerful, and evolutionary science supporting this approach, and you'll learn how real patients have benefited.

You may have heard of HBOT, ozone therapy, cryotherapy, and interval training. You've certainly heard of fasting. But it's unlikely you've heard of the science behind each of these therapies, their study-supported appropriate uses, and how to pair them correctly to spark massive health transformation. **It's time to get educated.**

Ground Zero: Current Challenges in Health Care

It's where we start, but thankfully it isn't the end of the story!

Today's approach to "health care" is way off base. Instead of caring for health, we manage sickness. That mentality shows up in natural health practices almost as often as in conventional medicine. Sometimes natural medicine simply replaces pharmaceutical drugs with supplements. Sometimes alternative clinics get just as stuck in micro-specialization and can no longer see the whole person.

I believe there are four major factors that have fostered this perfect storm of "disease care":

1. We treat symptoms
2. We over-specialize
3. The drug industry limits our knowledge base
4. Research findings are poorly communicated

Symptom Patching: Pharmaceutical-based medicine inherently treats symptoms, but fails to address the underlying root cause of disease. Typically, patients progress in their diseases as their lists of pharmaceutical medications grow. We prescribe a drug for hypertension, surgically excise a tumor, or administer an antibiotic for an infection. But we fail to ask the more important questions: Why is the patient's blood pressure elevated in the first place? What lifestyle, nutritional, or environmental factors made it possible for the cancer to proliferate? What conditions made the patient vulnerable to developing a serious bacterial infection?

These questions matter. Yet our current insurance-driven system only permits brief office visits and by-the-book drug-based care. It doesn't allow the time investment that's required to truly understand each patient. We're all paying the price for the resulting "Band-Aid" illness care. We may be living *longer* now, but many of us are not living *better* in our later years. It may be hard to believe but **iatrogenic illness**, death caused by adverse reactions to medications and complications from invasive procedures, represents the third leading cause of death in the United States.[1] And there is good reason to believe that this category is under-reported.

Micro-Specialization: The vast majority of our physicians focus on a single organ system, but the majority of diseases affect multiple, if not all, body systems.[2] Diseases do not recognize "organ boundaries" in the body. Meanwhile, the degree of interaction between specialists is often poor at best. Most physicians also fail to focus on overall wellness or peak performance. **But disease reversal, longevity, and peak performance all exist on a continuum, and all health goals require a whole-body, whole-person approach.**

Under-Educated and Pharma-Educated MDs: The majority of physicians today actually practice 1980s medicine since most medical school curriculums are more than 30 years old and have changed very little.[3,4] After school, continued education for MDs often consists of pharmaceutical-company sponsored events. Knowledge about new health "breakthroughs" often comes in the form of medical journal advertisements, also backed by pharmaceutical companies. That means knowledge about non-drug breakthroughs, never gets into the hands of MDs. There's a massive gap between leading-edge metabolic and immune research breakthroughs and the practicing MD community.

Poor Communication within the Research Community: Research groups can be overly proprietary about their findings or simply siloed by highly specialized projects. Furthermore, research groups and individual researchers frequently don't talk to each other. Huge numbers of disconnected research projects, working on similar questions, often occur simultaneously. Researchers in one specialty commonly miss significant findings or developments in another specialty that could shed light on their own work.[5]

Where are the Medical Breakthroughs?

Despite technological advancements, there's little progress in disease care.

I am always amazed at the significant innovations in so many other fields—engineering, computer science, and the automobile industry—and how modern medicine has failed to keep pace with their advancements. Why do we have better skyscrapers, ever more capable smart phones, and the most technically advanced automobiles, but continue to suffer from the same dreaded disease states that have plagued us for decades? Consider these hard truths:

- The number of yearly deaths from cancer in the United States has almost tripled from 63 per 100,000 people[6] to 187 per 100,000 people[7] in the past century.
- According to American Cancer Society data, childhood cancers have been increasing steadily by 0.6 percent since 1975, a fact that cannot be explained by improvement in diagnostics.[8]
- The "War on Cancer" was started in 1971 with the founding of The National Cancer Institute. NCI's budget has increased over thirty-fold, from 150 million to now over 4.6 billion.[9] Yet we're nowhere closer to a cure.
- Diabetes incidence in the US has increased 400 percent in only two decades.[10]
- One in every three American adults is diagnosed with high blood pressure[11] and about 15 million have coronary heart disease.[12] Another 93 million are considered clinically obese.[13]
- 1 in every 5 American adults struggles with chronic pain,[14] and, on average, about 115 Americans die each day from opioid overdose.[15]
- Death from Alzheimer's disease increased by 50 percent from 1999 to 2014[16], and the disease now affects 5.7 million Americans.[17]
- The incidence of autism was 1 in 10,000 in the 1970s[18]. In 2010, 1 in every 110 children was diagnosed with autism spectrum disorders; now it is 1 in 59.[19] The increase in the past decade cannot be attributed solely to improved diagnostics and awareness.

Our modern health care system in the U.S. is the most costly in the world.[20] Yet its quality is ranked 37th overall by The World Health Organization.[21] While we fall behind the rest of the world in terms of efficacious care for common conditions, we also have new "mysterious" diseases showing up. Conventional medicine has virtually no solutions for conditions like fibromyalgia, chronic fatigue, and multiple chemical and food sensitivities.

That's the state of U.S. health care right now. Thankfully there are options. There is a path away from "disease care" and toward restored health. But it's going to take serious effort from all of us, both physicians and patients, to solve these problems.

Time to Change Our Medical Thought Process… Again

Imagine a high-speed, out-of-control, freight train about to careen off the tracks. It took tremendous energy to get that train moving initially, but because of its weight, it possesses tremendous inertia. Once the train has momentum, it picks up significant speed and becomes challenging to stop. So much must be done to avoid an impending disaster! Something similar happens when the body is out of balance for years, can no longer compensate, and finally has major symptoms of disease. So much uphill work must be done to reverse that momentum, to extinguish destructive fires in the body, rebuild damaged tissues, and re-create a healthy state. Effective change is hard work.

The first major task in our paradigm-shift involves shedding the "single-symptom-single-pill" mindset. This outdated perception—that we can take a pill to fix a medical problem—dates back to modern medicine's inception. Back then, we did not appreciate basic germ theory. Humankind suffered for millennia from countless infections including malaria, measles, leprosy, tuberculosis, and polio. With advancements in microscope technology and the first widely available antibiotics in the early to mid 1900s, our quality of life and longevity improved dramatically. We finally had the skill sets to investigate and understand the previously unseen world of disease-causing organisms. Modern medicine, the pharmaceutical industry, sanitation standards, and sterile technique, were born from this new understanding of germ theory. At that time, improved sanitation or one round of antibiotic medication really could be the difference between life and death. Even so, it took time for all practitioners, clinics, and patients to embrace the new understanding of communicable diseases.

It was a major shift that did usher in many good changes in health care. **But, along the way, we made the mistake of thinking that this one-pill mentality would continue to ensure our health indefinitely**. The medical establishment continues to believe that it can treat almost all diseases with pills. Yet today we face a completely different set of medical problems that respond poorly to drug-based protocols. Pharmaceuticals and invasive procedures are not fully effective for cancer, heart disease, diabetes, obesity, autoimmune conditions, asthma, ADHD, depression, cognitive decline, anxiety, allergies, infertility, chronic pain, and aging.[22] We also need to recognize that invasive medical procedures rarely correct the underlying imbalances in the body, and they certainly don't help with actual rebuilding of healthy tissue.

We need a different approach, a true paradigm shift, as dramatic as the shift at the time of Louis Pasteur and his contributions to germ theory. Let's first look at the well-researched (though not so well-known) root causes of today's metabolic, immune, and neurological diseases. Once we grasp the true causes, we can take the first effective steps toward reversing the processes that made each disease possible.

Resiliency: The Body's Double-Edged Sword

Our resiliency gives us hope that we can improve our current level of health and quality of life. Ironically, human resiliency is also a major factor in why the medical industry is so slow to change. To put it bluntly, the human body puts up with a lot of bad medicine. Our bodies tolerate countless harmful inputs before manifesting obvious symptoms.

It can take years for researchers and physicians to discover that a certain protocol was actually harmful all along.[23] That stands in sharp contrast with the prompt consequences experienced in any other field of study. Consider a poorly engineered building, faulty circuitry in a new smart phone, or a failed airbag system, all of which can have dramatic and disastrous immediate consequences.

It's time to quit taking our resiliency for granted. Why not harness that resiliency instead? Why not channel it into the safe, natural, functional medicine therapies that can restore health?

What Really Causes Today's Major Health Problems?

Discover the common threads between cardio-metabolic diseases, immune disorders, and neurological challenges

How does disease happen? This is an important question. If we can better understand what is occurring in the body, from the cellular level outward, we can take steps to prevent and potentially reverse disease progression. Too often, both patients and practitioners focus only on the outward symptoms and try to fix those very obvious problems. But if we don't know what's going on at a cellular level, we never get to the root cause. Life becomes a losing battle of patching new symptoms.

Take a close look at my Disease Progression Model. It begins with a seesaw balancing act between health and four common, unavoidable modern day stressors: **Nutrient deficiency, toxicity, hormonal imbalance, and psychological stress**. These are challenges we all battle in today's world, and they set the stage for disease. In addition to these stressors, **low cellular oxygen levels** also play a fundamental role in setting us up for disease.[24] Oxygen is crucial. Our cells require it to produce energy. If that process is impaired, we become disease prone. I've seen these foundational issues set the stage for disease or poor athletic performance in most of my clients.

VHC Disease Progression Chart

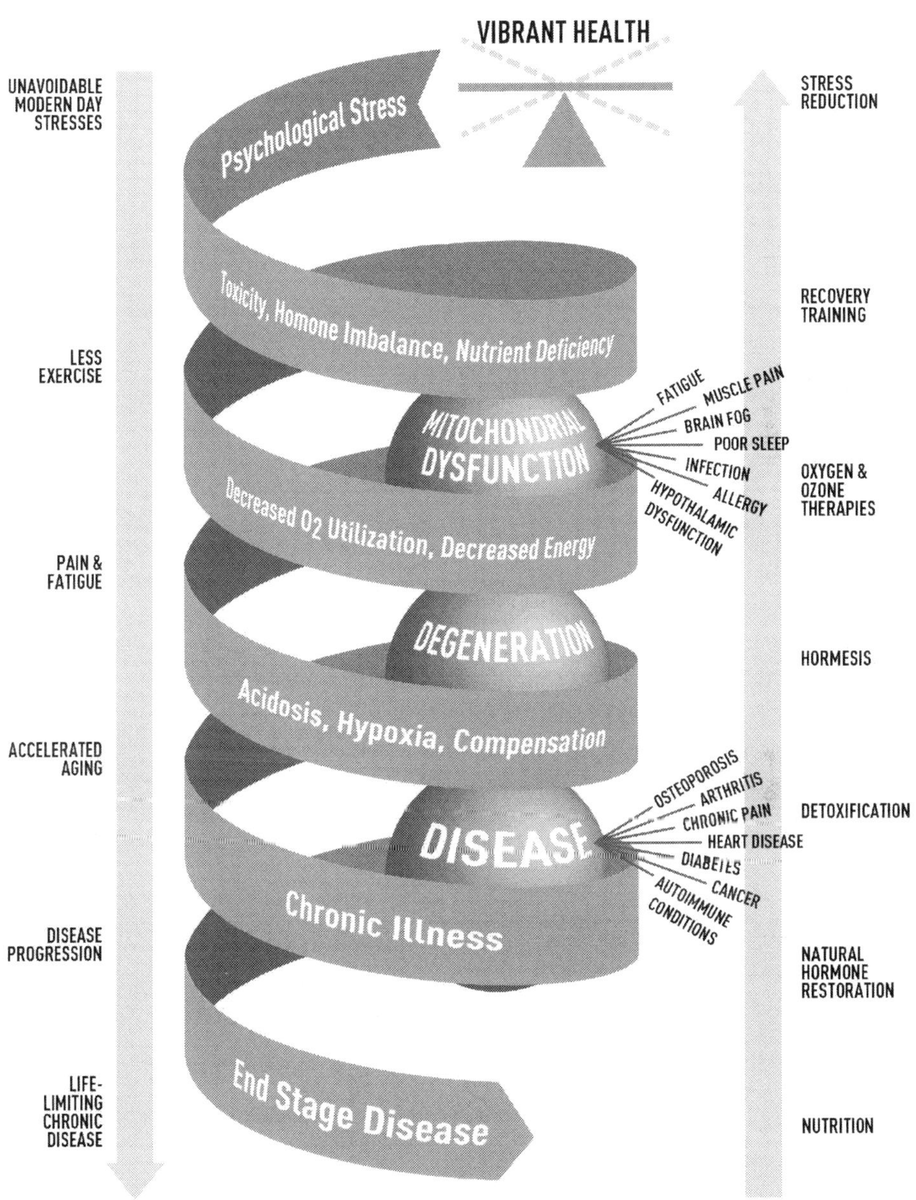

The Disease Progression Model is illustrated as a downward spiral. Those common stressors at the top can lead to a shift that makes us disease susceptible. This occurs when we begin to use oxygen less efficiently.[25] This may seem like a minor issue but it has far reaching implications on cellular health. When cells don't get enough oxygen, use oxygen less efficiently, or experience excess oxidative stress, they produce less energy.[26] Less cellular energy means that the cell is now vulnerable and threatened. Its basic functions can be impaired. These important functions include protein synthesis, cell repair, elimination, detoxification, antibody production, and hormone production. Just like any engine that begins to fail, we become prone to disease if our cellular engines falter.

Decreased oxygen utilization is measurable and detectable. In fact, how we use oxygen is perhaps our most important health determinant. Oxygen utilization testing is one of my primary screening and assessment tests for many of my clients. It can be studied non-invasively by analyzing how much carbon dioxide (CO_2) is produced relative to how much oxygen is consumed as a client progresses from rest to moderate and, if appropriate, more intense exercise. This ratio is referred to as the person's *respiratory quotient* (RQ). The RQ test involves use of a breathing gas analyzer, a computer program, and a stationary exercise device. Through this test, we can detect shifts in how our cells interact with oxygen before we even have symptoms of disease.

Oxygen's role in cellular energy production is focused in the *mitochondria*. These tiny organelles are often referred to as the cell's energy factories. Mitochondria use oxygen in the reaction that produces ATP—the molecule that all cells use as fuel to get their work done. As mitochondria become impaired from compromised oxygen levels, we can develop many seemingly unrelated symptoms. As shown in the Disease Progression Model, *mitochondrial dysfunction* predisposes us to a host of different medical conditions.[27] Even though the following symptom groups appear radically different, they all stem from a reduction in how the body uses oxygen at a cellular level. Examples include:

- **Hypothalamic dysfunction** leading to worsening hormonal imbalance, altered sleep, and brain fog[28]
- **Oxidative stress** causing diverse organ dysfunctions including the general symptoms of aging, cardiovascular problems, cataracts, and neurodegenerative diseases[29]
- **Imbalanced immune function** resulting in allergies and chemical sensitivities, autoimmune disorders, rheumatoid arthritis, frequent or un-resolved infections, and cancer [30]
- **General cellular exhaustion** manifesting as frequent muscle pain and fatigue[31]

It may seem hard to make the connection, but all of our degenerative diseases (including cancer, heart disease, diabetes, inflammatory diseases, autoimmune conditions, and chronic infections) share similar underlying mechanisms. You can see this relationship a little more clearly in the illustration of the Disease Progression Model. That downward spiral of disease is characterized by several factors, which we will explore in much more detail in coming chapters, but for now the Big Three are:

- Hypoxia – Compromised oxygen levels
- Fermentation – Abnormal cellular energy production
- Acidosis – An acidic state in the body

When this trio kicks in, the body attempts to compensate and salvage crucial body functions at a cost to other tissues. That means it's stealing nutrients from bones or muscle and other soft tissue just to maintain a basic survival state. That nutrient stealing is at the heart of all degenerative diseases—an organ, muscle group, bone structure, or connective tissue is literally being broken down (degenerated) for emergency use elsewhere in the body.[32]

For most degenerative states, hypoxia (compromised oxygen) is the lynchpin.[33] It's fairly easy to grasp that heart attacks and strokes stem from a lack of oxygen—either to the heart or to the brain. But so do all the major degenerative diseases. As an example, let's explore cancer a little more to discover what out-of-control cell growth has in common with a heart attack.

The scientific community has actually known the cause of cancer for decades. Dr. Otto Warburg, winner of the Nobel Prize in 1931, demonstrated that cancer is a direct result of oxygen deficiency and an acid state in cells. He also proved that a 35 percent reduction in cellular oxygen levels caused **any** cell to either die or become cancerous.[34]

It all goes back to cellular energy production. Essentially, we have two mechanisms to produce energy:

- **Respiration**: In a healthy body, this is the preferred method. In an optimal situation, our cells use oxygen to generate adequate levels of ATP (cell energy). This is the heart of *respiration*—not just breathing, but using oxygen to make energy.
- **Fermentation**: This less efficient method is triggered when our cells face insufficient oxygen levels. Instead of relying on oxygen, cells begin to *ferment* sugars to make energy. It works, but it creates a lot of unwanted byproducts that have to be detoxified out of the body.

If nature did not offer fermentation as a back-up plan, all of our cells would die the moment cellular oxygen levels fell. So it's good we have fermentation as an option. But it's not an ideal energy production method over the long-term.

If we continue to experience low cellular oxygen levels, a micro form of natural selection occurs: The cells that are good at fermentation remain alive, while healthier normal cells (which need higher oxygen levels) begin to die off.[35] Unfortunately, the cells that are fermentation experts are using a primitive survival tool. These cells can survive, but they're not thriving. And their survival comes at a grave cost. These cells have highly limited functions. Essentially they can only manage to survive and reproduce. They no longer have the ability to differentiate and specialize and contribute to the intelligent blueprint the body once had.

The stage for cancer is set. Healthy cells that cannot survive in a low oxygen environment die off. An unhealthy subset of cells persist using a primitive survival mechanism. These primitive cells are limited in all functions except cell division. The body's plan for law and order is gone. Worse, as these primitive cells divide and spread, other body functions are threatened. Cancer is not an invader from the outside world. It stems from a lack of cellular oxygen and a reversion of cells to a non-intelligent survival mechanism.[36]

Oxygen is that important.

Again, back to the Disease Progression Model, all of the degenerative diseases that we face today represent states of hypoxia, fermentation, acidosis, and resulting degeneration. Those states are fueled by those unavoidable modern day stressors: Poor nutrition, toxicity, hormonal imbalance, and psychological stress.[37] The body's default attempts to compensate, further exacerbate the downward disease spiral. Fermentation increases, tissues become even more acidic, and more oxygen is driven out of the cells—which only encourages *more fermentation.* It's a self-perpetuating cycle at that point! The downward spiral progresses. Until we intervene wisely.

Yes, the downward spiral can be hard to break, especially if we don't address the underlying causes. But just as degenerating factors encourage a downward spiral, **we can reverse engineer an upward path back to health.** We can introduce rejuvenating therapies that reverse the progression and begin to build real health along an upward spiral. There is hope. That downward Disease Progression Model can just as easily be viewed as an upward Disease-to-Vitality Continuum. We all can choose to move in the right direction. It takes dedicated effort, but the results are truly worth it.

The clients who come to me all fall into one of three goal categories as they travel on their continuum. Many come to me with **Disease Reversal** goals, some with **Longevity and Anti-Aging** goals, and others with refined **Athletic Performance** goals (see the Health Goals Triad illustrations at the end of Chapters 2 through 6). This may seem like a diverse and unrelated client base, but they're all confronting the same core modern realities. Many of the strategies that reverse a disease will also ensure longevity and promote peak performance. The specific therapies will differ dramatically from client to client, but the underlying principles remain the same.

The initial lifestyle choices that I require of my clients will look pretty familiar to you. There are literally thousands of books and resources available today that cover the following foundational needs in any health transformation protocol:

- Restore an **ancestral-style diet** (more veggies, healthy fats, raw and cultured probiotic foods, grass-fed animal protein)
- Promote whole-body **detoxification**
- Support natural **hormone balance**

While these three practices are foundational for all my clients, they're not my focus here. Instead, I'm filling in the complete knowledge gap. These pages will focus on novel therapies that enhance **oxygen delivery** throughout the body and **"hormetic therapies"** that enhance resiliency, strengthen the body, and make it more capable to respond to any new stressor. When a client is doing everything else right, these novel therapies are the ones that can break stubborn cycles of disease, fatigue, and poor performance. To start on this path, we must first define one unusual word: *Hormesis*.

Reversing Your Direction on the Disease-to-Vitality Continuum

Natural Medicine and Hormetic Therapies for Real Health-Building

For 99 percent of humankind's history, we have lived in the presence of frequent physical and environmental stress. Comfort was a rare treat in lives defined by the work of: Hunting, gathering, and farming; confronting seasonal temperature extremes without climate controlled shelter; and coping with regular, sometimes yearly, shortages in food supply. These challenges are still immediate realities for many populations. However, for the average adult in the developed world, life is no longer characterized by physical *challenge*. Instead, life is characterized by *comfort and convenience*:

- 24-hour access to favorite foods and snacks
- 24-hour climate control
- Mechanized transportation
- Sedentary office work

Modern life has resulted in some very real health benefits, from clean water access and basic sanitation to life-saving surgical procedures. But on a grand whole, many of our "advances" in convenience have created surprising new health risks. In centuries and millennia past, the greatest threats to human health were starvation and disease. We've exchanged those health risks for risks that appear far more subtle at first glance. Today, our most common health threats could be described as *diseases of comfort*. Since the mid-twentieth century, we have been living in a way that is radically different from the way any species has ever lived. We are the first to experience *continuous comfort*, and it is eroding our health in the process.

It all comes down to what medical researchers refer to as **hormesis**. That's an odd-sounding word that comes from a Greek term meaning "to set in motion or urge onward." In research, hormesis refers to how exposure to a mild or moderate stress can cause a positive effect in an organism, whether human or bacterial or any other lifeform.[38]

Too much of a physical stress can cause damage. There is a definite *hormetic zone*—not so much stress that you cause damage, not so little that you have no effect. But the right level of good physical stress (hard work, occasional fasting, exposure to cold temperatures) can trigger beneficial anti-oxidative, circulatory, metabolic, and repair processes in the body.[39] In fact, physical stress and environmental challenge are the only way to trigger many of those processes.

Hormesis: A Strange Word for a Common Sense Concept

Hormesis - noun. A cellular state of increased positive health-building activity following exposure to a mild or moderate stressor. The hormetic zone refers to the intensity of the stressor—not so much it induces damage, not so little that it causes no effect.

As humankind adapted to life on this planet, our bodies not only learned to cope with physical stressors, they began to **require** them. On a genetic level, our cells expect physical stress, and our systems suffer when we're not exposed to enough. There are major metabolic fat-burning processes that only turn on when we fast from food.[40] Many of our innate cellular systems for resolving inflammation initiate in response to challenging exercise.[41] Certain vascular muscles only flex in the presence of extreme cold exposure.[42]

Perhaps the simplest example of hormesis is the concept of cyclic exercise, which we'll study in depth in the next chapter. Exercise in short bursts—cycles of full exertion, followed by complete recovery—perfectly mimics the physical movement that was so common for tens of thousands of years of hunting, gathering, and farming. We may not have those hands-on food-gathering lifestyles anymore, but our bodies are still adapted for them. Without that regular burst-style exercise, there are certain tissues in the body that never get their needed nourishment and oxygen or reach their full potential. Cyclic exercise is one of the best ways to heighten metabolism, nourish the brain, and even ensure that the gut is digesting food efficiently.[43] This is a prime example of what I call a *hormetic therapy*. It's a physical stressor that turns on innate body systems that are crucial for health, resiliency, and optimal performance.

There are many more body systems that work efficiently only when we are challenged. Take away those physical and environmental challenges and you have a recipe for metabolic and immune disaster. We gain un-shedable pounds. We ache and feel fatigued. We're more susceptible to illness, autoimmunity, and cancer. We're living longer, but aging prematurely. Our bodies are completely coddled, but we're more mentally stressed than ever. Even if we think we're eating well, these strange health challenges keep creeping up. What's going on? The answer lies in the fact that we've lost touch with our innate hormetic systems.

We desperately need hard exertion and the extra oxygen delivery and countless other benefits that come from it. We need to feel hungry once in a while. We need to get cold and learn how to cope with that feeling too. Hormesis, put as simply as possible, means that **what doesn't kill you makes you stronger.** It turns out there's scientific underpinning for that saying. In fact, it's safe to take that sentiment one step further and note that **continuous comfort just might kill you**.

Here's the good news: It's completely possible to determine your personal hormetic zone—what constitutes too much stress, and what's just right. Many hormetic therapies are very simple. You can do them at home. Some require advanced technologies and the guidance of an integrative physician, but awareness and access are rapidly growing even with these more novel therapies.

In modern times, there's never been a better moment to decide you want to take charge of your health. Today, you have the option to get off the path of medicating your symptoms and coping with chronic health problems. It's also important to note that hormetic therapies aren't only for people with complex diseases. If you're in decent health and already enjoy a favorite sport, you've got the chance to reach a new level of athletic performance and recovery too. Remember, the hormetic therapies and principles that can usher us from disease to vitality, are the same principles that can supercharge an athlete from plateaued performance to new personal bests.

Get ready for some paradigm shifts, and get ready for some hard work. Hormetic therapies are about restoring a sense of physical challenge in your life. You really can access the innate restorative processes that lie dormant in all your cells. But it will take committed choices and lifestyle changes. **To get healthy, you're going to have to get out of your comfort zone.** Ironically, failing to make those strong choices now, choosing continuous comfort instead, can result in greater pain, disease, and suffering down the road.

Adaptive Homeostasis: Hormesis by any other name, is probably still hormesis

If you decide to self-educate extensively on hormesis, you'll quickly discover a small controversy in the medical research community regarding terminology. One of the most enlightening published reviews on hormetic principles is a 2017 *Journal of Physiology* article titled "The role of declining adaptive homeostasis in aging." In it, the authors provide a beautiful and comprehensive overview of how hormetic principles affect diverse conditions including: aging, blood sugar imbalance, cancer, cold shock, sarcopenia (muscle loss), inflammation, immune compromise, and even psychological stress.[44] However, in building their call for more research in these areas, they contend that the word *hormesis* is a misnomer.

Hormesis, in their opinion, should be reserved solely for discussing toxicology research—studies examining how minute doses of toxins can elicit positive effects in some organisms. The authors insist that *adaptive homeostasis* is a better term for discussing how environmental (not chemical) stressors can cause positive effects in an organism. *Adaptive homeostasis* is, indeed, a better term. It clearly describes how the body *adapts* to a stressor to restore *homeostasis* (a balanced healthy state). Point taken.

The challenge is, if you search academic databases for research about how the body adapts to stressors, you'll find most other researchers are using the term "hormesis" instead. *Adaptive homeostasis* might be a more appropriate phrase based on sheer semantics, but it's simply not in common use yet. Using it as a primary search term won't yield many results.

For my purposes in this book, know that I use the term *hormesis* to refer primarily to **the body's response to natural environmental and physical stressors.** Considering the current research pool, it's simply easier to use a word that other researchers are using as well.

One of the Most Researched Concepts in Medical Science—But Virtually Unknown Among Physicians

Curiosity about hormesis in the medical research community is exponentially growing in recent years. As one researcher noted, "In the year 2000 articles using terms 'hormesis' or 'hormetic' were cited approximately 400 times, while in 2016 articles using those terms were cited more than 8000 times."[45] Hormesis is widely studied by **more than 30 different scientific disciplines** including: microbiology, cancer care (oncology), nutrition, genetics, cardiology, anti-aging medicine, reproductive medicine, and hormone therapy.

I know of no other science that is more universally studied than hormesis. The concept that cellular stress can yield positive benefits is obviously captivating to research communities around the globe. I've found countless articles about hormetic principles in every major medical journal, and all those articles end with a similar sentiment: *It seems these findings could have significant impact for public health and addressing age-related disease processes.*[46,47] In other words, doctors should probably be recommending these concepts to their patients.

Yet, almost all of these articles are authored by researchers who never treat patients.

Over the years, I have asked numerous physicians within modern medicine if they know what hormesis is. Not one practitioner I spoke with knew the term. It's not common knowledge among integrative doctors either. And my patients have certainly never heard of it. Why the knowledge gap between the research world and the world of practical medicine? Why the disconnect?

I think the answer involves several factors. First, the concept of hormesis initially got tied up in homeopathy, a branch of natural medicine that has come under scrutiny in recent years. It's possible that there's a guilt-by-association factor for some scientists. Similarly, hormesis has also been associated with some alternative toxicology applications that are quite suspect—certain alternative practitioners have recommended micro-dose exposure to radiation or known toxins to achieve "hormetic" benefits.[48] I should make it clear that I never recommend exposure to damaging stressors like that. The only hormetic therapies I allow and encourage in my clinic are natural and scientifically proven therapies that involve physical or environmental challenges (exercise, fasting, cold exposure; see Chapters 2, 5, and 6) or use of substances that are naturally present in the body (oxygen and ozone; see Chapters 3 and 4). Regardless, few people outside the medical research community are aware of hormesis at any level at all, so these guilt-by-association issues can't be the only ones at play.

Ultimately, several other factors are probably responsible for the fact that you haven't even heard of this well-researched health-transforming concept. The challenges begin in the research world and trickle all the way down to what happens in your local general medical clinic.

Research: Hormesis is exceptionally well-researched at a *cellular* level, but it is admittedly challenging to research on a *human clinical* level. This is because the empirical research process prefers to focus on one single input and one single outcome: Take this one pill, measure a single effect. **Hormetic therapies are inherently more powerful and affect multiple body systems.** They involve complex cellular changes that result in diverse whole health effects. Studying something with that many layers takes a lot of time. And money.

Funding: Who might fund such massive years-long human clinical studies? The main corporate entities that fund multi-million dollar health-related studies are pharmaceutical companies. Why would a pharmaceutical company choose to fund a study that might put their drug brands out of business? There's no conspiracy theory here. It's pure economics. Many hormetic therapies are simple and lifestyle based. The handful of hormetic therapies that involve complex technology (i.e. hyperbaric oxygen or exercise with oxygen) or ozone infusions and injections (i.e. Prolozone) still use natural substances that cannot be patented or trademarked. There's no major profit potential. So who's going to foot the bill on the large-population flagship study?

Publicity: Even when university-based, NIH, or foundation-funded studies have filled the gap, there are no publicity machines lining up to get the word out on a national or global scale. Pharmaceutical influence is involved there too. As mentioned earlier, most doctors receive the bulk of their continuing education through efforts funded by pharmaceutical companies. Those companies aren't going to provide seminars on new medical therapies that could effectively replace drug-based health care.

Application: Despite industry resistance to publicizing hormetic research findings, there have been some significant

> human clinical studies on the efficacy of specific therapies. You'll find several of them summarized at the end of the therapy-spotlight chapters. But even when physicians are made aware of such studies, they're not always quick to adopt these modalities into their practices.

The reality is that effectively administering hormetic therapies requires significant additional training and certification. It takes a high level of critical thinking, assessment, monitoring, and design to create a hormetic therapy program for an individual patient. *How much, how intense, and how often should this patient perform a given hormetic therapy? Does this patient need "pre-conditioning" prior to hormetic challenge? What type of activity would be best?* There is no quick-reference dosage chart to answer these questions as there is for pharmaceutical drugs. Instead, it takes detailed and nuanced understanding of individual patients, their pasts, their current challenges, and their goals. **That level of awareness is uncommon between physicians and their patients today.** Indeed, the application of hormetic therapies holds us, the practitioners, accountable to breaking the cycle of fifteen-minute office visits and single-pill fixes.

All of the above factors have made it challenging to incorporate hormetic therapies into conventional clinics. But the integrative world is beginning to catch on. We can all benefit from these therapies. Hormesis is our most ancient and powerful science. It's an adaptive process that's knit into all our cells, and it's shared by every lifeform on the planet, from plants and single-celled organisms to humans and all other animals. Unlike fad diets and other fresh medical theories that show up, only to be discounted a year later, hormetic principles are ancient, proven, and here to stay.

Evolution designed us to respond intelligently to physical challenge. As mentioned earlier, our bodies need environmental and molecular challenges to "turn on" certain cellular processes. We can flip those hormetic switches by exposing ourselves to small challenges and then work up to bigger ones. Whether it's cyclic exercise or cold exposure, simple therapeutic practices re-acclimate our bodies to healthy stressors. Re-training your body to be more adaptable can make you more resistant to lifestyle stress, disease states, and anything else life throws at you. Hormetic therapies awaken powerful cellular functions that can:

- Upregulate antioxidant defenses[49]
- Enhance detoxification systems[50]
- Activate damage repair systems[51]
- Optimize the stress response[52]
- Reduce inflammation[53]
- Promote healthy gene expression[54]

That's everything we need to address the most common health challenges today. It's true that our lives look nothing like those of our hunter-gatherer ancestors. But we do have the ability to mindfully choose habits and therapies that induce hormesis. We can reintroduce the ancestral physical challenges that our bodies need to function well. These practices tap directly into our greatest health asset: the human body's resiliency.

In my practice I often refer to hormetic therapies as challenge therapies. This term is a little easier to grasp for a patient who is completely new to the concept. Challenge therapies are medicine. They are core to all my treatment programs. Instead of sending my patients home with a list of symptom-silencing pharmaceuticals, I address root causes. "Prescriptions" in my medical model fall under three categories: **Foundational care** (as described earlier in this chapter) plus the **oxygen therapies** and **challenge therapies** explored in this book. This is strategic, personalized, health-restoring medicine that can reverse—not just mitigate—degenerative conditions.

I should mention one note of caution. Hormetic therapies are inherently physically challenging. Each of the following chapters will address the "pre-conditioning" processes necessary for those with complex and physically limiting diseases. It might not be possible to immediately undertake every hormetic therapy if you are struggling with certain medical conditions such as chronic pain, severe fatigue, or major metabolic disorders. But, yes, even if you are facing serious limitations, hormetic therapies can become part of your health journey over time. Indeed, I believe these therapies are crucial for full health restoration. One of my greatest passions is designing the programs that pre-condition, strengthen, and prepare people who are not yet ready for a hormetic challenge.

How To Use This Book:
You've got the general principles, let's dive into the therapies!

Chapters 2 through 7 are each dedicated to one of the game changing functional medicine therapies that I routinely use in my practice. I've focused on five therapy categories that are lesser known, or virtually unknown, in both conventional medicine and alternative care clinics. Lesser known does not mean unproven. In my practice, I only use therapies with strong scientific support and published studies backing them. I want you to feel as confident about these therapies as I do. Each chapter will provide you with a solid knowledge base. The first half of each chapter provides a description of the therapy's history, its common and appropriate uses, and how it affects the body and organ systems. I'll explain the therapy's specific health benefits, citing studies that demonstrate those results.

After that core description, there are four more sections you'll find in every chapter:

- **Meet the Patients** – Multiple case stories covering real people who have benefitted from the therapy. General factual description of a therapy can only go so far. Most people need to "see" the therapy at work within a real narrative. Through detailed patient stories, the therapy and its actual health-changing effects come alive!

- **Try It** – Detailed instruction on how to try the most accessible therapies at home and how to find and screen a provider for tech-dependent or IV/injection therapies. Of course, this section does not constitute personalized medical advice. It only deepens your understanding so you can work with your own practitioner to develop the plan that works best for you.
- **Health Goals Triad** – How the therapy interacts with *Disease Reversal, Longevity*, and *Athletic Performance* goals. By the end of this book, you'll be able to see how the therapeutic principles that can transform a metabolic disease, are the same principles that can help performance athletes reach their next level.
- **Further Science** – Summaries of several featured studies investigating the therapy. While this is not the comprehensive list of cited references for the chapter (that appears at the end of the book), these selections will help you deepen your understanding. I encourage you to self-educate by visiting PubMed, the primary online database for accessing published scientific articles. Google "PubMed" or visit directly at: **https://www.ncbi.nlm.nih.gov/pubmed/**.

If you are interested in one therapy category more than the others, you certainly may read the chapters out of order. But realize that each chapter builds on principles outlined in preceding chapters. To ensure your best understanding of biological and medical concepts, please read at least the core therapy descriptions in the first half of every chapter.

At the end of the book, Chapter 7 describes how multiple therapies enhance each other's effects. You'll discover sample protocol recommendations for certain health goals. Again, this isn't meant to give you definitive medical advice for your own unique situation. Rather, I hope you'll use this chapter as a discussion guide when speaking with your own primary care provider. You'll also have the concrete tools for trying a few hormetic therapies on your own and taking your first steps towards health transformation.

Welcome to Health Building

I wrote this book to stand in the gap and become a voice for a better approach to health care: An approach that blends foundational wellness practices with strategic hormetic therapies. I draw from the best of both conventional and complementary worlds for a truly integrative approach. I don't rule out the use of pharmaceutical medications when appropriate, but they're not usually my starting point. Instead of patching over symptoms with chemical drugs, and managing the side effects with more drugs, why not access the body's innate ability to self-heal using its most powerful cellular capabilities? Instead of juggling pills for disease management, we could actually restore health.

This book is for everyone. If you are committed to health and wellness, there is much here to deepen your journey. If you are new to this work, you'll acquire a roadmap to chart a highly transformative path. If you are an athlete who wants to naturally enhance performance, you'll get to develop a fresh game plan. If you are struggling with a disease, you'll find new solutions you may wish to incorporate as stand-alone therapies or as therapies that fit seamlessly into an existing treatment plan. Regardless of where you stand right now, the core principles in each chapter will have application in your life. If you need additional support, I am here for you. My practice and website can offer more structured guidance to anyone who needs it.

Chapter 2

Cyclic Exercise & Interval Training

Simple exercise routines to transform your health and revolutionize your existing athletic program

The vast majority of my clients come to me with a major presenting symptom. For over 60 percent of them, that concern is pain-related. They're dealing with a new or old injury or a degenerative condition like arthritis. Something hurts, and it's finally gotten to the point where it's limiting their ability to move, especially their ability to enjoy favorite activities. You might find one of these scenarios familiar:

- It's impossible to lift over ten pounds anymore.
- I can't play with my grandchildren like I used to.
- I've completely lost my edge on the tennis court.
- My mile timer is consistently 20 seconds worse than last year.
- I can swim and bicycle, but running is out of the question.
- I've quit exercising entirely.

Sometimes we're not aware of how much an old injury has limited us. Year after year, we slowly give up another activity and cope with a new limitation. We accept it as a normal part of getting older. But when pain eats away at our ability to exercise, it's not just the loss of an enjoyable pastime. It's a serious blow to overall health. Exercise is that important. It's not solely about weight management and heart health. **Exercise influences the function of every body system: digestion, detox, mood, cognition, mental health, immune response, bone density, circadian rhythms.**[1] Every system.

You've got to be able to move.

What if I genuinely can't exercise?

I've worked with clients who come to me so debilitated by new or chronic pain that they cannot begin even the lightest exercise program. Others are barely coping with obesity or immune and metabolic disorders that diving into a full-effort exercise program could be dangerous. It is priority one at Vitality Health Challenge to address severe disease states first, so the client can at least begin regular movement.

If you fall into this category, there is a path for you. Pre-conditioning for exercise might involve oxygen and ozone therapies—the subjects of Chapters 3 and 4. Pay close attention to the section titled "Restoring Movement" later in this chapter and also the second Case Story. That Case Story shares an example of how I've helped people work up to exercise, even when it seemed impossible. There are solutions, and you **can** begin moving again with the right preparation. Stay positive and hopeful. Fully resolving many of your health issues will depend on your ability to get your body moving again!

On a practical level, exercise can be simple: A fifteen-minute protocol, three times a week. But the whole health effects are way more complex than most people know. Let's look at what exercise actually does for the body, how pain and injury compromise our ability to move freely, and how we can restore movement in severe situations. Then we'll learn about the concepts of Cyclic Exercise and an Interval Training technique that releases your body's own internal supply of growth hormone. You will see how these simple, easy-to-incorporate methods can transform any exercise program you already follow—or followed in the past and want to re-incorporate.

Seven Exercise Benefits Your Doctor Never Explained to You

Everyone knows that exercise helps with **weight management**. That's easy to understand. You're up and moving and burning calories. It's also easy to comprehend the central benefit for the **cardiovascular system**. When you exercise, your heart is working harder than usual, which helps maintain the strength of the heart muscle itself. (There's another significant benefit for the heart, but we'll get to that when we look at Heart Rate Variability later in this chapter.) During exercise your blood vessels also expand to accommodate increased blood flow, and that's good for keeping your vascular system pliable, clean, and healthy.[2] From there, it's easy to extrapolate the cascade of metabolic benefits. Maintaining a healthy weight and cardio wellness through exercise means you're at less risk of diabetes, high blood pressure, heart disease, stroke, and related conditions.[3] That all makes sense.

Here's where things get interesting. Exercise has several other whole health effects that make it the tipping-point therapy in treating many seemingly unrelated conditions.

1. Mental Health and Focus: Exercise not only produces happy-feeling endorphins and leaves you feeling accomplished—a great mental health benefit in itself—it's also vital for routing fresh blood and nutrients to the micro-capillaries in the brain. It oxygenates the brain, creates positive shifts in brain chemistry, and enhances neurotransmitter release.[4] Regular exercise is a must for anyone dealing with depression, anxiety,[5] cognitive decline,[6] and ADD/ADHD,[7] as well as anyone who simply wants to heighten mental sharpness and reduce day-to-day fatigue.

2. Restorative Sleep: Cyclic Exercise is vital for people who struggle with insomnia or poor sleep quality (feeling "still tired" in the morning). Exertion creates an outgo of energy that can make the body naturally tired and primed for deeper sleep later on.[8] Cyclic Exercise can help to restore the circadian rhythms that are disrupted by modern stress, blue light exposure from computers and cell phones, and modern electric light usage.[9]

3. Digestion: Digestion can be disrupted by food sensitivities or allergies, poor diet, probiotic imbalance, infection, and stress. While each of those root causes require individualized treatment themselves, they're all also aggravated by a sedentary lifestyle. Even if you eat well and have no dietary restrictions, exercise helps with optimizing digestion (and therefore optimal energy throughout the body). Gut motility, the ability of the gut to literally move things along, is enhanced by exercise.[10]

4. Bone Density: Bone growth and maintenance is enhanced by movement. All those micro-impacts felt by our bones during appropriate exercise can trigger the mechanisms by which the body builds and maintains bone structure. It appears that weight-bearing, moderate-impact exercise and sports have the most positive effects on bone density.[11]

5. Detoxification: Exercise makes you sweat! The skin is the body's largest detoxification organ, and sweating is one of our innate systems for getting rid of environmental and food-born toxins. Sedentary living leads to toxin build up, which makes you feel fatigued—which makes you even less likely to exercise. It's a vicious cycle with one solution: Get up and get moving.[12]

6. Healthy Aging: It's a positive self-reinforcing cycle. Fit people stay active longer. There is definitely a simple use-it-or-lose-it factor involved. But there is also growing evidence that intensified exercise can increase anti-aging effects on a genetic level. At the end of each human chromosome is a protective end-cap called a *telomere.* Shortening telomeres are associated with aging.[13] As telomeres shorten, it can lead to altered cell division that results in slight mutations in our genes.[14] These mutations aren't lethal, but they are responsible for the common signs of aging.[15] Intense exercise appears to protect and maintain telomere length, preventing those minor errors when cells divide.[16] The research is still growing, but it seems that protecting telomere length can slow the effects of the aging process.[17]

7. Immune Function: On a biomechanical level, exercise moves our lymph around. The lymph system, which is a major transportation system for our white blood cells, has no circulatory pump. The lymphatic system flows through different channels that are not part of our main circulation system for blood flow. Only physical movement can cause flow in these lymphatic spaces. Along with promoting lymphatic flow, healthy levels of exercise can also reduce CRP levels (a marker for systemic inflammation) and increase healthy white blood cell activity.[18]

All these benefits seem unrelated on the surface, but if you remember learning about hormesis in Chapter 1, you might see a pattern at this point. You're right. Appropriate moderate exercise, especially the Cyclic Exercise and Interval Training methods we'll look at soon, are hormetic therapies in and of themselves.

Exercise as Your Own Built-In Hormetic Therapy

For millions of people, exercise is likely the only hormetic therapy they utilize on a regular basis. If you're not able to move well, or exercise in a way that challenges you, you lose one of your greatest built-in hormetic inputs for health and wellness. When someone has debilitating pain and can't exercise, that's a setup for developing other diseases. **People who quit exercising often have no hormetic stimulation at all.** A sedentary lifestyle is the most dangerous existence of all. It's a failure to activate the greatest inborn cellular machinery we have for growth, repair, resilience, and stress recovery. So yes, it's pretty important!

Exercise, like any hormetic activity, depends on that fine line between "optimizing stressor" and "damaging stressor". Jogging for half an hour at 50 percent of your peak capacity doesn't actually induce hormesis. It's too mild. On the other end of the spectrum, frequent endurance running can swing the pendulum past the hormetic zone and into a state of vulnerability to injury and illness.[19]

Achieving optimal hormetic effects from exercise involves intensified exertion and appropriate rest and recovery. That dual focus is key. In short, the Cyclic Exercise that we'll look at in-depth in the second half of this chapter is "Hormetic Perfection".

Where's the line between good-stress exercise and pushing yourself to the point of injury? There are some common sense realities here. Obviously, the answer will vary for each person. Someone who has maintained fitness over the years will be able to exercise more often and more aggressively with less risk of injury, compared to someone who has been sedentary for decades. But whatever your age and athletic performance level, there are a few questions you can ask yourself to get a sense of whether you're over-exerting:

- Does your exercise invigorate you and leave you feeling stronger, or does it always leave you exhausted, weak, tight, sore, and less alert?
- Do you look forward to exercise?
- Do you have rest days built in, and do you work on training for recovery as much as performance?
- Are you making gains and performing better anytime you commit more time to your sport?

"No pain, no gain" can be an appropriate sentiment when starting a brand new exercise program or pushing yourself to reach a new level of performance. But if your exercise regimen is only depleting, if you don't bother with rest days, if you have neve for recovery, if increased training no longer yields or if you simply don't look forward to exercising b these are signs of over-exertion. Take some serious time t implement the recommendations in this chapter. Incorpora minutes of Cyclic Exercise (to be described in detail soon) into y current weekly training schedule. It will likely be your game changer.

On the other end of the spectrum, there are plenty of people who regard themselves as allergic to exercise, or their exercise is limited to using the stairs instead of the elevator or walking from the far end of the grocery store parking lot. I hope this chapter helps you discover the role of exercise in experiencing a possible breakthrough with many of your other health goals. Cyclic Exercise is the most enjoyable and least time-consuming introductory exercise form that you could possibly engage in.

Inflammation: The good, the bad, and the chronic

The most common reason for plateauing in athletic performance, or giving up exercise completely, is pain. Without commitment to an athletic training and recovery program, most of us naturally lose about one percent of our joint mobility and motion every year beginning around age 30.[20] That sounds minimal until you think of it as a 20 percent loss between age 30 and age 50. That's significant. Add in the effects of a poorly healed injury, with some associated pain and restriction, and now you have serious limitations. That's why by age 50, many have simply given up the activities they used to enjoy in their twenties.

Over time, it's normal to experience some limitation and change in pace. But fully losing access to your favorite pastimes should not be considered a normal effect of aging. It doesn't have to be that

. Understanding how to reverse that process, and re-build health, gins with a quick overview of the inflammatory cascade.

Inflammation is not inherently bad. In fact, as part of a healthy balanced healing process, inflammation is intended to call the immune system into action. Ideally, it's an alert system that rallies protective immune cells toward the damaged or stressed tissue. From there, inflammation should progress to a mending and rebuilding phase. Ideally that tissue-rebuilding phase should be paired with mindful movement (physical therapy), so the new tissue is trained to stay supple, flexible, and strong. Eventually, we reach a state of fully restored function and range of motion.

If only it always worked that way!

The challenge is when the inflammation cycle gets stalled—perhaps through repeated re-injury, lack of appropriate PT, excess scar tissue formation, or even poor nutrition and psychological stress. Sometimes a conventional treatment can cause problems too. Steroid injections for pain and even over-the-counter pain-killers used for too long, can compromise the immune system and harm the long-term healing process.[21] Any of these factors can result in a joint or muscle injury that never fully resolves. Instead of a healthy healing process, we're left with a bad back, a bum knee, or a wrist that can't hold a baseball bat without pain.

Old injury isn't the only source of chronic pain. Chronic inflammation is at work in standard osteoarthritis. The inflammatory process can also go astray when it's involved in damaging autoimmune conditions such as rheumatoid arthritis.[22] Unhealthy systemic inflammation is likely a factor in chronic fatigue and fibromyalgia.[23]

Whatever the chronic inflammatory state, the greatest irony is that if you can restore some level of healthy exercise, the exertion itself helps metabolize many of the pain mediators.[24] **Turning more sedentary only worsens pain in the long run.**[25] Like any disease spiral, joint pain can become exponentially self-reinforcing: More pain leads to less movement, which leads to more pain and restriction.

We are meant to move freely and get our heart rates up. Exertion benefits every organ system. If pain has limited your access to exercise, or simply limited your performance, it's vital to address and resolve that before you resume or expand your exercise regimen.

Restoring Movement: When exercise isn't possible

If clients come to me expressing that pain has limited their ability to exercise, or cut them off from exercise entirely, that issue is a top priority. **These clients must be able to get back up and moving in order to support all their other body systems**. If you're in that boat, you may need a team of professionals like the one we utilize at Vitality Health Challenge to help you break through and resolve this limitation.

Even many integrative physicians may not fully appreciate the importance of comfortable movement and exercise in relation to other health challenges. You'll need a practitioner who can craft a complete rehabilitation plan, including small preliminary steps to *pre-condition* your body for regular exercise. At the very least, you'll need access to restorative oxygen and detoxification therapies (See Chapters 3 and 7).

It is crucial for your physician to acquire a complete picture of the source of your pain and your health before pain took over. If you were generally fit before the pain cycle began, your treatment strategy will likely differ from that provided for someone who was living a sedentary life and then began to struggle with pain. Your current and past diet, family history, hormonal balance, major life changes, and stress levels come into play too.

As I build that full picture of a client's health, I develop a pre-conditioning plan. Whether I'm helping someone with old injury pain, arthritis, autoimmune conditions, fibromyalgia, or chronic fatigue, the pre-conditioning plan will incorporate many of the same elements. I find that each client often needs a period of intensified oxygenation (see Chapters 3 and 4), nutrient infusion, and detoxification before I even start this individual on rehabilitative physical therapy (PT), and Cyclic Exercise. Part of the pre-conditioning plan will involve getting the body to sweat again and detox through several sessions in a specialized sauna. Sauna time might be paired with an oxygen therapy. The initial ventures into movement might involve simply stretching in the sauna or a heated room. I often pair oxygen therapies with the initial efforts of PT too.

I also make recommendations for structural therapies like chiropractic care. If there is an underlying subluxation in the spine, or another joint, that misalignment is not likely to spontaneously correct itself. Subluxation refers to mild *misalignment* of a joint—not a complete and immediately disabling *dislocation*, but a joint that is not optimally aligned. Over time a slight misalignment can lead to muscle dysfunction, pinched or impeded nerves, and more subluxations in other parts of the body as associated muscle groups tug at each other. A good sports chiropractor will care not only for the spine, but also for the minor subluxations that can occur in all joints. Skillful chiropractic manipulation is an additional synergistic therapy to correct such issues when they're present. This is vital for full recovery. Otherwise we're always trying to calm the muscles that are irritated from being constantly pulled out of alignment.[26]

Carefully and strategically, we restore movement and support overall health. When a client has been stuck in a chronic pain state for a long time, there can be new or intensified pain as we recruit those joints and muscles for restored movement. It's vital that we listen to this pain and not over-train, reinjuring an old injury, or aggravating long-standing arthritic conditions. But working through the pain wisely and strategically, we can often restore both strength and range of motion.

If chronic pain is your main obstacle preventing you from exercising, please take this seriously: you will need medical help.

Don't dive into a major exercise program if you need a series of oxygen therapies, nutrient therapy, chiropractic care, and PT first. If you're not sure, get in touch with a regenerative functional medicine physician (see the Resources section at the end of this book). Get that holistic assessment first. Restoring your ability to exercise is crucial, but you've got to do it in a way that doesn't cause re-injury.

What's the Best Workout For Me?

Whenever I discuss exercise with my clients, I'm careful to use the terms "appropriate" and "strategic." What's the ideal workout regimen? That answer will vary widely for each person, depending on current fitness level. But everyone, from performance athletes to mall walkers, can benefit from Cyclic Exercise.

It's not a replacement for the exercise activities you already engage in. You don't have to dump the sport you love. If you're already athletic, Cyclic Exercise will only enhance what you're already doing. If you're living a mostly sedentary life, Cyclic Exercise will dramatically alter your health and day-to-day energy levels. And if you are struggling with a disease, you may be surprised at how significantly that condition improves or resolves fully. This type of exercise will provide you the most crucial benefits of regular exercise with a minimal time commitment. Let's explore this concept and find out how you can apply it immediately.

Let's "Cause Health" Instead of "Treating Disease"

We constantly hear about miracle drugs and invasive surgical procedures providing new approaches to "managing" a disease. Over time, most modern medical patients retain their illnesses, while their lists of pharmaceutical medications grow. It's exceedingly rare to hear of a patient taken off prescription drugs because the drugs were no longer needed, or to learn that a chronic condition was cured by pharmaceutical medicine alone.

Perhaps it's time to ask some fresh questions: Can we cause health instead of treating disease? Could something as simple as exercise cause health? I believe the answer to both questions is yes. Now that we have reviewed the vast benefits of exercise in general, it's time to dive deeper and discover what Cyclic Exercise can specifically offer offer us in terms of maintaining health and possibly even reversing disease.

One of the first individuals to contribute to this line of research is a physician named Irving Dardik. In addition to significant contributions in his chosen field of vascular surgery, Dr. Dardik was also a running enthusiast and trained many top U.S. Olympic track and field athletes. When one of Dr. Dardik's closest friends experienced a fatal heart attack immediately following a long-distance run, the physician decided to hone his career focus on athletic training and recovery strategies.[27]

Post-exertion heart attack is not unheard-of. Not long before Dr. Dardik's dear friend passed away, another long-distance runner and noted fitness author, Jim Fixx, also sustained a fatal heart attack after a long-distance run.[28] In fact, the word *marathon* comes from the Greek legend of Phidippides who suffered the same fate after he ran the almost 26 miles from Marathon to Athens to spread word of a military victory. Shortly after sharing this news, he too, is reported to have collapsed and died of a heart attack.

You'd think there would be a little more scientific curiosity about this phenomenon. Shouldn't we wonder why these incredibly fit individuals would die, not during, but *after* a distance run? There are indeed certain exercise regimens that can compromise health. Conversely, there are other exercise methods that fully optimize health. Dr. Dardik was the first to study why these post-exertion heart attacks happen and to offer significant insight into the very nature of how we ought to exercise. We can cause greater health through a simple but specialized exercise protocol.

What could possibly explain why death associated with exercise typically comes *after* the individual stops an activity and not during the exertion phase? In nature, sustained exertion is rare throughout the animal kingdom. Burst activity is much more common in almost all animals studied. Cheetahs, the fastest animals on earth, only sustain those high speeds for short periods of time. Humans in their most intuitive forms of play are similar. Think of children playing on their own, how they typically exert for short periods of time and then rest, as in a game of tag or musical chairs.

We now know that exercise is intended to be cyclic, and to consist of **two equally important parts**: exertion and recovery. Initially Dr. Dardik tested this theory with heart rate monitoring of long-distance runners. He had them perform a short sprint and then fully stop. Their heart rates increased to 140-150 beats per minute (BPM) during their sprint, but when they immediately stopped and sat down after the sprint, some of their heart rates suddenly dropped from 150 to 40, 30, or even lower. Dr. Dardik saw how dangerous the fall in heart rate could be for these long-distance runners. Typically, these athletes exerted for long periods of time, and then they would often need to keep moving or jogging when they finished to prevent their heart rates and blood pressure from plummeting to dangerous levels. Of equal concern, some of these well-conditioned, long distance runners had heart rates that remained elevated for some time after a brief sprint.[29]

These athletes were over-trained in one part of a crucial two-part cycle. Specifically, they were *over-trained* on the exertion/performance phase, but completely *non-trained* in the recovery phase. This explained why some athletes, immediately following exertion, had heart rates that remained quite elevated for several minutes and others had heart rates that fell dangerously low. **Both conditions represented untrained recovery physiology.** As stated by anthropologist Roger Lewin, PhD, "down-regulation of a revved up system is an active physiological process that also requires exercise." We have to train our bodies for recovery, just as much as we train them for performance. [30]

Just as we might create a several-month training plan to achieve specific athletic performance goals, we should be just as diligent with creating and implementing training plans that condition our bodies to recover, to smoothly return to resting heart rate. We can all benefit from training both phases of the exercise cycle—*performance* physiology and *recovery* physiology.

Dr. Dardik eventually found that training for recovery had whole health implications reaching well beyond cardio function. It seems, if we over-train the performance side of the equation, it can lead to a disruption or a "flattening" in our natural rhythms and physiology. It's possible this physiological disruption can set up some people to develop or aggravate a chronic disease.[31] Introducing Cyclic Exercise can be a breakthrough change that restores natural rhythms in the body. Recall the countless benefits of exercise. Cyclic Exercise optimizes all those benefits. It's an especially course-altering method for those at the extremes: People who do not exercise at all and those who over-train for performance.

What a Cyclic Exercise Protocol Looks Like

Before starting any exercise program, please check with your health care provider. Certain disease states may prevent you from exercising in any fashion. Other conditions will limit the types of exercise and degree of exertion you can perform. Additional modifications may be required. At Vitality Health Challenge we specialize in several exercise protocols, including Cyclic Exercise. We typically employ both heart rate monitoring and oxygen saturation monitoring during a client's initial Cyclic Exercise experiences. We also make sure that clients are warmed up and have stretched prior to any exercise challenges. Please partner with a practitioner who can do the same for you.

When working with any hormetic therapy, it is crucial to start slow and ensure that the stress is strong enough to register as a *challenge,* but not sustained enough to cause *damage.* Cyclic Exercise addresses both requirements and is a great starting point to experience hormesis.

Cyclic Exercise is not complicated. It consists of exercising in any fashion that rapidly gets your heart rate into the range of your maximum. As a rough guide, maximal heart rate is 220 minus your age. For example, a 35-year-old would have a max heart rate around 185, and a 50-year-old would have a max heart rate around 170.

To reach this target rate, you might use common exercise equipment like a stationary bike, elliptical machine, or a jump rope. You could also simply sprint in place. After an appropriate warm up, the exertion phase will last between 30 to 60 seconds. After that brief exertion, stop the exercise, immediately sit down, and focus on your breathing with one goal: Get your heart rate down to baseline. That baseline, or resting heart rate, is the rate you had before you began to exercise. Stay seated until you reach that resting heart rate. Once baseline heart rate has been reached, the second exertion cycle begins, and the process starts over again. A typical protocol may contain four to five of these cycles, resulting in an entire workout lasting about ten to fifteen minutes. Ideally this should be done two to four times per week, depending on your other fitness workouts and goals.

This is a short duration exercise protocol that anyone can find time for. It can be helpful to record the time interval that it takes to have your heart rate return to normal. Initially, it may take several minutes—though it may be much faster for some. That recovery time will vary between cycles and over weeks of practice.

Your thirty-second recovery time following a maximal effort may represent one of the single greatest markers of fitness and health. It is one of my most sensitive measures of optimal health, and it's a more valuable data point than many lab tests. We will explore how to integrate this type of exercise into your existing exercise regimen if you have one. And if you don't, this may be the best option to start with or work towards.

Causing Health Through Hormetic Effects and Restoring Natural Rhythms

I want to make an analogy between what Dr. Dardik refers to as waves or cycles and the concept of hormesis. I believe that they are one and the same. Dr. Dardik's exercise cycles represent gentle hormetic stimulation—cycles or waves of stress and recovery. This method is equally accessible to those who have limited or no exercise capacity, as well as those who already exercise but in a fashion that does not offer maximal hormetic stimulation.

As outlined in the previous chapter, there is a continuum from chronic disease to wellness to peak performance. The protocols we need to recover from a disease state are the same ones we need to maintain health, wellness, and longevity. The same protocols also help us continue on toward peak performance and athletic recovery. Although the specific therapies will differ, the underlying physiologic principles remain the same. Cyclic Exercise makes this concept easier to understand. The physiology that optimizes athletic performance also supports disease reversal. Just as the heart rate can become inflexible in its ability to quickly accelerate and decelerate, our cells, tissues, and organ systems can also become inflexible and poorly responsive to stressful challenges. That state of inflexibility can result in disease or simply poor physiological function.[32,33]

This isn't just an interesting parallel between cardio flexibility and the flexibility of other organ systems. These are completely intertwined realities. Training for cardio recovery can affect the entire body's ability to respond well to diverse stressors. With so many chronic stresses in our modern life, it makes intuitive sense that training the body to relax and recover from exercise stress can also help us to recover from other stresses. This is the very definition of hormesis.

In the Western mindset, we tend to think of the body's organs and systems as independent entities, when in fact everything is highly interconnected and cyclic. To understand this interconnectedness, it might help to consider the countless circadian rhythms and daily fluctuations that normally exist in our bodies. We have daily cycles for hormones,[34] pulse rates,[35] blood pressure,[36] and much more. For example, cortisol—a key adrenal hormone—peaks around five a.m. and helps us wake up. Levels fall consistently throughout the day, reaching their lowest point around ten p.m., as we prepare to sleep.[37] We also have daily rhythms for practically every behavior and psychological measure including sleep-wake cycles,[38] body temperature,[39] hand-eye coordination,[40] mental alertness,[41] and athletic ability.[42] Even our diseases often follow a daily clock. Heart attacks,[43] strokes,[44] headaches,[45] hay fever,[46] and arthritis[47] tend to cluster in the morning, while asthma,[48] gout,[49] colic,[50] gastric ulcers,[51] and heartburn tend to occur more at night.[52]

We will continue to expand on this concept in coming chapters. For now, realize that Cyclic Exercise is a highly effective way to restore a sense of natural rhythm and a deep aptitude for recovery in all the body's organ systems and daily cycles.

A Note About Media Coverage of Dr. Dardik's Work

Back in 1991, an article about Cyclic Exercise was featured in *New York Magazine*. The article noted Dr. Dardik's speculation that:

> "when a person makes large waves of energy expenditure and recovery, the body's immune chemistry and repair processes are activated. In turn, they're prompted to make their own healthy waves and to do their work more efficiently." [53]

I believe that Dr. Dardik tapped into an early understanding of the science of hormesis, prior to the identification of the exact biochemical pathways and messenger molecules. He was way ahead of his time, and it took decades for others to catch up to him and his way of thinking.

That *New York Magazine* article featured several patients who made significant disease-state recoveries while using Cyclic Exercise protocols. The stories included an individual with enteritis (intestinal inflammation resulting in frequent diarrhea), one with pain and depression, and another with Multiple Sclerosis (MS). All benefitted significantly from Cyclic Exercise. Dr. Dardik never claimed this method to be a panacea, a cure-all. He believed in its life-altering role within a larger treatment scheme. Unfortunately, after this article was published, an MS patient came to Dr. Dardik for consultation, initially experienced significant benefits from Cyclic Exercise, and then had a symptom relapse. She blamed the MS relapse on Dr. Dardik's protocols and filed a complaint against him to the Medical Board. After a series of meetings, his license to practice medicine was revoked. He was fighting an uphill battle back then.[54] In the early nineties, there was no real support for alternative medicine, and the medical establishment did not like being challenged.

It's more than unfortunate that so many have responded to that situation by patently throwing out all of Dr. Dardik's findings. His data-supported findings were profound and deserve our continued attention and research. Ignoring his contributions only leaves us at a loss. Again, Cyclic Exercise is not a cure-all. But it is a crucial component in any whole health or condition-related program. Cyclic Exercise paired with many of the other therapies we rely on at Vitality Health Challenge can trigger powerful synergies. I've taken a scrutinizing look at the findings of Dr. Dardik and other similar researchers, and I use the strongest studies to influence my protocols. I've also adjusted my strategies and therapy-combinations as I learn more from my own clients' feedback. That's what any good researcher and physician ought to do.

Cyclic Exercise and Heart Rate Variability (HRV)

A powerful marker of true health

We used to think that the heart beats in a regimented and fixed manner. We now know this is far from the case. For example, when your doctor palpates your pulse and notes it as 60 or 70 beats per minute (BPM), that number is accurate only for the few seconds that your pulse was taken. However, if your doctor continued to track your pulse for a full minute, it would actually vary quite a bit. In fact, heart rate increases with each inhale and falls with each exhale.[55] Heart rate variability (HRV) is a comparative measure of the time interval between successive heart beats.

This normal variation in time between beats stems from the two independent branches of the autonomic nervous system. The **autonomic nervous system** controls vital functions such as our breathing, blood pressure, temperature, and essentially all organs and systems that generally function without conscious control. (We will explore some of the conscious influences we have over the autonomic nervous system in Chapter 6.) The two components of the autonomic nervous system are:

- **The Sympathetic Nervous System** – Commonly referred to as the fight or flight system, which dominates in times of trouble or stress. It prepares your body for physical and mental activity, making your heart beat faster and stronger, opening airways so you can breathe more easily, and inhibiting digestion.
- **The Parasympathetic System** – Responsible for rest, digestion, repair, and relaxation. It lowers heart rate, calms your breathing, and prompts digestive processes to resume.

These two systems are in constant communication and balance, and HRV is a direct measure of their interplay.[56] The interaction of these two systems is crucial and allows for instantaneous changes in our cardiovascular function to respond to constantly changing internal and external environments. The greater your HRV, the more dynamic, flexible, and adaptable you are.

Low HRV has been established as a marker of biological aging and is also associated with increased risk of future health problems and premature mortality.[57] In fact, chronic diseases, including heart disease, cancer, autoimmune conditions, and even behavioral conditions are all characterized by lowered HRV.[58,59] Did you know that labor and delivery units continuously monitor fetal heart rates of the unborn baby? Immediate concerns for the baby's life occur if there are changes to HRV. These changes are the most sensitive and specific measures we utilize to monitor the unborn baby's status, and lifesaving interventions are based on these findings.

As you might have guessed, Cyclic Exercise has been found to improve or maintain healthy HRV. Adopting a Cyclic Exercise program for as little as eight weeks was shown to result in a 9 percent increase in HRV.[60] We will look at this valuable health indicator again in Chapter 6. For now, we can appreciate HRV as a measure of overall health, fitness, and our ability to adapt.

Additional Diverse Findings in Cyclic Exercise Research

A study in the *American Journal of Medicine and Sports*,[61] which found a connection between Cyclic Exercise and healthy heart rate variability (HRV), also found:

- A 15.5 percent increase in VO2 max, a measure of aerobic fitness
- A 7 percent drop in diastolic blood pressure
- Significant improvements in immune defense
- Better sleep and improved mental health

Interval Training: Exercise Induced Growth Hormone Release

CAUTION: This is a taxing form of exercise that can result in injury. You may need weeks to months of preparation and pre-conditioning before attempting this workout. Make sure you find an integrative or regenerative practitioner who has experience preparing people for this type of exercise. Your physician should customize your pre-conditioning program as well as oversee your first attempts at Interval Training, always monitoring heart rate and adjusting performance goals when needed.

Most performance athletes are aware of the ideal exercise regimen components: Strength training, aerobic training, endurance training, hand-eye coordination, and flexibility. Those are the basics. But with my clients, I include three more vital additions. The first two should be familiar to you by now. Let's take a closer look at the third:

- Recovery training
- Hormesis
- Natural growth hormone release

Inactivity is a set up for disease and early demise, and vigorous exercise has tremendous benefits in terms of longevity, reduced cardiovascular risk, and much more. Another powerful component in the exercise equation is anaerobic exercise. **Anaerobic exercise** is quick burst, high intensity activity—such as sprint running, sprint biking, and sprint swimming—at maximal effort and maximal speed. It's the kind of exercise that gets you out of breath quickly. And it's tied to the release of your body's own natural growth hormone (GH).[62] Releasing our own store of GH may be the single greatest goal we can strive for in our exercise programs.

To appreciate the power of GH, consider this summary from a landmark 1991 study done by Daniel Rudman in which they injected GH into men ages 61-80 three times per week for six months. The study found that, "The effects of six months of human growth hormone on lean body mass and adipose tissue mass were equivalent in magnitude to the changes incurred during ten to twenty years of aging."[63] The GH injections effectively left the study participants looking 20 years younger.

I include this study only to demonstrate the power of GH. Of course, anytime we can do something naturally in the body, we should. I have yet to see any health condition managed better in an artificial manner than with the method nature intended. Releasing your body's own supply of GH naturally is no exception to this rule.

By age 45, most of us have 50 percent of the normal levels of vitally important hormones in our cells.[64] Anti-aging medicine is based on the replacement of these deficient hormone levels. Adrenal, thyroid, testosterone, estrogen, and progesterone replacements are appropriate when levels are documented to be low and clinical symptoms are present.

As for GH, most adults rarely release any at all.[65] Endogenous (the body's own natural supply) of GH is the fitness hormone for adults. It is the only known substance that can burn fat and build muscle naturally.[66] No other substance can do this. We are not talking about injecting recombinant GH, which can be dangerous and is a banned substance for all professional athletes.[67] Rather, we are talking about helping the body release its own stored supply of GH from the pituitary gland into the bloodstream. This is no easy task.

Light intensity workouts like walking or jogging, or anything that does not involve a hormetic challenge, will not prompt this release, no matter how long we try. Even though popular lifestyle magazines and blogs frequently tout the benefits of the fifteen-minute walk, low-intensity exercise like this is only slightly better than doing nothing. The reality is, to experience true *disease-reversing* benefits, you need some hormetic challenge in your life. Looking at the most recent research, multiple published studies have concluded that low intensity exercise does little to prevent death from heart disease.[68,69] Only true interval training can tap into the body's GH release system and, in turn, let you access all the metabolic and cardiovascular benefits of a natural GH increase.

When done correctly, it is possible to increase your GH by 530 percent over baseline. GH is released in the body in direct proportion to exercise intensity. That GH level can remain elevated for hours after exercise, serving as a fat-burning and muscle-building catalyst.[70]

It is important to understand the four requirements for the body's natural GH release:[71]

1. **Oxygen debt.** We must make a maximal, or near maximal, effort during our sprint windows; that's exertion that leaves us winded and breathing hard to recover.
2. **Muscle burn.** This comes from intense effort resulting in accumulation of lactic acid in the muscles. We produce lactic acid when our intense exercise exceeds the supply of available oxygen in the muscle.
3. **Increased body temperature**. In fact, if the room is too cold it can stop the GH release.
4. **An adrenal response**. Our adrenal glands release stress-related hormones in response to this sprint-type workout, and this is the final requirement for a natural release of the body's own GH.

Our regimens must be individualized and address: our goals, any physical limitations or setbacks, our energy reserves, and our interests. I have clients who train year-round to stay fit to perform well in the activities they love. Their programs are customized to address all these issues. Given that understanding, it's a "next level goal" to work up to Interval Training and the associated Exercise Induced Growth Hormone Release. It should become a component of your routine if at all possible. But it takes time and pre-conditioning to work up to it. It's imperative that you find the integrative doctor or fitness advisor who can legitimately tell you when you're ready to take the plunge.

What it Looks Like
An "Exercise Induced Growth Hormone Release" protocol

This is adopted from Phil Campbell's Peak 8 workout.[72] You may use any device that allows for quick changes in intensity such as an elliptical trainer or stationary bike. Sprinting works too. After adequate warm-up, you engage in a series of eight intervals:

Performance – Consisting of maximal effort (85-95 percent) for up to 30 seconds
Cooling – Consisting of a 90-second period of reduced exertion at fifty percent effort

This series is completed up to eight times. If you do a three-minute warm-up, your first interval would start when your stopwatch reads 3:00 and run until 3:30. Then you would have 90 seconds to recover until the stopwatch reads 5:00. So, as the workout progresses, at minutes 5, 7, 9, 11, 13, 15, and 17, you would begin your next thirty-second max effort interval.

I know of no one who can make a maximal effort for the full 30 seconds of each of the eight intervals when they first begin this workout. That is fine; the benefits are still occurring. If you can go beyond 30 seconds your first time, most likely you are not making a maximal effort. And max effort is the key.

You will build endurance quickly. You can also help sustain your GH levels for a longer period of time if you limit sugar and other carbohydrates for up to two hours after this workout. It's ideal to work up to incorporating this Interval Training component two or three times per week. This workout is hormesis in action!

We have featured two types of workouts in this chapter. Cyclic Exercise and Interval Training are markedly different. Each offers significant health and medical benefits. Many of my clients incorporate these two workouts on a regular basis in different proportions. Some athletes with major peak performance goals will do Interval Training up to three times per week, while others stress the Cyclic Exercise routines instead. It all depends on your personal goals.

Exercise is perhaps the best-known example of hormesis. We'll explore several other lesser known examples, synergistic combinations of multiple hormetic therapies, and strategies to further maximize hormetic effects. We can layer on different hormetic therapies at the same time to achieve enhanced results for those who are ready and capable of greater challenge. Imagine doing the Interval Training workout with limited carbohydrates in your system, or in a fasted state, or while breathing less oxygen for brief periods. Chapter 7 will explore those advanced and highly personalized challenges.

Meet the Patients Who Have Benefitted

It can be hard to imagine how such brief exercise routines could result in improvements in so many crucial symptoms. Reading the stories about the people who have experienced exercise-related transformation can be far more illuminating than sheer data.

Case Story #1
45-Year-Old Woman Dealing with Severe Fatigue

Terry lived a stressful life as a busy professional, wife, and mother of two small children. She came to see me for fatigue that was worsened by exercise. This was problematic for her since she had always been a sports enthusiast and really valued her exercise time for stress reduction. When questioned further during our intake session, she also noted some irregular sleep patterns for several months. As part of a comprehensive analysis we saw that she was low in both free levels of thyroid hormone (T3 and T4), and her adrenal profile was consistent with a stressed state. Specifically, her Four Point Salivary Cortisol test showed elevations in all samples taken throughout the day. Recall that cortisol ought to be elevated in the morning, but should gradually decline through the day. We also looked at her 30-second recovery from max exertion, as well as other exercise testing. Her heart rate with exercise elevated quickly, remained high throughout exercise, and stayed high too long into her recovery period.

Because of her time constraints, Terry's current workouts mostly consisted of running for about 45 minutes to an hour. I asked her to wear a heart rate monitor during her next run and every time she exercised thereafter, so we could track changes and progress. I have my clients use the Myzone Heart Rate Monitor as I like the fact that it transmits data in real time to a smart phone where it is stored and can be reviewed later on. It negates the need to look at a wrist monitor during exercise. For our purposes here, the bar graph is in black and white. But the real app provides easier-to-read color graphs.

Here is a typical heart rate graph during one of Terry's runs before we began her treatment protocol:

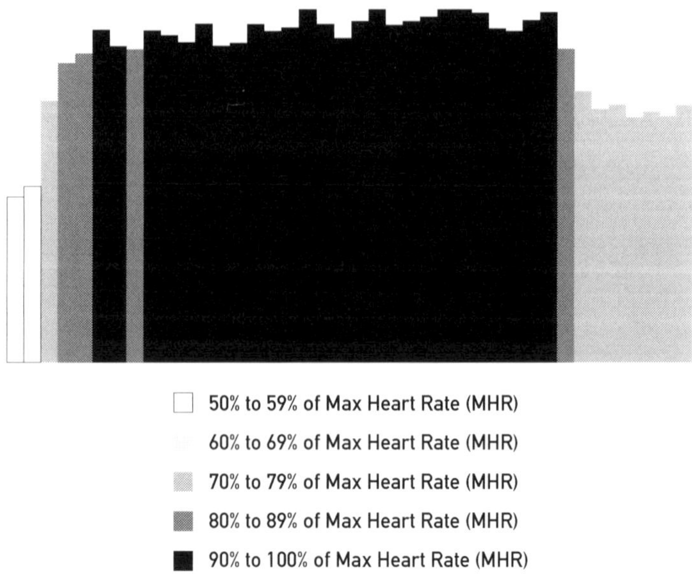

This sustained exertion (solid black) for the majority of the 47-minute workout was not serving her well. While it is good that she could elevate her heart rate into the range of her maximum heart rate, her exercise was further depleting her. We addressed a host of different factors that included dietary and nutritional supplement changes based on feedback from her lab tests. She also started some herbal adrenal support. Then we introduced Cyclic Exercise two to three times per week as the sole exertional exercise activity on those days.

Terry responded well to those changes. She felt stronger and noted a better sleep pattern. To complement her dietary and lifestyle shifts, I also placed her on low dose compounded T3 and T4, which she started taking every morning. Her self-reported energy levels went from a 5 out of 10 to an 8 or 9. She now generates heart rate tracings like the one shown below at least twice a week. What I like the most in the following graph are the two transitions from black to gray—that is hugely significant for anyone, and especially this client. To go from a near max heart rate down to around 70 percent of max heart rate in less than 30 seconds is considered "active recovery".

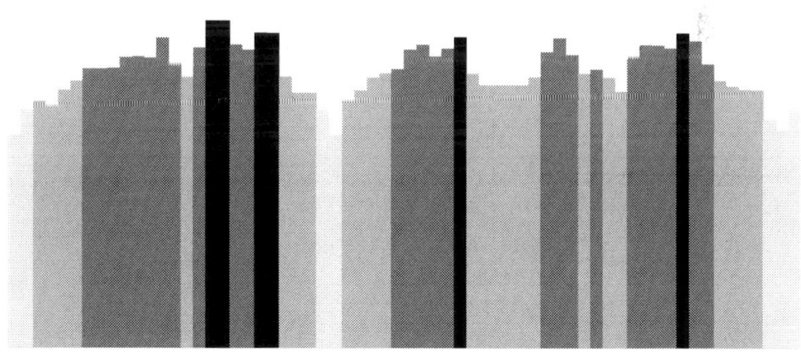

- 50% to 59% of Max Heart Rate (MHR)
- 60% to 69% of Max Heart Rate (MHR)
- 70% to 79% of Max Heart Rate (MHR)
- 80% to 89% of Max Heart Rate (MHR)
- 90% to 100% of Max Heart Rate (MHR)

Case Story #2

54-Year-Old Man with Severe Metabolic Challenges

Chris had a history of hypertension, obesity, and mild sleep apnea. He was active years before, but had no current exercise regimen when he came to me. His wife suggested we meet and talk. I informed him that these were serious conditions and that, if left unaddressed, he was a setup for further deterioration. We talked through the Disease Progression Model shown in the first chapter of this book. He paid the most attention when we discussed medication side effects and confided in me that he was having erectile dysfunction from the antihypertensive medications he was prescribed by another physician. This is a common side effect and a major reason for medication noncompliance. We talked about how an erection is a vascular event under neurologic control, and both hypertension and impaired oxygen delivery from obesity and sleep apnea can interfere with these processes.

Chris was in very poor health, but he was willing to work. That's what matters most. We started slowly. In addition to our targeted nutrition and detoxification approach, he agreed to start with some gentle stretching and quickly progressed to trying hot yoga. The hot yoga was effective and helped him to sweat regularly for the first time in years. We complemented this gentle training with a series of sessions in the ozone steam sauna to support his flexibility and reduce some muscular pain.

It's important to note how long Chris stayed in this preconditioning phase. It took about four months total. Then he was ready to exercise on his own. I started him with Cyclic Exercise three times per week for a month. He felt better, had more energy, and his weight improved. In consultation with his primary care physician and cardiologist, we made reductions in his antihypertensive medications. After a few sessions with a chiropractor, he started to try Exercise Induced Growth Hormone

Interval Training two times per week. Chris was shocked at how challenging this workout was. It took him almost ten weeks to get to the point where he could complete the workout as directed.

The ultimate goal of Interval Training is to perform a 30-second interval at maximum effort for the full-time period. Thirty seconds may not sound like a lot but making a maximal effort for that long is no easy task. The full workout consists of eight such intervals, each separated by a 90-second period of recovery at 50 percent effort. That's not a total rested recovery; you're still moving during those 90 seconds. It's hard!

Interval Training transformed this client's body. Chris lost fat around his middle and developed a much more muscular physique—likely due to the release of his body's own supply of GH. His body mass index (BMI) went from 37 to 31, a very significant change in only six or seven weeks. More importantly, he felt good and enjoyed his improved health. After a year of our working together, he came off both of his blood pressure medications—an impressive accomplishment!

Try It! Incorporating Cyclic Exercise into YOUR Life

Game-changing exercise, low-impact time commitment

While Interval Training is more involved and ought to be pursued only under pro guidance and monitoring, it is possible to experiment with Cyclic Exercise on your own. Always speak with your primary care physician or personal trainer before starting any new exercise routine. If you have any cardiovascular or respiratory challenges, it's crucial that you speak with your doctor before trying Cyclic Exercise.

There are a few modest preparation steps before incorporating Cyclic Exercise into your routine:

- Purchase a heart rate monitor. This tool is a necessity; stopping to take your pulse or trying to take it while exercising only results in errors. You can start with a basic wristwatch style heart rate monitor. I personally use a MyZone monitor, though I've heard that FitBit can provide similar data. The MyZone monitor straps around your chest under your shirt and transmits data to a smart phone. I like this because your phone can be propped up in front of you. The colored bar graphs are visible from several feet away and provide easy-to-read live feedback on your current heart rate zone.
- Decide on your preferred exercise activity—something you can do easily to get your heart rate up to max quickly: stationary bike, elliptical machine, jump rope, or sprinting in place. If you have any joint pain, lower impact exercises will be best (stationary bike or elliptical).
- Determine your target max heart rate: 220 minus your age.
- Determine your resting heart rate while seated before any exertion. This is your baseline.
- Start a performance tracking log in a digital document or notebook. Record your target max heart rate and baseline resting rate on the first page.

Starting out, try Cyclic Exercise only **two times per week**. Work up toward incorporating it three to four times per week. The cycles are simple:

Warm Up: Do a two to three-minute warm-up at a gentle pace. Go longer if you're working out in a cool room.

First Cycle: Head into your first max heart rate cycle. Up your pace to reach towards your max heart rate.

- When you're starting out with Cyclic Exercise, your goal is to simply reach near your max heart rate and then stop—don't continue exertion at your max. (Weeks or months into this program, you might work with your trainer to determine when you're ready for holding max heart rate for 15 to 30 seconds.)

- Whether you hold at max heart rate or not, you should limit the entire exertion phase to no more than a minute.

First Recovery Break: Immediately cease exertion. Sit down on a chair and focus on breathing to bring your heart rate back to baseline.

- Use this time to train your whole self for recovery. Use meditative breathing to calm both mind and heart. The two are entirely connected. Reaching a meditative state at this point in your workout provides powerful whole-person training for your stress response.
- **Log how long it takes for you to return to your baseline.** This is how you'll track your progress. Over weeks of practice, this recovery time will shorten.

Repetitions: Once you've reached baseline, get up and start another max heart rate cycle.

- Your first time trying Cyclic Exercise, repeat the cycles only three or four times. Over the coming weeks, work up to completing five cycles per session.

That's it. The entire routine takes ten to fifteen minutes depending on your baseline recovery times and number of cycles.

Cyclic Exercise & Interval Training

HEALTH GOALS TRIAD

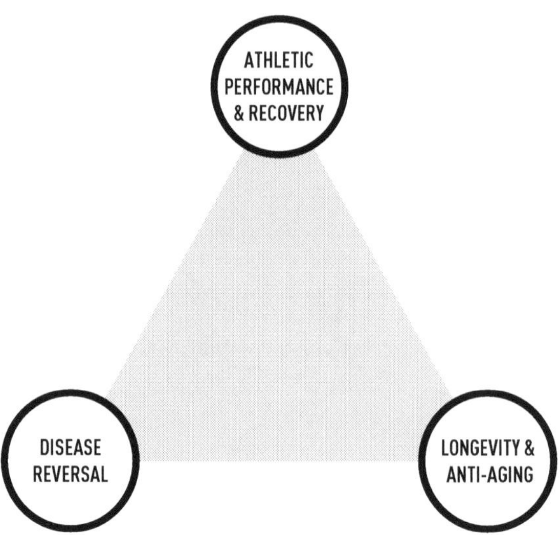

DISEASE REVERSAL Cyclic Exercise and Interval Training are ideal for both preventing and reversing metabolic conditions by engaging the body's innate hormetic response systems. Cyclic Exercise is beneficial for cardiovascular challenges, neurodegenerative disorders, diabetes, chronic pain, and chronic fatigue. Its simplicity makes it perfect for people who have not been exercising recently.

LONGEVITY & ANTI-AGING Cyclic Exercise quickly increases quality of life, and appropriate Interval Training further enhances anti-aging effects. These hormetic exercise forms engage innate antioxidant and repair systems. Interval Training can promote natural human growth hormone release, which benefits joints and muscles, hair and skin, and cardiovascular function, and can also improve overall cellular energy.

ATHLETIC PERFORMANCE & RECOVERY Even performance athletes benefit from Cyclic Exercise and Interval Training. Many endurance athletes are over-trained for exertion. Training for recovery and healthy HRV is key to maintaining heart health. My clients also find Interval Training useful for preventing injury, optimizing immune response, and enhancing performance in the exertion phase too.

SIMPLE EXERCISE ROUTINES TRANSFORM YOUR HEALTH OR REVOLUTIONIZE YOUR CURRENT ATHLETIC TRAINING

Further Science

Read the Research for Yourself

The following provides just a few highlighted studies that can help you expand your understanding of the material in this chapter. Comprehensive chapter References & Notes are found at the end of the book. To read more about these studies, search for "PubMed" online, the world's largest medical library. Reach PubMed directly at: https://www.ncbi.nlm.nih.gov/pubmed/

1.
Pingitore A, et al. "**Exercise and oxidative stress: Potential effects of antioxidant dietary strategies in sports**." *Nutrition.* 2015 Jul-Aug;31(7-8):916-22.

This review article explains how regular moderate training has beneficial effects on oxidative stress and overall health through the principle of hormesis and results in antioxidant upregulation, cellular adaptations, and increasing stress resistance. The authors describe how over-training is shown to result in an over-production of reactive oxygen species. The authors conclude that, since athletic performance is tied to so many different variables including training, adaptation, and mindset, optimal nutrition and supplementation need to be individualized for each person and timed appropriately.

2.
Cadet P. "**Cyclic exercise induces anti-inflammatory signal molecule increases in the plasma of Parkinson's patients**." *International Journal of Molecular Medicine.* 2003 Oct;12(4):485-92.

This study analyzes Cyclic Exercise and its effects on patients diagnosed with the autoimmune condition, Parkinson's Disease. The authors' results show how Cyclic Exercise was effective at reducing chronic inflammation known to be part of the Parkinson's Disease process. Specifically, there were measurable increases in the cellular mediators that are responsible for a reduction in inflammation. Patients also demonstrated enhanced motor skills and mood elevations with Cyclic Exercise protocols.

3.

Stokes KA, et al. "**Growth hormone responses to repeated maximal cycle ergometer exercise at different pedaling rates.**" *Journal of Applied Physiology.* 2002 Feb;92(2):602-8.

This article examines growth hormone release during sprint exercises. Consistent with other literature, a single 30-second sprint window is shown to produce a near-maximal Growth Hormone Release that remains elevated for at least 60 minutes post exercise. This study also provides additional evidence demonstrating that a maximal effort results in more Growth Hormone release than a non-maximal effort. The time frame in which Growth Hormone remains elevated after sprint activity is also presented.

Chapter 3
Oxygen Therapies

HBOT and EWOT for greater energy, anti-aging effects, and optimal athletic performance

Oxygen is essential. We all know that. Every biological activity, including healing of any kind, requires ample oxygen delivery to the tissues. Nothing is more vital to the life process of every cell. The human body can survive a few weeks without food and days without water, but brain function is fully lost within four to six minutes without oxygen. We easily understand that total oxygen deprivation equals death. It seems strange that we don't appreciate that *compromised oxygen* equals *disease*. The reality is, low cellular oxygen is a hallmark of every major degenerative disease.[1-5] Shouldn't we pay attention to that?

In daily life, oxygen supply is nuanced. It's on a continuum, and most of us simply don't get quite enough. We're not going to die today from this compromised supply, but we're not going to thrive either. The body is highly adaptable and capable of coping with sub-optimal situations. That's the reality for most people today. Our environments are not as oxygen rich now as in the past, we breathe in extra pollutants, and our bodies experience a lot more work-related stress on a day-to-day basis. These stressors are compounded by nutrient-poor diets. So, we're chronically in a state in which we need more oxygen, but we're getting less.

Research has confirmed that the amount of available oxygen in our air has been decreasing for millennia, but that decrease has accelerated dramatically in the past century. We're able to assess this through examining the air trapped in the historic layers of Antarctic pack ice. Taking air samples from the prehistoric ice layers, as well as from layers in the past century, and comparing them with air samples from today, it's clear that today's air contains more toxins and less oxygen. We have gone from oxygen levels above 21 percent in prehistoric times, to below 21 percent presently, and certain city environments show readings below 17 percent oxygen.[6,7] Yet, we only provide supplemental oxygen to the sickest of the sick hospitalized patients, the elderly with end stage disease, and elite athletes after extreme exertion.

If oxygen is so good and necessary for these populations at the extreme ends of the health spectrum, why wouldn't it be considered essential for preventive health and vitality? The reality is, whether we are seeking peak performance, longevity, or hope to recover from a disease state, additional oxygen is crucial to accomplish all these goals. Why isn't Oxygen Therapy a major branch of medical specialization, and why don't we have Medical Oxygen Clinics? Some integrative practitioners are beginning to face these questions in the U.S. But trying to bring restorative and empowering oxygen therapies into the mainstream remains challenging. Let's take a closer look at how oxygen is used in the body so we can understand why therapeutic oxygen provides such health-changing breakthroughs.

Oxygen is Essential

No Oxygen = Death

Compromised Oxygen = Pain and Disease

Active Oxygen Therapies = Restored Vitality

Remember that Disease Progression Model, which also shows the path from Disease to Vitality? Everyone exists on this continuum, and your "location" may correlate best with cellular oxygen levels—the amount of oxygen in your individual cells. The higher your cellular oxygen levels, the healthier you are. Conversely, our degenerative diseases are characterized by low cellular oxygen and acidity. To understand that reality, it helps to take a quick review of cellular biology.

Oxygen and Human Metabolism: Your Vital Internal Fuel Burner

Primordial life came about in a low-oxygen environment. Most microbes—bacteria and some fungi—possess *anaerobic* metabolisms. That means they don't require oxygen to thrive; in fact, oxygen can even harm them. They produce their own energy molecules through the process of *fermentation*, which operates best in a low-oxygen environment. Chapter 1 discusses the difference between respiration and fermentation.

The cells in complex mammals, including humans, are totally different. We require oxygen to make the same energy molecule. That energy molecule is referred to as ATP, or *adenosine triophosphate*, which is what cells use to get work done. Scientists and practitioners often refer to ATP as the cell's *energy currency*. Both microbes and animal cells need ATP, but they use different processes to create it. Many microbes use *fermentation*; human cells use *respiration*. This is an important difference. For us, "low oxygen" equals "low energy".

When we experience conditions with compromised oxygen supply, our bodies cope. They have a system for regressing into a lower, primordial-looking state. Our cells start to act like microbes, producing energy, when needed, through fermenting sugars.[8] This is definitely not ideal. Over time, two major challenges ensue when our cells use fermentation to get their energy needs met:

1. **Fermentation itself is inefficient.** It produces less ATP. For example, in a healthy oxygen-based **aerobic metabolism**,

one molecule of glucose will yield **38 ATP molecules.**[9] In **fermentation**, one molecule of glucose yields only **2 ATP molecules.**[10] Low-oxygen fermentation produces only 1/19th of the energy your body really needs. This translates into fatigue and reduced ability to meet all your cells' metabolic needs for repair, growth, immunity, and more.

2. The longer the body relies on fermentation, the more acidic it becomes. The byproducts of fermentation can create an acidic state in the body, called *acidosis.*[11] Acidosis triggers a self-reinforcing cycle of poor health. If a cell is acidic, this actually drives oxygen out of the cell. This happens because an acidic solution can bind only 1/100th of the oxygen that can be bound by an alkaline solution.[12]

You can see the cycle now:

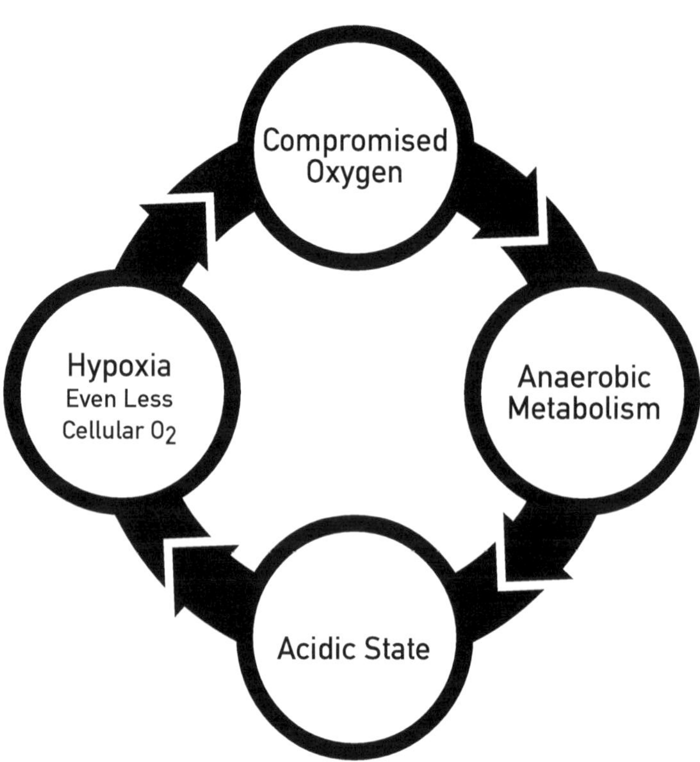

These are subtle changes that occur over years of cellular coping. We're not talking about strangling someone; we're talking about a decades-long fall in cellular oxygen levels. The longer a body remains in this coping metabolism, the greater the susceptibility to pain and disease.

As the body persists in this sub-optimal state, it develops even more coping mechanisms. The body cannot allow tissue acidity to affect the pH of the blood, so the body prioritizes maintaining alkaline mineral balance in the blood first and foremost. That's because deviations in the blood pH can cause death quite quickly. Your ideal blood pH is 7.4 (slightly alkaline), and it's considered a medical emergency if blood pH falls below 7.2. So the body will "rob" bones, connective tissue, muscles, and other tissues to acquire alkaline minerals for the blood.[13]

This self-degenerating process is at the heart of all degenerative diseases—from cancer to heart disease to type 2 diabetes.[14] As tissues become dysfunctional and diseased, cellular oxygen levels fall, acidosis worsens, and tissue breakdown accelerates as part of the degenerative disease process. Reversing a degenerative condition at this point is no easy task. Intensive oxygen therapies can be part of the integrative solution.

Oxygen and Immune Response: Your Natural Pathogen Fighter

We just looked at the difference between how human cells create energy and how anaerobic microbes make energy. That major difference in metabolism results in an interesting side benefit of oxygen therapies.

Unfriendly bacteria and other disease-causing pathogens don't like oxygen. In fact, too much oxygen can kill them. They have no antioxidant systems for dealing with rich oxygen exposure. These microbes definitely prefer low oxygen environments, and when a person is chronically in a state of compromised cellular oxygen levels, it leaves the body more susceptible to microbial infection.[15] Conversely, when patients start intensified oxygen therapies, they will often eradicate chronic low-level infections from unfriendly microbes.[16,17] Oxygen annihilates these problem cells, while it's harmless to healthy human cells.

Interestingly, cancer cells tend to possess anaerobic metabolisms just like lower, primordial life forms. As we explored in Chapter 1, cancer cells thrive in low oxygen situations. We've known this for decades. Otto Warburg was awarded the Nobel Prize in Physiology in 1931 for his discoveries related to the anaerobic nature of cancer cells.[18] For a time, it was believed that this anaerobic activity was the trigger that turned the cell cancerous. Since then, the cancer research community has concluded that the anaerobic metabolism in cancer cells is the *result* of an earlier genetic shift in the cancerous cell, rather than the *cause* of the cancer.[19]

That conclusion turned research to focus more on cancer genetics instead of exploring the possibility of utilizing oxygen therapies to weaken cancer cells. That's unfortunate. While oxygen therapies aren't a cure-all, they can be powerful adjuvants. The logic is pretty simple. Because of its anaerobic state, a cancer cell can't thrive in the presence of oxygen. Saturating that cell with extra oxygen will cause extreme stress and leave it vulnerable. That vulnerability makes other treatments more effective against the cancer.[20,21] Meanwhile the surrounding healthy human cells only benefit from the extra oxygen boost.

Whether we are dealing with mild low-level infections or confronting a challenge as big as cancer, the reality is this: Oxygen therapies are lethal to many of the entities that damage us, but they're totally supportive and safe for healthy cells. There's nothing else in modern medicine that behaves quite like this.

Oxygen and Detoxification: A Built-in Toxin Neutralizer

Oxygen is also needed in our innate detox systems. We often think of the liver, kidneys, colon, and skin as the star players in neutralizing and excreting the toxins we encounter every day. But we don't often think of *how* those organs neutralize the waste products to begin with. Yes, oxygen is involved.

The waste products of normal metabolism and the toxins we encounter each day are excreted through urine, feces, sweat, saliva, and mucous. There are four major components of this waste: Hydrogen, carbon, nitrogen, and sulfur. During waste processing, the body combines each of these four elements with oxygen.

- Hydrogen + Oxygen = H_2O (water)
- Carbon + Oxygen = CO_2 (carbon dioxide)
- Nitrogen + Oxygen = NO_2
- Sulfur + Oxygen = SO_2

Here's the kicker. If these waste products don't combine with oxygen, they don't come out of the body. If they don't leave the body, these toxins begin to stockpile and cause disease. Thus, without sufficient oxygen, waste toxins build up.[22] The body always wants to rid itself of toxins. Compromised oxygen levels delay or halt that natural process.

Oxygen is vital for both transforming food-derived nutrients into energy, and also for assisting with the clean-up stage of metabolism. You might think of it as a healthy forest fire that burns cleanly, releases stored energy, and thins the forest. When you don't have enough oxygen, it's like trying to burn wet wood. It's not a complete burn and there's a lot of ash left.

The Crucial Roles of Oxygen

Oxygen is vital in these primary metabolic and immune roles: [23,24]

- **Energy Production**: Burning food and turning it into energy (ATP) efficiently
- **Waste Clean Up:** Binding and excreting day-to-day metabolic waste products (toxins)
- **Immune Support:** Beneficial to healthy cells, but harmful to unfriendly pathogens and diseased cells

Compromised oxygen levels can lead to: [25,26,27]

- Poor cellular energy and generalized fatigue
- Constant, low-level infections
- Waste toxin build-up
- Degeneration of soft tissue and bone
- Overall predisposition to disease

Can't I Get Enough Oxygen Through Deep Breathing?

The Oxygen Cascade, from the air we breathe to individual cells

The short answer is no. Deep meditative breathing can help a little, but the truth is that most of us simply need more oxygen than the air around us can provide. It's also important to recognize that oxygen levels dilute at over half a dozen points in the journey from the atmosphere to our cells. This is referred to as the Oxygen Cascade.

The heart and lungs work together to circulate the oxygen we breathe. Veins collect oxygen-poor blood and deliver it to the right side of the heart. The blood then enters the lungs, gets oxygenated, and heads to the left side of the heart. The left ventricle pumps that oxygenated blood through the arteries to all of the body's cells, before the process starts over again. All along this complex pathway, oxygen levels continually fall. Multiple stages exist where oxygen levels dilute dramatically from the amount found in the atmosphere.

Oxygen is measured in partial pressures in the body. At sea level, air has a partial pressure of 760. Since air is 21 percent oxygen, oxygen's partial pressure at sea level is 160. This partial pressure measurement drops as oxygen is transported through the body. Looking at these partial pressure figures helps us appreciate how pathology (dysfunction) anywhere along the Oxygen Cascade can result in low tissue levels of oxygen: [28]

- We breathe oxygen from the environment at a partial pressure of **160.**
- We humidify and reduce that oxygen in our trachea down to a pressure of **150.**
- By the time oxygen gets to the alveoli in our lungs, the pressure is down to **105.**
- Oxygen diffuses into the arterial blood supply at a pressure of **100.**
- Oxygen diffuses further into smaller blood vessels (capillaries) with a pressure of **45.**
- There's another round of diffusion to enter our cells, reducing pressure to **10-20.**
- Oxygen pressures in the mitochondria, our energy factories, are in the **single digits**.

Oxygen really is a precious resource in limited supply once it reaches the inside of our cells. These are **normal** reductions as oxygen travels from the environment to our cells. Imagine now if we have issues along that pathway: inflammation, toxicity, or infection. The cascade helps us appreciate how such a vital pathway can be interrupted and severely compromised by disease.

Even in a relatively healthy body, what's in your lungs is not equal to what's in your blood. What's in your blood is not equal to what's in your soft tissues. Then, at the cellular level, you need to have the right fatty acid composition to transport the oxygen correctly.

Essential fatty acids make up 50 percent of our cells' membranes and help shuttle oxygen in and out of each cell.[29] From lungs, to veins, to capillaries, to tissues, to individual cells, oxygen gets depleted at every transition. Oxygen delivery and utilization in the body is a complex and multi-stage process. All those stages present potential setups for disease or dysfunction. That's why active forms of oxygen can have such powerful effects for so many conditions.

Oxygen Utilization Can be Tested

We don't have to guess at how well a body utilizes oxygen. Back in Chapter 1, I mentioned the importance of optimal oxygen utilization and how I test for this regularly as part of my primary health screening for new clients. Remember, the *respiratory quotient* (RQ) refers to the ratio of how much carbon dioxide (CO_2) is exhaled relative to how much oxygen is consumed as an individual progresses from rest into moderate exercise. To test a client's RQ, I use a breathing gas analyzer, a computer program, and a stationary exercise device.

This analysis is exceedingly valuable in assessing an individual's overall health, since it can detect detrimental shifts in oxygen utilization before there are even symptoms of disease. Carbohydrates and fats have different RQs when burned for energy, so RQ data can indicate when a client has shifted from optimal aerobic energy to compromised anaerobic energy production on a cellular level.[30] This test also provides several other useful insights that can help an individual shift from disease to vitality:

- **VO2 Max**: The maximum amount of oxygen consumed as exercise becomes more intense.
- **Maximum Oxygen Utilization**: The maximum amount of oxygen consumed just prior to entering anaerobic metabolism.
- **Anaerobic Threshold:** The moment when exercise intensity surpasses the aerobic system's ability to keep up with the energy demand; lactate levels increase sharply in the blood from the intense muscle use.

- **Maximum Energy Produced from Fat and Glucose:** Ideally we want to burn stored fat as our preferred fuel source. Reductions in fat metabolism are detectable prior to development of disease symptoms or signs of accelerated aging.

These are important measurements that can be followed over time. Knowing these measurements gives my clients an edge in their preventive health protocols and athletic performance goals.

Oxygen Therapies: A Brief Overview and Personal Experience

Oxygen therapies have actually been around for a long time. They can range from inhaled forms, usually through a mask, to hyperbaric oxygen therapy (HBOT), which involves sitting inside a sealed pod of soft fabric or steel, with oxygen or air pumped in. We'll explore these individual therapies more in the next section, but for now it's good to know that hyperbaric principles have been used since the 1600s. Ozone therapy, a more active form of oxygen that we'll cover separately in Chapter 4, has been in use since the late 1800s.

Oxygen therapies have been used for generations. They're well-researched and proven. But the majority of hospitals don't even have HBOT machines. The handful that do, only offer it for fourteen FDA-approved conditions. It's strange to offer HBOT only to these extreme conditions but deny it for the broad range of chronic diseases and infectious states that could benefit. Thankfully, there is a growing community of integrative providers throughout the U.S. who offer diverse oxygen therapies outside the hospital system (see Resources section).

Personally, I began my own education about oxygen therapies more than two decades ago. As a Johns Hopkins trained anesthesiologist, my specialty centers on oxygen delivery. Anesthesia is all about maintaining vital functioning and oxygen delivery during surgical procedures. It's our job to keep patients unaware, safe, and comfortable, and to ensure constant oxygen delivery through a breathing tube or supplemental oxygen. We are constantly assessing the adequacy of oxygen delivery throughout each procedure.

In the early 2000s, I had several family members who had medical problems that weren't improving through conventional medicine. I'd just come out of training at one of the best medical universities in the world. I was baffled that I could not come up with solutions for chronic fatigue, fibromyalgia, and congestive heart failure linked to medication side effects. So, I started to read. I realized I'd had a fantastic education about the nuts and bolts of conventional medicine, but there was a whole world of integrative practice that was completely unknown to me.

My innate curiosity about oxygen eventually led me to HBOT and ozone therapies. In 2008, I sought formal training in ozone administration, regenerative medicine, and HBOT. I've been involved in the integrative community offering life-changing oxygen therapies and other integrative therapies on a private-client basis for more than 10 years. I come from a unique vantage point as both a modern medical and alternative physician who continues to practice both disciplines. Let's take a look at how these specific therapies work and meet some of the clients who've benefitted from them.

Hyperbaric Oxygen Therapy

What is it and how does it work?

What if we could oxygenate body tissues and fluids that don't normally carry significant amounts of oxygen? What if we could boost the amount of oxygen all along the Oxygen Cascade including the most important cellular levels? This would be a proactive and direct step toward combatting underlying problems instead of treating symptoms.

Hyperbaric Oxygen Therapy (HBOT) accomplishes all the above and more. HBOT utilizes the principle of increasing atmospheric pressure to allow all the body's tissues and fluids—including plasma, lymphatic fluid, and cerebrospinal fluid—to absorb additional oxygen.[31] This extra oxygen is available to promote healing, aid detoxification, fight infection, and help the body achieve a state of optimal wellness or *homeostasis*, a balance of all the body's many tasks and processes.[32]

The power of HBOT rests with its ability to bring extra oxygen to all regions including places where our blood circulation has been compromised. Think about that for a moment. HBOT can bring oxygen to places that our body can't. Many medical conditions interfere with our blood supply: infection, inflammation, stroke, peripheral vascular disease, diabetes, poor wound healing, and more. HBOT is not limited by these issues; it enhances oxygenation without reliance on a compromised circulatory system.[33]

HBOT supports oxygen delivery independent of our heart, lungs, and circulatory system. The pressure in an HBOT unit "pushes" more oxygen into body fluids that do not normally carry significant amounts of oxygen.[34] For example, if a patient has a wound or infection that is not healing because of poor or compromised circulation, HBOT can bring oxygen directly to the problem, bypassing the damage and without depending on blood flow from the diseased artery. [35]

Over time, a course of HBOT can help heal damage to the body's tissues. It can encourage *angiogenesis*, the growth of new blood vessels.[36] As you can imagine, this has positive implications for supporting brain health. That includes helping with recovery from stroke,[37] and Traumatic Brain Injury (TBI),[38] along with general support for maintaining cognition and mental clarity.[39]

HBOT is also a powerful therapy for those who are in good health but want to work on enhancing athletic performance and quality of life. Athletes looking for a competitive edge and those seeking longevity and wellness, have turned to HBOT to flood their systems with extra oxygen. The additional oxygen enhances athletic recovery, reduces lactic acid accumulation, reduces fatigue, and supports all of the body's energy requiring tasks.[40,41]

Understanding Hyperbaric Pressure

You've likely heard that the air is "thin" at high altitude. It's not so much that the air is "thinner" but, as the atmospheric pressure decreases with altitude, the partial pressure of oxygen is less, and there is less oxygen available for us to breathe. As we go below sea level, atmospheric pressure increases and the partial pressure of oxygen is increased. Sea level is defined as *one Atmosphere* and each 33 feet of sea water is considered another Atmosphere. As pressure increases, more gas (oxygen) can dissolve in a liquid (body fluids). HBOT works by increasing the pressure surrounding us, which drives and dissolves more oxygen into our body's fluids.

Consider a can of soda. Carbon dioxide gas is dissolved in the soda under pressure. Before opening, the CO_2 bubbles are present, but they are tiny and fully dissolved in the soda. We do not see the bubbles because the pressure has made them small enough to dissolve into the solution. Once we open the can of soda and release the pressure, the volume of each individual bubble enlarges and carbonation appears.

Similarly, during an HBOT treatment, pressure increases and drives more oxygen into our plasma. Our bodies use all the extra oxygen dissolved into our plasma, so there is no concern when the pressure is released. In fact, HBOT can be life saving for those suffering from decompression sickness or the "bends". When people SCUBA dive at depth, the high pressure causes more oxygen and nitrogen to dissolve into their blood. Their bodies consume the additional oxygen, but the additional nitrogen remains. If the diver surfaces too quickly, that nitrogen can bubble out, block small blood vessels, and cause pain. The treatment is HBOT to dissolve the nitrogen back into solution.

Normally, 98 percent of our oxygen is bound to a transport molecule called hemoglobin, found in our red blood cells. Less than 2 percent of our oxygen is dissolved in our plasma.[42] But under hyperbaric conditions, that math changes significantly, as our plasma becomes saturated with oxygen. **This highly oxygenated plasma is molecularly smaller**; it can reach and deliver oxygen to areas that larger red blood cells can't reach. In terms of molecular size, comparing plasma to red blood cells is like comparing a marble to a baseball.

During HBOT, a small amount of oxygen is absorbed directly through the skin, but most of the oxygenation power is in relation to HBOT's ability to drive oxygen into the plasma[43] (See Table 1, later in this chapter). The human body is 70 percent water, and much of that water exists as plasma in the bloodstream. Plasma is also what becomes lymphatic fluid, cerebrospinal fluid, and tissue fluid. It's ubiquitous, everywhere throughout the body. Oxygenating the plasma translates into oxygenating every part of the body. Put simply, HBOT increases the overall amount of oxygen that can be delivered to all body tissues.

A Brief History of HBOT and Its Uses

The first recorded use of hyperbaric therapy actually predates the discovery of oxygen. In the mid 1600s, a British clergyman by the name of Nathanial Henshaw, believed that certain lung conditions could benefit from increased air pressure. In 1662, he designed a sealed chamber and manipulated air pressure in the unit through a bellows.[44]

Oxygen was discovered in 1775, which laid the groundwork for eventual understanding of the medical value of both higher air pressure and supplemental oxygen. In the late 1800s, a hyperbaric operating room was built in Europe, and in 1928, a six-story hyperbaric hospital was built along Lake Erie.[45,46] The more familiar single-person, soft fabric HBOT units were developed in the late 1990s. Today,

HBOT is an FDA-approved medical therapy (for limited uses) and is recognized by both alternative and conventional medicine.[47] Despite its dual discipline acceptance, HBOT remains the most powerful and most underutilized therapy I know of. This is despite ample scientific evidence supporting its efficacy.

Though the FDA has acknowledged several of its uses, HBOT is not commonly used in modern medicine. Its formally approved uses are limited to a handful of rare conditions that the vast majority of us will never experience. But what about blood vessel diseases, strokes, infections, chronic fatigue, and other fairly common conditions that affect millions? Having such a powerful and effective therapy limited to only rare conditions is like refusing to use an available supply of water at the scene of an inferno.

As you can imagine, augmenting oxygen delivery to the tissues has tremendous healing potential. Reviewing the 12,800 HBOT-related published studies found on PubMed, one finds an abundance of information supporting use of this therapy for wide-ranging conditions. Based on this robust research, conventional medicine recognizes HBOT's benefits for these conditions: [48]

Acute mountain sickness
Air or gas embolism*
Anemia (severe)*
Bacterial infections
Brain infections
Carbon monoxide poisoning*
Compartment syndrome
Compromised skin grafts and flaps*
Crush injuries*
Cyanide poisoning
Decompression sickness*
Gas gangrene*
Intracranial abscess*

Osteomyelitis (bone infections)*
Radiation injury*
Soft tissue infections (necrotizing fasciitis)*
Thermal burns (from fire or heat)*
Sudden deafness*
Wound healing (arterial insufficiency)* and diabetically derived illnesses (diabetic ulcers, diabetic foot, retinopathy, nephropathy)
* - FDA-approved use.

Based on hundreds of other studies and clinical reports, integrative practitioners have also successfully utilized HBOT for many more indications including: [49]

Athletic recovery
Autism
Chronic fatigue
Fibromyalgia
Infection
Insomnia
Lyme's disease
Migraine
Neurodegenerative conditions
Stroke recovery
Traumatic Brain Injury (TBI)

Again, we come back to our Disease Progression Model. The amount of cellular oxygen available is a primary factor that allows us to transition from disease to health. The more we augment oxygen delivery, the more we can shift from disease to better function, and then onward to longevity and peak performance.

The HBOT Experience: Chamber Styles and What a Session Feels Like

HBOT units can be designed for one person or for multiple patients at a time. The outer shell can be made of steel, which is much more costly but capable of reaching higher pressures. There are also soft fabric shell options that have the advantage of being transportable and much more affordable. They reach pressures up to 1.3 atmospheres (ATA).

The pressurized gas is a big distinction. Most commercial units are filled and pressurized with 100 percent oxygen. This provides additional oxygen for breathing during a treatment. However, it introduces other concerns, most notably the fact that oxygen is flammable and significant care must be taken to reduce the risk of fire. Specifically, clothing restrictions, make-up restrictions, and lighting restrictions exist for these 100 percent oxygen HBOT units.

I prefer soft fabric chambers pressurized with room air for the vast majority of my clients. These units have no fire risk, there are no clothing restrictions, and they can be set up in a way that offers clients the ability to breathe supplemental oxygen during a treatment. They are safe for home use and easy to self-administer treatments once you have some basic training. I have set-up and trained many clients with this type of unit over the years with no problems.

What it feels like in a HBOT chamber: You don't feel different once pressurized during a HBOT session. Most clients find that they simply feel relaxed and comfortable during a session. However, acclimating to the pressure changes takes a little getting used to. It is like beginning a scuba dive in that you need to equalize pressure across the inner ear as the pressure builds. This is easy to manage by opening your mouth, yawning, or swallowing. For the soft fabric units that pressurize to 1.3 ATA it takes about three to four minutes to reach pressurization, and clients typically need to clear their ears two or three times. With these units, you can always stop or slow the process if you are having difficulty clearing your ears or begin to feel uncomfortable. Once at pressure, clients often read, relax, sleep, or listen to music. There are some activity restrictions placed on units that pressurize with 100 percent oxygen, to avoid fire risk.

Typical treatments take 50 to 60 minutes. Depending on the condition, best results are seen with regular use of at least 4 to 5 sessions per week. Some clients experience such a significant energy boost after treatments they prefer to complete their sessions in the morning. If I experience a busy 24-hour on-call hospital shift and I'm up most of the night, I often sleep in the HBOT chamber for about 90 minutes and then feel functional for the rest of the day until a normal bedtime. That is a powerful endorsement for the rejuvenating effects of this therapy.

Oxygen Cascade Table[50]

This table compares oxygen levels at sea level, at elevation, and in three different HBOT scenarios. As you can see, HBOT offers significant improvements in tissue oxygenation at all levels. These examples are considered mild HBOT conditions, not exceeding 1.5 ATA. In fact, most of the clinical protocols for HBOT therapy rely on pressures in the lower range, typically of 1.3-2.0 ATA. The bottom line of the table reveals that under these mild hyperbaric conditions the dissolved portion of oxygen in our plasma is increased six- to ten-fold over baseline amounts.

	10,000 Foot Elevation	Normal Conditions (Sea Level)	HBOT at 1.3 ATA and 24% O_2	HBOT at 1.3 ATA and 100% O_2	HBOT at 1.5 ATA and 100% O_2
Max O_2 Level mmHg	109	160	237	988	1143
Arterial O_2 mmHg	60	100	149	632	1036
Venous O_2 mmHg	29	39	58	246	404
O_2 in Plasma ml/liter	1.8	3.0	4.5	19.0	31.1

TABLE 1 Based on data from: Treacher DF, Leach RM. "Oxygen Transport-1. Basic Principles." BMJ. 1998 Nov 7; 317(7168): 1302–1306.

HBOT Challenges: Unit size and precautions

It can be challenging to enter an HBOT chamber; the units are typically small, and the soft fabric units can feel claustrophobic. If you do your research, you may also discover something referred to as oxygen toxicity, an extremely rare condition that can adversely affect the lungs, brain, and eyes. However, for this to occur, one would typically need to breathe 100 percent oxygen at 2 ATA for a prolonged period of time.[51,52] Vitality Heath Challenge only utilizes room air to pressurize the hyperbaric chamber, and we do not typically use pressures above 1.75 ATM. I have never seen a case of oxygen toxicity.

As for possible side effects, when I discuss HBOT therapy with clients I like to break down the side effects into two categories—those related to pressure and those related to oxygen.

Pressure Effects: There are a few absolute contraindications for use of a hyperbaric chamber. As prerequisite to any HBOT therapy, you must be able to clear your ears. This can be difficult if you have a cold, sinus infection, active allergies, or an ear infection. You cannot undergo HBOT treatment if you have a collapsed lung (pneumothorax). A very small percentage of patients experience reversible myopia, a slight change in vision from pressure effects on the lens. This side effect usually goes away within a few weeks of completing treatment. It is recommended that patients do not get a new prescription for their eyewear while they are receiving HBOT treatments.

As mentioned previously, HBOT's pressure-driven oxygen can support new blood vessel growth, called *angiogenesis*. This is advantageous in many medical conditions, but contraindicated (not advisable) for known soft tissue tumors. Patients with known cancerous tumor masses are encouraged to avoid HBOT and use another oxygen therapy instead, such as ozone (See Chapter 4).

Oxygen Effects: Oxygen is flammable and care must be taken whenever high amounts of oxygen are used in a closed space. This represents additional challenges for hospital/commercial units, and any other HBOT units that are pressurized with 100 percent oxygen. The practitioner must advise on spark resistant clothing, avoidance of flammable hair and makeup products, and lighting concerns.

In all, HBOT is a highly effective therapy with minimal risk when used with proper safeguards. Restricting the degree of pressurization to under 2 ATA and using room air as opposed to 100 percent oxygen further reduces the risk profile.

EWOT: Combining Oxygenation and Exercise

Another powerful oxygen therapy is called Exercise with Oxygen Therapy (EWOT). In this therapy, we are exercising while breathing additional oxygen. In some ways, EWOT is more powerful than HBOT, as it relies on the body's own circulatory system to deliver much more oxygen than normal while exercising. It's a completely natural therapy since we are augmenting our circulatory system to transport more oxygen to the body's tissues.

Recall that the air we breathe contains 21 percent oxygen. Now imagine breathing 100 percent oxygen while exercising. That's almost five times as much oxygen as we normally breathe. We also have to consider the exercise component. When we exercise, we increase our cardiac output two to three times more than when at rest. When you combine a nearly five-fold increase in oxygen with a doubled or tripled cardiac output, EWOT has the ability to deliver ten to fifteen times the amount of circulating oxygen that we normally experience. That is a huge oxygenation effect—even more than mild HBOT.

Not all EWOT systems are the same. Using just a five-liter oxygen concentrator with a nasal cannula will not allow for the profound oxygenation increases described above. You need a specialized set-up to accomplish this degree of oxygenation:

1. A large reservoir bag that can hold more than fifty liters of oxygen
2. One or two oxygen concentrators each capable of putting out at least ten liters of oxygen per minute
3. A large diameter anesthesia-style closed breathing circuit and facemask to accommodate breathing large volumes of oxygen during strenuous exercise

Why is this specialized system so effective? Recall the Oxygen Cascade showing the continual fall in oxygen levels as oxygen is transported into the body's cells. The beauty of EWOT rests with its ability to offer supercharged, highly oxygenated, and high velocity blood throughout our entire vascular system. In the process, we are flooding our tissues with the greatest and most natural anti-inflammatory molecule: oxygen. I personalize this work with clients, assessing basic exercise capacity, understanding limitations, and developing appropriate protocols to support each client's individual goals.

You do not need a lot of time to get major benefits. Incorporating EWOT two to three times per week can help maintain higher levels of oxygen in our tissues on a permanent basis.[53] Remember that low levels of oxygen are part of the degenerative disease cycle, leading to the downward spiral of disease. EWOT is one of the most natural and enjoyable ways to reverse disease progression and head toward vitality.

EWOT and Hormesis

It's the great paradox of complex life: We must have oxygen to live, and yet the body's use of oxygen inherently produces free radicals—the tiny highly active particles that can cause cellular damage. In popular health media, free radicals get a bad rap. They're considered purely damaging. *Oxidative free radicals* should be combatted with a diet rich in antioxidant foods, right? Well, yes. But in reality, the free radical-antioxidant relationship in the body is more like a dance than a war. We actually need some free radicals to trigger certain useful processes in the body. This is the heart of hormesis.

Oxygen free radicals are inherently hormetic. Our cells use oxygen, free radicals are a natural byproduct. Those normally-occurring free radicals create a moderate stress in the body that's actually a good thing. Healthy free radicals encourage cells to adapt, improve themselves, and increase their resistance to stress.[54] This is the definition of hormesis. In fact, many of the effects we see with HBOT are due to signaling from *reactive oxygen species* (ROS), which leads to positive changes in gene expression. That ROS signaling can also increase activity of the mitochondria—the organelles that make energy for every cell. Any oxygen therapy has at least a slight hormetic quality because of this reality. But we also have the option to further enhance the hormetic effect of EWOT.

Hormetically-Enhanced EWOT: The following is a medical procedure and peak performance training tool that should only be offered with oxygen saturation monitoring, heart rate monitoring, and medical supervision. I work with clients for some time before we consider this as a possible therapy. The personalized variations are endless.

When we breathe high amounts of oxygen while exercising, our bodies tend to relax because there is so much oxygen available. This is not a bad thing—it's an appropriate response to high amounts of oxygen. We can use that innate response to our advantage. Our EWOT systems offer a switch and a separate reservoir, which allows us to instantly change to a low oxygen setting for a brief amount of time. We can switch to an oxygen level that mimics a high altitude, lower oxygen environment.

Imagine that you have exercised while breathing high amounts of oxygen for five minutes. Because of the extra oxygen, your body is warmed up, but not significantly challenged even though you are exercising. We can now switch to a low oxygen setting and, for a brief time, you breathe air that contains only half the normal amount of oxygen. This is an immediate hormetic stressor. Within a few seconds, heart rate increases, and the work of breathing increases. You are quickly challenged. Significantly so.

Depending on the client's goals, medical history, age, heart rate, performance in the moment, and the oxygen saturation level, I may allow the client to breathe low oxygen for up to 30 seconds. It's hard work, but worth it. The rewards come when we switch back to 100 percent oxygen. Because of that 30 seconds of mild deprivation, now the client's heart and lungs are working hard and cardiac output is near maximal. With the fresh burst of 100 percent oxygen, high speed, high velocity, fully oxygenated blood is being pumped hard throughout the body, deep throughout the vascular network.

Imagine for a moment how most of us feel when we are winded from exertion. Our brains are often not focused, our breathing is challenged, our bodies are fatigued. All that changes quickly when you now circulate more oxygen than most of us have ever been exposed to. We feel great, often elated. We can focus differently. The fatigue fades. At the cellular level, all that high-speed oxygenated blood is delivering oxygen and removing waste in a profound manner. This is hormesis in action. After one or more low oxygen challenges, I always make sure to end this therapy with at least five minutes of mild to moderate exercise, then full recovery, on the high oxygen setting.

I want to stress that this is a specialized hormetic therapy, intensely challenging, and not for everyone. Regular, high oxygen EWOT can be used as often as you like with almost no downside potential. But these low oxygen challenges are typically implemented only once per week, unless I am working with a high-level younger athlete with a specific training goal. Chapter 7 will discuss this workout in much more detail.

HBOT and EWOT have different indications. Both are powerful oxygen therapies with significant healing and wellness potentials. In my practice, I often reserve HBOT for more established disease conditions or for clients who are not able or ready to exercise. EWOT and EWOT with Hormetic Challenge are superb for wellness, peak performance, athletic recovery, and for conditions in which exercise is not contraindicated. I also use EWOT as an athletic recovery tool. After a long run, or after a few days of strenuous activity, we often have accumulation of lactic acid in our muscles. A quick EWOT session can help wash out those waste products that otherwise would take the body a day or two to process. Oxygen is the ultimate waste remover.

Meet the Patients Who Have Benefitted

Oxygen therapies involve complex technologies, but their effects are based on core natural health principles. Complex multi-cellular organisms need oxygen to thrive, and today we simply don't get enough to meet our body's demands for maintenance, repair, and growth. Oxygen therapies can have major real-life implications for recovery from injury or disease and living at our best. Only case stories can make those implications come alive.

Case Story #1

Competitive athlete recovering from severe head injury

Randy is a competitive athlete who was hit by a car while biking. He sustained a closed head injury but made a full recovery—almost. When Randy began to work out again, he experienced an unusual limitation. As soon as he began to exercise vigorously at maximum effort, he would pass out. He had been to the two university hospitals in his town and seen many specialists. No one was able to solve his problem. I had heard about his situation from a mutual friend and asked a few questions. I wanted to know if he had any other current medical problems and what had been tried to date. Once I learned that he was otherwise healthy and I understood his present care, I made a rare and bold prediction that I could be helpful, and I did so prior to even meeting him.

Those close to me know that I never promise clients anything, and I almost never make predictions. My experience has taught me that it is crucial to not give false hope. But it is equally important to never limit a client's recovery potential either. So I never say to a client that any medical condition cannot be improved. Let me explain why I was so confident in Randy's case.

Often when people experience a brain injury with residual symptoms there is a portion of brain cells that are dead and that will never recover. But encircling the region of dead cells, are patches of cells that are alive but not functional. This area is called an "ischemic penumbra." This refers to an area around a stroke or injury that does not have enough blood flow to be functional, but remains otherwise intact. These "halo" cells are in a state of suspended animation. I knew the literature about this phenomenon. I also knew that HBOT had been effective at helping certain stroke patients regain neurologic function even long after their strokes.

Stroke and traumatic brain injury (TBI) have a lot in common. Both involve physical damage to brain cells and oxygen-starved regions. I viewed Randy like a stroke patient with one big exception—he was otherwise totally healthy, since his "stroke" was caused by an external injury. And the fact that Randy passed out with exertion told me that the problem area in his brain was simply not getting enough blood flow during the added strain of exercise. At rest he was fine; the injured area was not as stressed, and he could meet the oxygen demand possibly from collateral blood flow (from surrounding blood vessels). However, as the oxygen requirements increased with exercise, the compromised blood supply became inadequate to meet the demand of the area of his brain responsible for maintaining consciousness.

I knew that HBOT could oxygenate compromised areas of the body and, even more importantly for Randy, help to regrow new blood vessels over time. I also knew Randy was an athlete and had otherwise great health. These two facts allowed me to offer such a high level of confidence to Randy even though he had "tried everything". Randy was set up with a soft fabric HBOT unit in his home. He was trained and instructed to use it at least five times per week for at least 45 minutes each session.

Only ten days into this treatment protocol, Randy let me know he felt like he could push himself harder. He knew something was different. I had to remind him, "It's still important to keep your heart rate below 145 and pay close attention to your own sense of max effort. We don't want you to actually hit that point where you pass out again." As exciting as this immediate progress was, I wanted him to stay safe! He diligently reined himself in and kept to about 80 percent of max effort.

From week four to week eight, Randy continued his HBOT protocol and gradually began to increase his exercise exertion to what we considered 90 percent of max effort. He had no problems with that. After three months of regular HBOT treatments,

Randy's problem was fully solved. He was overjoyed. His wife told me that I had given him the greatest gift possible—the return of his ability to exercise and train as he likes, including sustained max effort. As Randy put it, he "couldn't believe this technology wasn't more available and well-known." Many viewed his case as a miracle. There are countless other potential miracles out there just waiting to happen!

Case Story #2

72-year old suffering from massive trauma and infection after car accident

Brad was a 72-year-old who was involved in a motor vehicle accident. He sustained many injuries, the most severe of which was an open fracture to the jaw bone. Open fractures occur when bone is exposed through the skin. There is increased risk for infection with this type of fracture and emergent or urgent surgery is needed. During Brad's initial surgery, a plate and screws were put into the lower jaw bone to reconstruct and hold the many injured pieces together. To ensure proper healing, his jaw was wired shut. He would not be able to eat normally for weeks.

I saw Brad in these earliest stages. My initial work consisted of helping with IV and oral nutrition to support his recovery. His condition worsened when we learned that his jaw bone was infected with MRSA. This is a dangerous hospital-acquired bacterial infection that is resistant to antibiotics. Now Brad's condition was much more dangerous. He was infected, his implanted hardware was failing, and powerful antibiotics were not working. His surgeons took him back to the operating room twice to attempt to clean out the infection deep in the bone. The primary problem was that the surgeons could not remove enough bone to cure the infection, and each time he returned to the operating room his healing started all over.

His doctors had nothing new to offer. At this point I informed Brad's wife that his best chance was to do a course of Hyperbaric Oxygen Therapy to address two main threats:

First, we needed to clear the infection, which was deep in the bone and preventing new healthy bone growth from interfacing with the hardware to stabilize the fractures.

Second, Brad was showing signs of the infection spreading to the soft tissues around the neck and possibly spreading into the bloodstream, meaning threat of sepsis, a dangerous systemic infection.

This was serious. It was clear that Brad was deteriorating. His condition was now life-threatening, and his nutrition was so limited because of his injury. His body wasn't getting the building blocks it needed for normal life, let alone fighting this severe infection. Multiple surgeries to remove infected tissue were not the best option—especially in someone who was now so vulnerable to any more trauma. He wasn't going to survive if something didn't change fast.

His university physicians were actually resistant to the idea of HBOT. Nevertheless, I helped his wife arrange for the HBOT services. Brad completed a seven-week course of HBOT sessions at 1.5 ATM at least five days per week. After the first few sessions he was able to tell that something was "different". He described it as a sense of comfort both in the unit during each treatment and afterwards. He felt stronger, slept better, and his appetite improved although he was still only consuming smoothies.

Then, he really made a turn for the best. He had two drains at the surgical sites, and within the first week of HBOT treatment, the drainage from the incisions began to turn clearer. There was less redness in the tissue at the surgical sites. He reported less pain across the whole jawbone. All were signs that the infection was responding to the HBOT treatment. By the second week, the redness was completely gone. His conventional physicians had the drains removed, and the incisions were able to close on their own without further stitching. The enhanced oxygen levels were clearly promoting healing in addition to helping resolve the infection.

By the third week, cultures showed that the antibiotic-resistant MRSA infection had, indeed, fully cleared. Within a month, new healthy bone growth was occurring for the first time. Brad and his wife were so surprised and appreciative that this one therapy had completely shifted his failing condition. He was truly brought back from the brink.

Case Story #3
Middle-aged man struggling with multiple metabolic health challenges

Jeff came to see me after his annual medical exam with his primary care doctor. His blood pressure was elevated, despite his medication, and his weight was up. He also struggled with lower back inflammation and tightness. Jeff wanted to address all this and more, but he wanted a natural approach. He stated that he was willing to work if I told him what to do.

In our initial conversation, we identified several areas to focus on. Jeff believed that he could overcome a lot with exercise. As we toured the Vitality Health Challenge Clinic, I demonstrated how some of the equipment and training tools work to restore health naturally. Watching Jeff work out and try some of the equipment gave me an opportunity to assess his conditioning, strength, and flexibility.

He was drawn to the EWOT type device and wanted to know more. I told him that whole-body oxygenation combined with exercise could help many of the health problems he was facing. We discussed how using the body's natural pumping mechanisms to circulate more than ten times the amount of oxygen usually in our system had far-reaching effects. Jeff appreciated how high velocity and highly oxygenated blood combined with exercise could reduce inflammation all throughout his vascular system. He also understood that his elevated blood pressure, cholesterol dysfunction, and back pain were all caused by inflammation. We discussed how these conditions seemed unrelated, but actually had common ties.

Jeff started a program that involved EWOT, intermittent fasting (Chapter 5), Prolozone injections (Chapter 4), and some more specialized work to address his lower back tightness. Ultimately, the synergy of all these treatments fostered his whole life transformation. But EWOT produced the most encouraging benefits early in the process. Jeff said he experienced a brief euphoric feeling immediately after the first session. I explained that doing EWOT regularly over time would increase oxygen levels throughout his body in a more lasting fashion. EWOT could deliver oxygen to some of his most oxygen-starved tissues. As a result, his overall day-to-day energy levels should go up. Over the next few months, that's exactly what happened.

Jeff committed to working out at least three times a week and also used our specialized saunas post-workout to further reduce his back tightness. After only two months, he began to feel that general increase in energy and a significant reduction in pain. He wondered how oxygen therapies could provide anti-inflammatory effects—even better than aspirin or NSAIDs. I explained that all the components that make up smog (hydrogen, carbon, nitrogen, sulfur) are the same waste products that the human body produces. The body desperately needs to excrete these wastes, and it does so by first binding them to oxygen. "If those wastes aren't combined with oxygen, they accumulate," I said. "And as toxins accumulate, they cause pain and disease." Providing extra oxygen helps the body clear waste from chronically inflamed areas. That leads to general pain reduction, without side effects.

"Why did they give me drugs first?" he asked. "The side effects kept me from exercising, which is what I needed to do in the first place."

It's always hard for me to answer that question. The reality is that most of conventional medicine is set up on a profit-from-disease model. Jeff should have been placed on natural therapies first. In my opinion, prescribing pharmaceutical medication as first-line therapy is a true disservice to most patients with metabolic and inflammatory health conditions.

Ultimately, Jeff was able to stop his blood pressure medication and had greatly improved energy. We set him up with some home equipment to further incorporate oxygen therapies into his training, which he continues on his own. He is a prime example of using natural therapies to restore total health, instead of constantly medicating symptoms and coping with side effects.

Try It! Incorporating Oxygen Therapies into YOUR Life

High tech therapies with an option for the DIY health hacker

CAUTION: Always discuss new exercise programs with your current physician, or look in our Resources section for a clinic that specializes in oxygen therapies. You'll want personalized professional guidance to create an EWOT exercise program that works best for you, keeps you safe, and helps you meet your health goals.

HBOT definitely requires partnership with a professional medical provider. Even if you invest in a soft-sided home unit, you'll need training from a pro on how to use it safely. EWOT, on the other hand, can be accessed and utilized by anyone. It's possible to purchase an EWOT oxygen concentrator and facemask system from online manufacturers and distributors. The Resources section provides a few reliable sources for you to research.

The best benefit will come from a high-flow oxygen concentrator that supplies 8 to 10 liters of oxygen per minute, paired with a non-re-breather facemask, or a facemask with a large reservoir bag. Having a large reservoir to pull oxygen out of at peak effort makes a big difference in terms of tangible oxygenation benefits. Make sure your system also comes with one-inch diameter tubing to connect the reservoir bag to the mask, to ensure you get to inhale appropriate air volumes.

There are low-flow units available that supply less than five liters of oxygen per minute. They supply oxygen through a small cannula that sits in the nose. This results in delivery of only about 2 to 3 liters of oxygen per minute. The actual benefits are definitely compromised with these lower quality systems.

For those capable of exercising on their own, a high quality EWOT system is a great way to experience an oxygen therapy at home. Most people use their EWOT system while working out on a stationary bike. This is definitely the easiest setup. There's no real downside to using EWOT, whether you're pedaling gently to warm up or exercising hard. If a client is fully unable to exercise, I do recommend utilizing HBOT or ozone first. But the hope is always that they can work up to EWOT.

Oxygen Therapies
HEALTH GOALS TRIAD

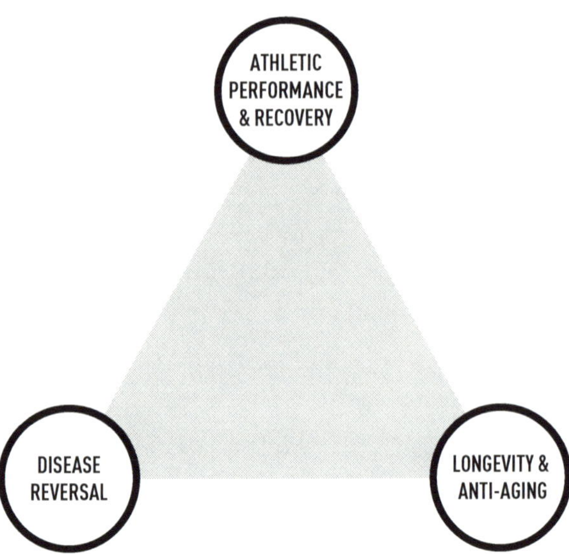

DISEASE REVERSAL Human cancer cells and our degenerative diseases thrive in low oxygen environments. Oxygen therapies can be game-changing additions to immune-support protocols. Oxygen therapies are also vital for helping the body rebuild after major trauma and injury—from restoring connective tissue injuries to helping the brain awaken and rewire after injury and stroke.

LONGEVITY & ANTI-AGING Oxygen therapies provide endless anti-aging benefits. These therapies readily enhance quality of life through an overall energy boost. Key to cellular metabolism, oxygen affects the energy and function of every body system. These hormetic therapies also help build our stress resistance and resiliency. This benefits cardiovascular health, the musculoskeletal system, cognitive function, dermal health, and more.

ATHLETIC PERFORMANCE & RECOVERY Many performance athletes already utilize oxygen therapies for post-exertion recovery and performance. Oxygen is just as valuable in post-injury protocols to promote healthy tissue repair. It's key for detoxing and clearing lactic acid build-up. EWOT can also tap into a highly hormetic state that boosts endurance and performance.

HBOT AND EWOT ENHANCE ENERGY, PROVIDE ANTI-AGING EFFECTS, AND BOOST ATHLETIC PERFORMANCE

Further Science
Read the Research for Yourself

The following provides just a few highlighted studies that can help you expand your understanding of the material in this chapter. Comprehensive chapter References & Notes are found at the end of the book. To read more about these studies, search for "PubMed" online, the world's largest medical library. Reach PubMed directly at: https://www.ncbi.nlm.nih.gov/pubmed/

1.
Kahle AC, Cooper JS. **Hyperbaric, Physiological And Pharmacological Effects of Gases.** © 2018, StatPearls Publishing LLC. Creative Commons Attribution 4.0 International License. Bookshelf ID: NBK470481.

This e-book provides a basic scientific understanding of hyperbaric oxygen therapy, pointing out that plasma oxygen levels can reach more than 20 times the levels we normally obtain breathing room air. The authors also discuss known mechanisms of HBOT which include angiogenesis (new blood vessel formation), reductions in tissue edema (swelling), and modulation of the immune response. The article also notes that when oxygen is pressurized and used to treat disease, it is classified as a drug and subject to proper dosing protocols, a therapeutic index, and side effect profiles that must be respected.

2.
Rossignol DA, Rossignol LW, Smith S, et. al. "**Hyperbaric treatment for children with autism: a multicenter, randomized, double-blind, controlled trial.**" *BMC Pediatrics.* 2009; 9:21. Published online, March 13, 2009.

For many years, parents of autistic children have believed that HBOT is the single most effective therapy for their children. However, prior to this investigation, there had never been a double blind and controlled study looking at HBOT's efficacy for autism. It is important to point out that the hyperbaric treatments used in this study were at 1.3 ATM and 24% oxygen, demonstrating again the effectiveness of mild HBOT therapies and room air pressurization. Autistic children who received the HBOT treatments demonstrated significant improvements in overall functioning, receptive language, social interaction, eye contact, and sensory/cognitive awareness compared to autistic children who did not receive the HBOT treatments. This study design is the gold standard of medical research.

3.

Efrati S, Fishlev G, Bechor Y, et. al. "**Hyperbaric Oxygen Induces Late Neuroplasticity in Post Stroke Patients - Randomized, Prospective Trial.**" *PLoS One.* 2013; 8(1): e53716. Published online 2013 Jan 15.

This article discusses how most stroke rehab programs are only partially successful and a need exists to focus on new therapies, like HBOT, to target the stunned areas of brain tissue that can exist around the area of a stroke. The article explains that these non-functional but alive areas can remain for years after the original stroke. The authors point out that hyperbaric pressure provides the key element required to repair these stunned areas of the brain. This study is among the first to demonstrate that HBOT provided significant clinical improvement in neurologic function post stroke and encouraged *neuroplasticity*, the ability of the brain to reorganize synaptic connections following injury.

Chapter 4
Ozone Therapies

The least understood but most health-changing therapies

In 2015, international soccer sensation Christiano Ronaldo suffered a patellar tendon injury that was clearly affecting his performance. Ronaldo had played for Manchester United and Real Madrid, as well as the Portuguese national team. Noted by *Forbes* as the highest paid professional athlete in 2017, clearly he could arrange for any medical care needed to address his injury.[1] The professional sports rehab community was definitely intrigued when Ronaldo choose to utilize *ozone therapy.* He not only fully recovered, he went on to win the FIFA Best Player award in both 2016 and 2017.[2]

It's time to shed some light on this unique "activated oxygen" therapy.

Of all the alternative modalities I've researched, ozone therapy is the most misunderstood and potentially the most therapeutic. The difficulty begins with confusion over what ozone actually is. Patients and practitioners alike usually regard ozone therapy with great skepticism at first, often asking, "Isn't ozone a chemical in air pollution?" That question is a good opportunity to clarify several matters.

First of all, ozone is simply O_3—three oxygen molecules bound together, albeit in an unstable union—as opposed to the more common O_2 form of oxygen in the air all around us. Even though it is unstable, ozone is actually naturally-occurring in the environment. It's responsible for the sweet smell in the air after lightning storms. It occurs near highly charged moving water, such as waterfalls and ocean waves. Ozone is concentrated in the stratosphere, the upper layer of the earth's atmosphere, and protects us by filtering out some of the sun's harmful UV radiation.[3] As a bluish tinted gas, ozone is responsible for the natural color of our daytime sky.

Ozone is also naturally present in our bodies. The immune system makes ozone in some of its reactions. Like all naturally-occurring molecules in the body, there are appropriate levels for ozone. Believe it or not, even water and salt have levels at which they are considered dangerous. The body tightly regulates water and salt, and severe consequences result if the concentrations deviate in either direction from the safety zones. Similarly, ozone has its own safety range. But ozone itself is not a toxin. Ozone's unfortunate connection to toxic pollution readings is misleading, but also easy to clarify.

When we burn carbon-based fuels, there are several highly toxic byproducts. When the sun's rays interact with some of those air pollution chemicals, ozone can be formed. Therefore high ozone levels in urban air tend to indicate the presence of dangerous smog levels. But it's not the ozone component that causes health problems—it's the hydrocarbons and nitric acids that are trouble. Ozone is simply a "flag" that's easier to measure than all the other components of smog. Unfortunately cautions about high ozone levels have translated into a guilt-by-association relationship for ozone.[4] Far too many people hear the term "ozone" and immediately think "toxin."

Nothing could be further from the truth. At correct and strategic dosages, ozone provides the benefits of oxygen therapy, in a more focused and longer-acting fashion.[5] Let's look at how ozone interacts with the body at a molecular level.

How Ozone Works

You might remember that the surface of each human cell is covered with receptors. The common analogy provided in school is that of the key that fits in a lock and opens a door. A natural hormone or a synthetic drug can "fit" into one of these receptors. Once latched onto the receptor, it causes an immediate change in the cell's activity. Much of the pharmaceutical world depends on these simple cause-effect receptor relationships. The concept is referred to as a Direct Mode of Action.

Ozone does not fit that model. That might be one of the reasons the medical world finds it so startling. There is no cellular receptor for ozone. It doesn't bind to cells. Its activity involves multiple "direct" and "indirect modes of action", but none of them involve a cell receptor-based effect.[6]

Still, you don't need a PhD in molecular biology to get the basics. Ozone therapy acts in two routes. The first involves **direct oxidation** with immediate tangible effects on pain and inflammation. The second route is through an **indirect chain reaction** in the body causing a cascade of effects that can last for several days, after a single treatment.

Ozone's Immediate Direct Effects: Ozone is an *oxidant.* This means that it is highly charged and energetic and can easily donate its extra molecule of oxygen. As we mentioned in Chapter 3, oxidation is not always bad. In fact, most oxidative reactions are exceptionally good and necessary. Oxidation is how you turn your morning smoothie into cellular energy. Every bodily function requires oxidation reactions. All the food we eat gets oxidized, broken down into smaller components that can be used in individual cells.

Ultimately those oxidative steps convert food into ATP, which is the body's energy source at a cellular level.[7] ATP is the energy currency that the body uses for all its metabolic goals, from movement to repair, from immune function to protein synthesis. That's why your body absolutely requires oxygen every minute of your life.

Oxygen and oxidation are crucial to life. Got it. Now, back to ozone, as a form of oxygen. That third oxygen molecule in ozone is unstable and ultra-ready to launch off to donate itself in an oxidative reaction. So, in the initial minutes of an ozone therapy treatment, multiple oxidizing reactions occur in fast sequence.

When focused on a joint or muscle group affected by chronic pain and inflammation, **the extra oxygen molecules immediately oxidize pain and inflammatory mediators**, the chemicals at the root of the sensation of pain. In chronic pain, the body gets "stuck" in a cycle of producing these inflammatory mediators. The pain itself causes more irritation, which results in more inflammatory mediators, which fuels continued pain, and so on. Oxidizing the mediators immediately halts their activity.[8]

Depending on the administration method, **ozone's initial activity can also oxidize microorganisms like bacteria and viruses**. While human cells have systems for managing and recovering from oxidation, microbes do not. Research has found that ozone's ability to oxidize pathogens provides an efficient leg-up for the immune system cells, which can jump straight to playing clean up on the neutralized threat.[9]

None of these reactions involve cell receptors, but they are still considered *direct modes of action*. That's because they are immediate and can produce a tangible change in pain level and immune status within minutes. These effects occur as soon as ozone comes into contact with biological systems.[10]

Ozone's Long-acting Indirect Effects: Ozone has even more impressive Indirect Modes of Action. These indirect activities explain how ozone can have such profound and long lasting effects in our tissues. After the initial direct oxidation reactions, ozone continues to interact with other molecules in the body. Through lengthy chain reactions, it combines with *messenger molecules*. These are substances that influence the activity of red blood cells, white blood cells, platelets, bone marrow cells, the endothelial cells that line our blood vessels, and more.[11]

Ultimately, these messenger molecule chain reactions result in several powerful shifts throughout the body:

- A moderate uptick in free radical levels – Similar to free radical production during and after moderate exercise (potentially hormetic)[12]
- Heightened production of the body's super antioxidants, including glutathione [13]
- Increase in genetic expression (transcription factors) involved in cell repair and regeneration[14]
- Immune cell activation and stem cell release[15]
- Improved function of mitochondria, the energy-production factories in every cell[16]
- Heightened levels of growth factors[17]
- Increased nitric oxide (NO), which dilates blood vessels and improves oxygen delivery to all tissues[18]

Look back at that first bullet. At the beginning of the cascade is, once again, that principle of *hormesis*. Ozone, like exercise and oxygen, definitely has a hormetic quality. Like all hormetic therapies, the amount of exposure is key. Too much ozone and you get excess oxidation in the body. But when the dosage is optimal, you hit that *hormetic ideal* that upregulates all of the body's systems for repair, regeneration, and strengthening.

As you can also see in the list above, ozone is not a single-molecule-single-effect therapy. Its effects are broad—not just systemic, but *multi*-systemic. Ozone influences the activities of cells throughout the body, though not in a cell receptor-based fashion. Instead it changes the foundational chemistry of the body in multiple complex chain-reactions.[19] That's why it can convey benefits for so many diverse conditions and continue its effects for days, or even weeks, after a single treatment.

Ozone therapy results in increases in oxygen delivery, immune activation, release of growth factors, and even release of stem cells.[20] While it is not imperative to understand all the science involved when ozone interacts with body systems, it is crucial to appreciate that this is a truly unique molecule with profound and far-reaching effects. It is equally important to understand that these effects are natural and consistent with how our biochemistry is designed to function. When we use ozone for medical purposes, we are stimulating these natural processes to accomplish certain goals including reduction of pain and inflammation, treatment of infection, and enhancement of growth factor release for stem cell therapies.

How Ozone is Administered

Ozone has widespread appeal for health, wellness, and disease management. Ozone is administered in several ways. Ozone must always be used with precise instruments that ensure a closed system and accurate ozone outputs.

1. **Ozone can be administered directly into sites of pain and inflammation through Prolozone injections.** Prolozone provides both ozone and a series of nutrients. I routinely use this method with my clients and have seen success with almost every joint in the body. In chronic pain situations, the pain often develops in areas of reduced blood flow. Cells in these areas are compromised and do not produce energy from oxygen normally. Ozone injection has an immediate effect on the chemical mediators that cause pain, and the

additional nutrients provide what the ailing cells need to produce energy more efficiently.[21]

2. **Ozone can be administered as an IV therapy.** It is mixed with an individual's own blood and then re-infused back into the body. This is a powerful tool as it provides whole-body effects unlike Prolozone, which targets a local area. IV ozone is called Major Auto Hemotherapy (MAH).

3. **Ozone steam saunas are exceptionally helpful for detoxing and oxygenating.** The patient sits in a comfortable pod that encloses the entire body except the head. Steam fills the cabinet, causing sweating. Ozone gas is then added, and it is absorbed through the skin, the body's largest organ of elimination. This therapy oxygenates tissues and cells, stimulates the immune system, increases white blood cell (WBC) count, and increases tumor necrosis factor. It's a powerful detoxer as well, helping the body purge accumulated toxins and waste products. Ozone steam therapy is helpful in a wide variety of situations, from diabetes to fibromyalgia to athletic recovery.[22,23]

4. **Ozone can be given via rectal insufflation**. While this may not sound pleasant, it is one of the most common methods since it is noninvasive and can be done easily. It isn't typically uncomfortable either, though it can cause a light cramping or gassy sensation. Ozone administered by this route provides whole-body effects similar to MAH.

5. **Ozone can be applied directly to arm or leg wounds.** The affected limb is enclosed in an ozone resistant material, such as a silicone bag, and ozone gas is introduced into the sealed bag. This is referred to as *limb bagging*. Ozone administered in this fashion is incredibly effective at killing infection in

wounds, as well as promoting the healing process through tamping down inflammation and oxygenating the wounded tissue.[24]

6. **Second Generation PRP is a novel ozone use**. This technique involves the drawing of blood and the isolation of the platelet rich plasma (PRP) portion. This material is then ozonated. Ozone has a remarkable ability to augment growth factor release from the platelets.[25] This material can then be injected into joint spaces and serves as an activated stem cell therapy specific for each individual. This activated stem cell material can also be turned into a three-dimensional gel and injected into the face, serving as a non-invasive, living, ozone stem cell facial with remarkable results.

Combination MAH/UBI

A lesser known therapy with intensified synergy

This combination therapy is extremely powerful because it combines two synergistic therapies. Like MAH, the process involves removal of a small portion of blood, suspending that blood in normal saline, adding ozone to the suspended blood, and re-infusing the intravenous mixture back into the patient. But in this combo therapy, just before the IV fluid goes back into the vein, it passes through a glass tube and gets exposed to ultraviolet light. This is called ultraviolet blood irradiation (UBI).

There are multiple synergies at work here. The oxygen-ozone mixture of the blood causes an initial oxygenation and oxidation, and if the dosing is appropriate, prompts a hormetic effect in the body.[26] As we've already discussed, that leads to adaptations, cellular repair, and multiple immune enhancements. The UBI portion of this therapy heightens those effects.[27]

UV light can inactivate bacteria, viruses, fungi, and other infecting organisms. This therapy can help clear multiple low levels of infection that can be quite challenging to treat with any other modality. Recall that cancer is an immunodeficiency state, a condition characterized by lowered immunity. Many cancer patients suffer from multiple low levels of infection that can aggravate their downward spiral of disease.[28,29,30] UBI can help eliminate these low-grade infections and, unlike antibiotics, it's effective against pathogens that aren't bacterial (viruses, molds, etc.) and doesn't create any bacterial resistance.

The UBI portion of the therapy inactivates infecting organisms in the treated portion of the blood. Those inactivated pathogens are then injected back into the body. These inactivated cell wall components of the pathogens are more presentable to the immune cells. They enhance the ability of the immune system to identify, tag, and create antibodies to these bacteria, viruses, or molds.[31] This tilts the scales in the patient's favor, making it more likely that the body can mount a proper immune response and clear many hidden low levels of infection.

It's easy to see why MAH/UBI combined therapy can have such dramatic and powerful potential results for so many diverse problems. This complementary natural medical therapy can benefit diverse conditions including cancer, heart disease, infections, and autoimmune conditions. We'll look at more synergistic therapy combinations like this in Chapter 7.

Ozone Horizons: O_3 Therapies and Autoimmunity

The Disease Progression Model (Chapter 1) showed how it takes numerous imbalances in the body to result in tangible signs of illness. Autoimmune conditions are no exception. Many natural health practitioners believe that autoimmune conditions begin in the gut with pathology that allows gaps in the intestinal *tight junctions* (the spaces between individual cells in the single-cell lining of the gut). These gaps can allow undigested protein and other materials to leak through the lining, gaining access to the blood stream. This is often referred to as *leaky gut*.[32]

The immune system attacks these undigested materials, thinking they are foreign invaders. Our immune system does what it is designed to do: it generates an antibody response and activates other immune processes. The antibodies bind the foreign material, considering it an *antigen*—a bacteria, virus, mold, or other problem particle. That's where the immune process goes wayward. These antigen-antibody complexes deposit into different body sites causing specific autoimmune conditions. Deposits in the thyroid could result in thyroiditis, deposits in the kidney could result in Lupus, deposits in the central and peripheral nervous system could cascade into multiple sclerosis.

There are now over one hundred different autoimmune conditions. Some of the more common ones include rheumatoid arthritis, lupus, inflammatory bowel disease (IBS), Type 1 diabetes, celiac disease, myasthenia gravis, Parkinson's, Alzheimer's, and psoriasis. Collectively, they represent a leading cause of disease, especially in younger women who are more likely to contract an autoimmune condition.

A dangerous cascade occurs in autoimmune conditions. Immune activation, oxidative stress, and inflammation combine to generate an over-accumulation of reactive oxygen species (ROS) and decrease every cell's ability to generate antioxidant resources to maintain balance.[33] These imbalances create the pathophysiology that damages healthy tissues of the body, leading to the various autoimmune conditions. The scientific evidence is quite clear: Excessive oxidative stress and inflammation affect countless systems of the body including, but not limited to: the cardiovascular, respiratory, and nervous systems, as well as the skin, joints, kidney, liver, and thyroid.[34]

Numerous pharmaceutical agents have tried to combat the oxidative stress and inflammation typical of autoimmune conditions. These medications include corticosteroids, biologics, antibiotics, and immunosuppressive agents. The key to overcoming these conditions rests in increasing the body's natural defensive antioxidant enzymes. In 2017, the *International Journal of Biological Macromolecules* published an article titled, "Role of enzymatic free radical scavengers in management of oxidative stress and autoimmune disorders." The authors discussed how to address the imbalance of reactive oxygen species and inflammation: "The imbalance can only be combatted by supplementing natural defensive antioxidant enzymes such as superoxide dismutase and catalase."

This is precisely one of the effects of ozone, and it explains why ozone is so effective in helping to normalize the imbalances associated with autoimmune conditions. Ozone has a remarkable ability to combat oxidative stress and boost antioxidant defenses. That explains why ozone conveys benefits for many different medical conditions. You can read more about this process in the Further Science section at the end of this chapter.

Ozone Horizons: Dental Care and Whole-Body Health

Ozone's impact on the field of dentistry is just as noteworthy as any of the other applications we've discussed. MDs and other primary care providers should be concerned about dental health. We now know that the germs responsible for tooth decay also are present in the plaques that line our arteries and contribute to vascular and heart disease. These cavity-causing germs found in dental infections get into our blood stream and can attack our joints and can even target implantable devices such as joint replacements and pacemakers. In addition to these infections, pathogenic dental bacteria also promote significant inflammation and make us vulnerable to a host of other inflammatory-based medical conditions.[35]

Ozone therapy for dentistry is already a major treatment modality in Europe, South America and many other countries. Since the primary goal of dentistry is to treat and prevent dental cavities, dental ozone therapies represent some of the most powerful and natural tools for this treatment. Often, deeper dental infections are also curable with ozone helping to give knowledgeable dentists the upper hand in treating conditions that may directly predispose patients to other major medical disease states.

The root of a tooth branches out much like a tree root system and contains tiny nerves, blood vessels and connective tissue. In conventional dentistry, during endodontic therapy (root canal work), small tools are used to remove this tissue, clear infection, seal, and fill this area. The problem with this technique is that it can be challenging to remove all the infection and fully seal off all of the minute canals of the remaining tooth structure. These hard to reach places often harbor bacteria and their toxins.

The use of ozone as a gas offers significant advantages over all other forms of conventional therapy, since the ozone gas can penetrate to deeper tissue layers and reach more hidden sites of infection. In dental application, ozone is administered using a syringe. It is not inhaled or directly injected into the bloodstream, both of which are never advised. Rather it is injected with a small tip applicator, directly into a tooth's root system. As a gas under pressure, ozone will naturally travel to the farthest reaches, effectively neutralizing microbes in the smallest tubules.[36] It's highly effective and, unlike antibiotic usage, or dental fillers, there is no risk of causing antibiotic resistance when utilizing ozone.

Meet the Patients Who Have Benefitted

Whatever the administration route, ozone is being used for a wide variety of health conditions and athletic recovery goals. Ozone interacts with pain pathways, inflammation cascades, and immune cell activity. That's why it's used in such diverse conditions including: chronic pain, heart disease, diabetes, autoimmune issues, athletic injury, and more. To get a sense of the scope of applications, it's easiest to meet some of the clients who have utilized ozone therapies.

Case Story #1
80-year-old Man with Severe Chronic Neck Stiffness

A colleague asked if I could help a friend of his who had significantly reduced range of motion in his neck. The client was in his eighties and, when I met him for the first time, I was amazed at how limited his neck range of motion was. He needed to turn his whole body in order to turn his head. He literally had no neck range of motion from side to side, and he was also quite limited in his ability to move his neck up and down as well.

I was shocked to learn that he had this problem for quite some time. In fact, his wife who was present as well, told me that she could not remember a time that his neck movement was normal. She believed the condition was present for over forty years. The patient did not have pain, and there was no traumatic event they could recall that caused the condition many years back. We discussed how joints can fuse over time, how minor problems can continue to erode our health if not properly addressed, and how muscle rigidity can occur in the body. The man's neck muscles were so tight that I was surprised he was not in some degree of pain.

After our discussion we scheduled a Prolozone injection in the neck area. I explained that this procedure would involve a two-part injection: first, ozone gas and then a mixture of nutrients. I mentioned that a series of injections might be needed, as this was a serious and long-standing problem with major structural involvement. I told him a positive response would involve a 20-25 percent improvement after the first one or two injections and that we should plan to do these weekly for up to four injections. I also let him know there could be some muscle soreness for a day or two afterward, especially since his neck was so stiff.

I recall examining the man's neck and upper back and feeling amazed how tight his muscles were. My plan was to inject several "trigger points" in the upper back and neck area and see what his initial response was. In line with my usual procedure, I gently manipulated the area of injection after the ozone and nutrients were injected. This helps to spread the ozone and nutrient mixture in the tissues. I remember noticing that the muscles had some improvement almost immediately after the injection.

The following day I received a call that I remember to this day. The client's wife told me that she came down the stairs that morning and was blown away when her husband was able to turn his head to greet her from his chair—without turning his body. They were amazed that a single injection could fix such a long-standing problem. So was I. The man followed up with me a week later. His range of motion was 80 percent improved, and the muscle tightness was essentially gone. We did one more injection. That was all that was needed. Ozone, a charged form of oxygen, and common nutrients overcame a long-standing condition that affected how this client had lived and functioned for decades.

Case Story #2

Metastatic Breast Cancer Patient

Video testimonial at www.VitalityHealthChallenge.com

An ICU nurse, whom I've known for many years, was diagnosed with breast cancer in 2010. I offered some alternative medical advice initially after her diagnosis, but she was not interested at that time. She elected to follow a conventional medical approach and, unfortunately, her cancer failed to respond favorably to surgery, chemotherapy, and radiation. She contacted me, having been informed her disease had progressed to Stage IV, the worst prognosis, with evidence that her tumor had spread to her bones, liver, and lungs.

I recall her coming to see me with her husband and one of her sisters. We talked for a while. It was clear to everyone that she was exhausted, frustrated, and close to giving up. I explained that cancer is an immune deficiency state and that all of her treatments to date, although well intentioned, posed further insults to her immune function. I explained that she should now focus on therapies that would enhance her immune function and address some of the underlying problems that likely made the cancer possible to begin with.

It was clear that she wanted to do something, but was very limited in her energy. Essentially I had to pick one strategy for her to try. My choice was a combined IV therapy using MAH/UBI. Simplicity was key. My choice was also influenced by the fact that she was a specialized nurse, and she already had a surgically placed port that had been used for her chemotherapy sessions. The IV treatment would be easy to administer through this port.

I did offer other therapies too but, at that time, she was only able to commit to the MAH/UBI treatments. She scheduled to start these powerful therapies two times per week, using a very low concentration of ozone. She completed her first few sessions and quickly noticed some small improvements in her energy levels. Understandably, as a Stage IV cancer patient, who had failed aggressive conventional treatments, her physical state was quite compromised. Having a little more energy was an incredible encouragement.

I had bigger hopes for her. I knew the MAH could induce a hormetic effect in her body, which would lead to adaptations, cellular repair, and immune enhancements from cytokine inductions. Meanwhile, the UBI could bolster her exhausted immune system. Remember, as mentioned earlier, cancer is an immune deficiency state (lowered immunity), and most cancer patients also suffer from multiple low levels of infection that support the disease progression cascade.[37,38,39]

Even in light of my hopes for her, what happened over the course of the next six months was quite miraculous. We gradually increased her ozone doses and, after each therapy, we added in a second intravenous infusion of some basic nutrients and trace minerals. Her metastatic lesions reduced in size and eventually disappeared. Her serial PET scans (imaging scans to look at potential whole-body cancer involvement) normalized.

Her doctors at the university hospital where she went for chemo were amazed. They did not want to know what she was doing, but told her to continue doing it. Which she did. As of writing this, she has been cancer free for more than five years. She continues to have imaging scans every six to twelve months. She still does the MAH/UBI treatments, although less frequently. And I am glad to report that she now does more natural healing therapies and has a much more nutritious diet.

She is in great health, active, and enjoys a fantastic quality of life. Last summer I was invited to go boating on the Chesapeake Bay with her. Watching her back on the water, enjoying the sunset with her husband, is a memory I will always cherish.

Case Story #3
50-year-old Male with Athletic Injury
Video testimonial at www.VitalityHealtChallenge.com

A very healthy and active Chiropractor had a devastating injury on the tennis court. He fell and injured his right hip flexor tendon. Immediately after his fall, he could not lift his leg or externally rotate it. He was in a very bad place for many reasons. First, his livelihood depended on his physical ability to adjust his patients. Second, he had devoted his life to health and wellness and highly valued his active lifestyle. He desperately wanted to make a full recovery that allowed for complete range of motion and strength.

Initial treatment of ice and rest helped to reduce some of the pain and swelling, but he was not able to ambulate normally. He wasn't using a crutch, but he was limping badly, his walking gait was slower, and he wasn't able to fully bear weight on his right leg. Adjusting his clients, and any other type of physical exertion, were not even on the radar.

We spent a lot of time talking about how the injured area needed to be saturated with oxygen to offer the best chance for fully functional and mobile healing.

As a chiropractor, he had an in-depth knowledge about the body's natural protective reflexes. He understood that these reflexes can take over after an injury, and that this can lead to healing with a *fixation,* an area characterized by stiffness and limited range of motion. When you have a serious injury like that, if you just let it heal as is, there will be contraction in the connective tissues. It heals, but without the best pliable characteristics of the tissue. However, if you intervene with strategic healing therapies and appropriate physical therapy, you can train those tissues to stay flexible.

Healing to the point of fully restored functionality requires both an oxygen component and a training component. I often add in a third component as well: Pulsed Electromagnetic Field Therapy (PEMF). This is another synergistic natural therapy that can introduce healing magnetic energy into the tissues and offer additional healing inputs (we'll discuss this more in Chapter 7).

I explained this three-pronged approach to my client. I also explained how rare it was to find such a holistic approach at any sports medicine clinic. All providers offer access to physical therapy, but only a few offer oxygen therapies in tandem. Meanwhile, PEMF is virtually unheard of. That's unfortunate because, as this chiropractor was about to learn, the synergy of all three is impressive.

First, we settled on a protocol that would utilize multiple synergistic oxygen therapies to promote healing. We injected ozone and nutrients into the injury area. He spent time in a hyperbaric oxygen chamber and an ozone sauna. Remember, oxygen is key to keeping soft tissue pliable. Over time he got stronger. He knew we were going in the right direction.

Once he turned the corner, and the joint showed some degree of tissue relaxation and healing from the oxygen therapies, we began training the healing tissue fibers to flex, bend, twist, and move without pain. This was accomplished by introducing the controlled functional movement of a physical therapy program. We remodeled the injured tendon through physical therapy and exercise, in the presence of continued oxygen therapies. He was highly motivated and wanted to get on a path that would lead back to restored—maybe even enhanced—range of motion. When timed correctly, these natural therapies can make the crucial difference between a fully functional recovery and recovery with limitations.

This client made more than a full recovery. You can hear from him and see video footage of him running on the tennis court on my website. For me, there really is no greater satisfaction than seeing an athlete (or any other patient who is told they'll never be the same) not only make a full recovery but wind up with better athletic performance than before the injury. It is an effort-dependent process, but it is possible.

Ozone Cautions and Historic Uses

As we have seen, ozone is a unique molecule with widespread effects in the human body. Ozone has been used to treat more than 114 major medical conditions.[40] It also has significant non-medical uses too. These include odor removal, disinfection, food storage, and purification of drinking water, aquariums, pools, and spas. Ozone is more common in day-to-day life than you might realize.

However, as mentioned earlier, all substances that are integral and basic to our physiology (even water and salt), still have safe and unsafe levels. Ozone is no exception.

1. Care must be taken not to inhale ozone, since its immediate oxidative effects can be damaging to delicate lung tissue.
2. Ozone should never be injected directly into a vein. In fact, the direct IV route was responsible for the majority of side effects from a 1980 German Medical Ozone Society Study. This route of administration is now no longer supported by any organization involved in medical ozone therapies.
3. Ozone should not be offered to patients with coagulation conditions or those who have experienced a recent heart attack.
4. Ozone should not be given to patients who are acutely intoxicated.

The limitations of ozone differ drastically when compared to pharmaceutical agents. The pharmaceutical agents have far greater restrictions and long side effect lists, even when used correctly. After over a century of use, appropriately administered ozone therapies are among the safest medical treatments available.

Medical ozone therapies must always be generated from medical grade oxygen and an ozone generator that is capable of precise ozone output concentrations. Since ozone should never be inhaled, it is imperative that ozone therapy systems contain ozone destruction devices, so that excess ozone is inactivated. Since ozone can degrade simple plastic materials, it is also important that ozone therapists use ozone resistant materials for all ozone-based medical therapies. Lastly, because ozone therapy is so different from conventional medical therapies, it is crucial that the ozone therapist possess significant training and knowledge. The standards for ozone administration are well-delineated in the Madrid Declaration on Ozone Therapies.

That said, ozone therapies have a surprisingly long history of safe and effective use. Few people know that medical ozone and ozone products were used widely in the mid 1800s, so their use actually predates the FDA's inception in 1906. In 1900, medical ozone was used in the U.S. by Nikola Tesla who formed the Tesla Ozone Company.[41] During World War I, doctors with knowledge of ozone's ability to treat infection used ozone topically to treat infected wounds.[42]

In 1980, The German Medical Society for Ozone Therapy commissioned the Institute for Medical Statistics and Documentation of Giessen University to begin an inquiry entitled "Adverse Effects and Typical Complications in Ozone Therapy." Questionnaires were sent out to all western German ozone therapists known by the Medical Society for Ozone Therapy. The replies showed 384,775 patients were treated with ozone with a minimum of 5,579,238 applications, and the side effect rate observed was only 1 in every 200,000 applications.[43,44] The report (mentioned in bullet 2 earlier) also stated, "The majority of adverse effects were caused by ignorance about ozone therapy (operator error)." Many have concluded that the proper use of medical ozone therapies represents the safest medical therapeutic we can offer.

There are over 10,000 articles published in medical journals discussing the activity, use, safety, and applications of ozone.[45]

A more recent publication from 2011 in the *Journal of Natural Science, Biology and Medicine* reiterates these assertions:

> "Ozone's effects are proven, consistent, safe and with minimal and preventable side effects. Medical O_3 is used to disinfect and treat disease. Mechanism of action is by inactivation of bacteria, viruses, fungi, yeast and protozoa, stimulation of oxygen metabolism, activation of the immune system."[46]

The most common reported "side effect" of systemic (MAH) ozone therapies is actually not a side effect, rather it's a sign of immune system activation. Because of ozone's ability to cause fast die off of certain pathogens, some patients do experience a Herxheimer reaction, also known as a "healing crisis."[47] If a patient has a persistent low-level infection at the root of his or her health challenges, ozone therapy can help their body finally clear that infection completely. That process can result in mild uncomfortable symptoms that one might associate with fighting a cold or the flu. The patient might feel fatigued or achy or even congested. But the sensations typically dissipate after a day or two and, afterward, the patient feels a noteworthy restoration of energy, now that the infection is finally cleared.

A similar healing crisis can occur in situations where the patient has been dealing with ongoing toxicity or chronic inflammation too. The body's processes for clearing toxins and inflammatory byproducts are similar to cleaning out infection. Immediately after the ozone therapy there might be a day or two of cold or flu-like symptoms. The effects of a healing crisis are manageable and transient—they don't last forever.

That's a big difference when compared to coping with ongoing side effects from a pharmaceutical drug. Some of our most commonly prescribed medications, such as statins and non-natural hormone replacement therapies, have lists of 60 to 100-plus side effects. Many of these risks are quite serious and, in contrast to ozone's transient "healing crisis," have no upside.[48,49]

What the Rest of the World Knows

And Why the U.S. is Just Starting to Catch On To Ozone Research

In Europe, the foundational research and standardization of contemporary ozone therapies has, by far, been led by the pioneering researcher Dr. Adriana Schwartz in Spain. Dr. Schwartz began her career in the field of obstetrics and gynecology before playing a key role in the basic science and research of medical ozone therapies. In addition to being one of the best clinicians and teachers that I have interacted with in my entire medical career, she has taken the lead in unifying the science and safe practices of ozone therapies across multiple countries.

Dr. Schwartz is the lead author of the Madrid Declaration of Ozone Therapies and is the President of the Spanish Association of Medical Professionals in Ozone (AEPROMO), the President of The International Medical Ozone Federation (IMEOF), and the Director of the Fiorela Clinic with facilities in both Madrid and Honduras. I have completed medical ozone therapy trainings with Dr. Schwartz in three different countries and can attest that her knowledge base and determination are most impressive.

In 2010, scientists from over twenty different countries met with Dr. Schwartz in Spain and adopted the Madrid Declaration of Ozone Therapies. This was a landmark proceeding, designed to standardize the science, reporting, and methods of administration for clinical ozone therapies. The Madrid Declaration noted that:

> "...since the discovery of ozone by the German chemist Christian Friedrich Schönbein in 1840, its medical use has increased in different parts of the world; there is more interest from health professionals to know how it works and what are its benefits; the number of ozone therapists keeps growing all around the world; and an increasing number of patients are benefiting from it."[50]

The declaration also identified the nations that have established standardized ozone uses and includes: [51]

Russia – Ozone therapy regularized by the Federal Service Public Health Control and Social Development (the first country in the world to do so in 2007)
Cuba – Ozone therapy regularized by the Ministry of Public Health in 2009
Spain – Accepted by the Balearic Islands and the Canary Islands (2007), Madrid (2009) and Galicia, Castilla-La Mancha, and Castilla y León (2010)
Italy – Also making significant advances toward standardizing ozone therapy and advancing its research.

While the U.S. medical system often looks down on Russia and Cuba, this might be one area where we shouldn't be so hasty in our judgments. For all the limitations of their forms of government, their medical systems are motivated purely by low cost and efficient results. It might be worth paying attention when they choose to invest in and normalize an alternative therapy. They're only endorsing it because it works.

While the rest of the world was furthering ozone therapy research, what was happening in the United States? As many countries were unifying the science and principles for the safe application of ozone, our FDA was still insisting that ozone has no medical therapeutic value.[52,53]

Did more than 20 other countries and 40,000 ozone practitioners worldwide get it wrong? Doubtful. Our country does not make it easy to offer ozone therapies. The medical establishment is a powerful business, and the pharmaceutical industry has deep pockets. Ozone is natural, inexpensive, highly effective—and not patentable. That last part is key. Because it can't be patented, ozone cannot become a significant and secure revenue-generating pharmaceutical drug. So there is no financial incentive for pharmaceutical companies to allocate the billions of dollars needed to route ozone therapy through the FDA-approval process. In the shadow of that reality, ozone remains a "fringe treatment" in the U.S., while it is a reliable go-to therapy for many European nations, Russia, and South America.

Thankfully, a handful of states do have medical freedom laws to protect both patients and physicians so that ozone, and other non-approved medical therapies, can be offered. At the time of this writing, the Maryland State government (my home state) will be considering a bill to protect physicians who want to use integrative, natural medical therapies to treat patients.

You can learn more about these issues through the citizen awareness group, National Health Freedom Action (**www.nationalhealthfreedomaction.org**). NHFA maintains a state list, noting those that have Health Freedom Safe Harbor Practitioner Exemption laws, those that are in the process of introducing similar bills, and those that have taken no action. Ozone therapies can also be offered in a limited fashion in other states when an individual provider is approved to administer it "for research purposes." To search for providers in your region, look online for the American Academy of Ozonotherapy.

I have attended trainings for ozone therapies in many different countries. I have seen countries with limited resources offer high-quality and cost-effective medical care using ozone therapies. I have also seen cutting edge ozone therapies invited into the operating rooms at major medical institutions in Spain, providing implantable, ozone activated, stem cell therapies for a variety of procedures including eye surgery, orthopedics, dental procedures, vascular surgery, and much more. In the U.S., such forward-thinking advances seem to be significantly more than a generation away, considering our intense suppression of natural therapies. It is up to patients and integrative physicians to self-advocate and lead the way. Ozone therapies are life-changing and worth fighting for.

Try It! Incorporating Ozone Therapy into YOUR Life
Challenging, but not impossible!

Right now, it's not easy to find a trained and reputable ozone practitioner in the U.S. But it's not impossible either. There are three major routes you can take:

- If you live in one of the Health Freedom states, you're set! You can learn your state's status through the National Health Freedom Action website (**www.nationalhealthfreedomaction.org**). If your state is on the list of Health Freedom states, a quick Google search should connect you with a nearby ozone therapist.
- If you do not live in a Health Freedom state, you may need to contact the American Academy of Ozonotherapy (see Resources section) to find the ozone therapist nearest you. You may need to travel a little to experience this well-worth-it treatment.
- You may also contact a state-based natural health association in your region and ask if there are any practitioners nearby who are administering ozone as part of a clinical research project.

Once you find a practitioner, be discerning. Ask where they received their training. It's best if they've been trained overseas in one of the countries that is already standardizing ozone administration, and even better if they've trained with Dr. Schwartz in Madrid. Chat with your practitioner about the "Ozone Cautions & Historic Uses" section in this chapter, and ask if their equipment has all the recommended safety features.

Beyond these three major paths for finding an ozone therapist, there is a fourth option. Consider contacting my clinic, Vitality Health Challenge, and ask if we're offering any therapies in medical freedom states. I occasionally set up ozone workshop weekends in safe states and can notify you about upcoming dates.

Ozone Therapies

HEALTH GOALS TRIAD

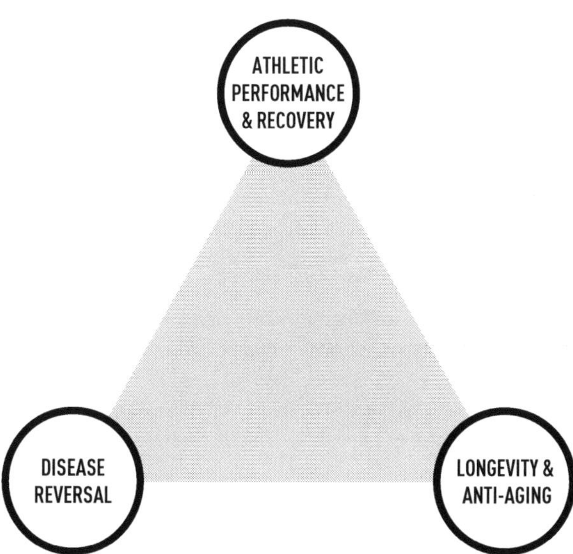

DISEASE REVERSAL Systemic ozone therapies are incredibly useful for pathogenic disease states such as cancer and chronic infections. Ozone can be used in combination with other alternative therapies in highly complex cases of autoimmune disease. Meanwhile, targeted, site-specific Prolozone is optimal for addressing chronic pain in muscles and joints.

LONGEVITY & ANTI-AGING It's intuitive to connect anti-aging medicine primarily with ozone's effects on joint health and range of motion. But ozone's longevity benefits don't stop there. Systemic ozone applications boost major antioxidant systems in the body. That has ramifications for overall energy and vitality, cardiovascular health, immunity, and detoxification.

ATHLETIC PERFORMANCE & RECOVERY Ozone therapies are incredible for recovery from athletic injury, restoring the body to pre-injury (or better) function without scar tissue, residual pain, or range-of-motion limitations. Athletes should look to ozone for performance optimization, too. Enhancing systemic oxygen and implementing other hormetic practices can boost reaction times. In sports where a tenth of a second can be the difference between first and second place, such therapies may be literal gold.

LESSER KNOWN, BUT WELL-RESEARCHED AND TRANSFORMATIVE FOR CHRONIC PAIN, INFECTION, AND INJURY RECOVERY

Further Science

Read the Research for Yourself

The following provides just a few highlighted studies that can help you expand your understanding of the material in this chapter. Comprehensive chapter References & Notes are found at the end of the book. To read more about these studies, search for "PubMed" online, the world's largest medical library. Reach PubMed directly at: https://www.ncbi.nlm.nih.gov/pubmed/

1.

Bocci V. **"How a calculated oxidative stress can yield multiple therapeutic effects."** *Free Radical Research.* 2012 Sep;46(9):1068-75.

Take a closer look at the biochemical chain reaction that ozone therapy triggers. At the end of that cascade is an increase in the synthesis of antioxidant enzymes. This article provides a detailed description of hormetic action: how a mild, appropriate stress (in this case ozone therapy) results in healthier function in the body.

2.

Sagai M, Bocci V. **"Mechanism of Action Involved in Ozone Therapy: Is healing induced via a mild oxidative stress?"** *Medical Gas Research.* 2011;1:29.

Learn the differences between "severe" and "mild" oxidative stressors. The inflammatory markers associated with mild stress and severe stress are completely different. Severe oxidation ultimately results in tissue damage, while a mild oxidative stressor will activate antioxidant systems that induce healing activities (hormesis). Ozone therapy, as a mild oxidative stressor, increases antioxidant enzymes including SOD and catalase, which help to reduce chronic oxidative stress.

3.

Muto M, Giurazza F, Pimentel Silva R, Guarnieri G. **"Rational approach, technique and selection criteria treating lumbar disk herniations by oxygen–ozone therapy."** *Interventional Neuroradiology.* 2016 Dec; 22(6): 736–740. Published online 2016 Aug 2. Doi: 10.1177/1591019916659266

Ozone injection is often used in Europe and Asia for chronic pain treatment. It is especially effective for low back pain associated with degenerative disc disease and disc herniation. This article reviews outcomes from existing literature data, proposes likely methods of action (how ozone interacts with back pain at a biochemical level), and makes protocol suggestions.

Chapter 5
Fasting and Time Restricted Eating Therapies

When you eat may be more important than what you eat

Clients can be somewhat resistant toward committing to regular exercise. But they can become borderline hostile toward the idea of fasting. Educating people about the value of fasting can be a challenge! Perhaps nothing threatens our sense of daily comfort and enjoyment like dietary limitation. Food is itself pleasurable, and it is often at the core of social interactions and family gatherings. Limiting what clients may eat or requesting that they not eat for a certain span of time can feel like I'm taking away their right to live a happy life.

Yet after that initial resistance, many circle back, curious about the therapeutic effects of fasting. This simultaneous resistance and curiosity point toward the ancient connection human kind has held with fasting as both spiritual and medicinal practice. We dislike it. But we do it anyway. Why?

Fasting in the animal kingdom is common practice. Many animals eat intensely after a successful hunt when food is available and fast in between. Fasting is also seen when battling bacterial infections. Most mammals will instinctively withdraw socially, rest, and water fast—not eating anything for days at a time and only drinking water occasionally. We now know that these actions conserve energy and enhance immune function.[1] Early humans doubtless retained similar instinctive "illness behaviors." Recently we have learned that force feeding, or simply bringing the glucose level to normal in mice can cause a non-lethal bacterial infection to become lethal.

Almost all cultures developed some form of ritualized fasting. As we became more socially and spiritually complex, fasting became a religious technology to evoke altered mental states, cultivate persevering characteristics, and make political statements of concern and solidarity with those who lack resources. Many subcultures still use fasting for these reasons.

In recent decades, with the emergence of the natural health care movement, some integrative practitioners have noted the cleansing and hormetic effects of fasting. It's a legitimate way to reset the entire digestive tract and immune system. When done wisely, fasting can enhance fat-burning and improve overall metabolism. On a cellular level, strategic fasting can provide a safe hormetic stressor that strengthens many body systems.[2]

Unfortunately, many who have tried fasting, have done so without an understanding of how to do it safely, how to build up their hormetic strength to deal well with a true water-only fast, and how to time fasting practices to align with circadian rhythms. They end up having a negative experience with no real benefits to show for it. That's too bad, because once you have those basic understandings in place, fasting is the easiest hormetic therapy to implement.

24-Hour Comfort is Not the Foundation for Long-Term Health

Hormetic therapies are all about embracing short-term challenge to enhance long-term strength and vitality, and there's never been a time in human history when it was more difficult to embrace such practices. We are trained from the day we can operate a light switch and a smart phone that if we want something, we can have it in a moment. We're wiring our brains to expect immediate satisfaction and the constant avoidance of discomfort.

Our lives are characterized by 24-hour comfort. We expect endless access to a steady supply of high caloric foods. Refrigeration, food preservation techniques, fast food corporations, artificial lighting, and climate control have collectively altered our lifestyles and eating habits more than any other technological shift in recorded history. What we may not appreciate is that we pay a hefty price for this 24-hour comfort.

Hearing a practitioner recommend even an occasional fast, can stir up strong visceral emotion. That strong emotion holds a clue as to why fasting is so powerful. On a cellular level, the sudden cut in caloric flow creates a strong biological response. That's not a bad thing. Fasting is so effective because of its ability to influence subconscious, autonomic systems—body processes we normally cannot control. It can alter our circadian rhythms and metabolic functions.

Remember, the cubicle worker sitting on a chair all day has a body very similar to the ancestor who worked hard at making stone tools by the light of a fire. Our bodies today still possess all the systems to survive occasional deprivation and survive it well. Those same body systems that kept us alive during frequent famines unfortunately wind up working against us when "times of plenty" turn into "a whole life of plenty." Our bodies are wired to hang onto fat and not let it go easily. In a world where we naturally cycled every year between harvest months and lean months and cycled on a larger scale between multiple years of famine or abundance, our bodies stayed alive by stockpiling fat for hard times. We shouldn't resent our bodies for doing that. We simply need to understand and accept that as long as there are *any* carbohydrates in our systems—yes, even that half-teaspoon of sugar in this morning's coffee—those carbs will generate an insulin release and ensure that we are not able to burn our stored body fat.[3]

That deserves some repetition. If you have any carbs in your system at this moment, you are physically not able to burn stored body fat for energy.

Because of this reality, intelligent well-timed fasting can fully alter your metabolism. The key is understanding how to do it well, safely, and effectively. Fasting is powerful, but it can be done inappropriately. It can make existing metabolic conditions worse. Like any hormetic therapy, it's all about finding that perfect balance: not so mild that it doesn't provoke any challenge, not so intense that it causes damage. Let's look at the cellular and metabolic benefits of appropriate fasting, then dive into the specifics of the fasting protocols that truly work.

What Happens When We Fast?

Fasting can have many variations. For the moment we'll look at the standard water fast, when you simply cease eating food, and drink only water for a certain span of time. When we fast, depending on the length of the fast, stored forms of energy are mobilized to meet our nutrient requirements. Once the available glucose (carbohydrate) supply is used up, the body will turn to *glycogen* for energy. Glycogen is the body's primary storage carbohydrate, and it is found primarily in the muscle and liver. As we continue to fast, glycogen reserves are typically depleted within 6 to 10 hours. As the fast continues further, the body accesses the largest energy reserve it has: stored fat. This produces both usable free fatty acids and *ketones* (also called ketone bodies).[4,5]

Ketones are byproducts of breaking down fat for energy; we make ketones by oxidizing fatty acids. When we fast for an extended period of time, the liver eventually stops burning carbohydrates and shifts into a fat-burning state. Ketone production begins. Ketones can be used for energy in the brain, heart, kidney, and muscle. In this fasting state, we can also produce a small amount of glucose from glucogenic amino acids, which helps supply glucose to the brain.[6] This all adds up to an enhanced metabolic state, one that relies on efficient fat-burning.

Fasting Vocabulary

- **Glucose** – Sugar derived from carbohydrates. The body's first line energy source.
- **Glycogen** – The body's main storage carbohydrate. A backup energy source when all readily available carbohydrates have been burned up.
- **Ketones** – The byproducts of breaking down fat for energy, made by oxidizing fatty acids. Used for energy by the brain, heart, kidney, and muscle.
- **Autophagy** – A state of cellular repair and "parts recycling" that can be induced by fasting. The process by which cells regenerate themselves.

Along with the positive metabolic shifts that occur when we fast, our bodies also enter a repair phase, not unlike the state we're in when we are sleeping deeply. A fasting state accelerates a process called *autophagy*. This Latin term translates as "self-eating". Autophagy is the body's maintenance and recycling system. It's a natural process by which individual cells break down dysfunctional components and, essentially, eat them. The cell processes the damaged organelles and proteins, breaking them down into usable material.[7] That raw material can be used for nutrition or turned back into building blocks for new cellular organelles. That includes repairing mitochondria, the energy-producing centers in each cell. Autophagy is cellular self-maintenance and repair.

In a state of long-term famine, autophagy can result in damaging muscle wasting. But when we enter autophagy for a limited time frame, it results in optimal cellular repair. It's actually a prime example of hormesis. Just enough challenge results in activating highly beneficial repair mechanisms throughout the body. Several animal studies have found fasting or calorie restriction to be linked to anti-aging effects and greater longevity.[8] Increased autophagy is likely the cause.

With all that said, once-a-year fasting probably won't cause any miracles for you. You may be surprised to learn that a four-day, water-only fast results in less than a 2 percent loss of stored body fat. That state of going-without is deep-rooted in our physiology, and we can survive quite some time by accessing stored fat.

This begs the question, why bother with fasting at all? It's true, if you only did a four-day water-only fast once a year, it wouldn't provide incredible metabolic gains as a sole hormetic therapy. Though it would provide some cleansing benefits. That one-time strategy is not one that I recommend. As a foundational fasting practice, I recommend a form of daily fasting called Time Restricted Eating (TRE). This incredibly easy hormetic therapy simply limits the times at which you eat and helps your body access a mildly fasting state on a daily basis. Let's explore the specifics of how TRE compares to other fasting strategies.

Defining Common and Not-So-Common Fasting Protocols

Calorie Restriction (CR)

For decades, we have known that there was one scientifically proven method to prolong life across multiple different mammalian species. That method is called Calorie Restriction (CR), and it is defined as eating approximately 25 to 40 percent fewer calories than recommended for your age and gender. This is a constant restriction in caloric intake over time. CR has been shown to repeatedly increase lifespan and reduce age related disease compared with *ad libitum* (unrestricted eating).[9-13]

Yet, CR has some significant drawbacks. Malnutrition is possible, as it can be quite challenging to limit calories to such a degree and still obtain optimal nutrition. There are also reports in the literature of low libido, infertility, and reduced wound healing associated with CR.[14,15] It's also difficult on an emotional level to constantly limit food intake. Despite the studies that show its associations with increased lifespan and anti-aging effects, I do not advocate CR for any reason. There are other fasting protocols that provide the benefits, while being associated with fewer potential side effects. They're easier to implement mentally and emotionally as well.

Intermittent Fasting (IF) or Fasting

This refers to occasional complete restrictions on eating. **When I refer to intermittent fasting (IF), or fasting in general, I am referring to a water-only fast of 24 hours or more.** The word "intermittent" implies that it's not forever. Typically, these fasts are one to three days in length. Outside that period, food is consumed *ad libitum* (when you wish).

Animal research has demonstrated that alternate day feeding (allowed to eat every other day, fasting on the off days) results in similar life extension as observed with calorie restriction (CR). The advantage of IF over CR is that IF does not require a continuous limitation on caloric intake to obtain the longevity benefits. These animal studies also showed metabolic benefits associated with IF, including improved glucose metabolism, enhanced cardio protection, and reduced risk of age-related diseases including neurodegeneration, cancer, and cardiovascular disease.[16-18] Again, this is similar to the effects of CR, without CR's complications. The benefits of eating and fasting cycles may represent an evolutionary adaptation to food availability—mammals adapted to thrive within a rhythm of nutrient abundance in times of plenty and starvation in between.

Unlike the animal and human research on time restricted eating (TRE, covered next), there are far fewer studies that look at well-designed outcome studies of fasting for greater than 24 hours. In 2015, *The American Journal of Clinical Nutrition* published a review article on this subject. The authors concluded that there is not enough data to answer the question of where the threshold of hormesis resides with longer-term fasting.[19] In other words, how much is just enough, and how much pushes the body past hormesis into damaging stressor? Clearly this will vary for each individual. Longer-term fasting regimens can offer benefits that push the hormesis envelope, but these need to be balanced. Harm can be caused from malnutrition and other risks.

Because of the potential risks, I view IF as a medical therapy reserved for occasional challenges (2 to 4 times per year) and implemented only with proper support and supervision. IF should be medically directed or supervised and is not for everyone.

Time Restricted Eating (TRE)

Time restricted eating (TRE) refers to eating during a defined period of time or "window". Each day, the TRE window begins with the first intake of food or any liquid other than water. Most of us eat freely for about 15 hours every day. In the most basic TRE lifestyle, one might restrict eating to a 12-hour window, perhaps from 8:00 a.m. to 8:00 p.m. An even more beneficial window would be to limit eating to a 10-hour window. This type of eating is more consistent with a normal circadian rhythm and can be followed as a lifelong, daily practice to enhance longevity and health. With TRE, there is no risk of malnutrition (as is seen with calorie restriction), and the eating window can vary.

When we eat matters, and it may matter more than *what* we eat! The timing of food consumption, independent of total calories and food quality, has emerged as a critical factor in determining our metabolic health.[20] Recall that, after eating, we process the glucose, fat, and protein in a few hours. Then, we rely on our glycogen stores for the next several hours. After 6 to 10 hours of not eating, we begin to rely on stored fat to meet our metabolic needs. As you can imagine, remaining in this fat-burning phase a little longer can be advantageous if we want to lose weight, burn fat, and further increase insulin sensitivity. We can also build muscle while in this fat-burning phase by combining fasting with exercise. We'll look at that more closely in Chapter 7. For now, let's take a closer look at the physiological science of TRE, beginning with a more thorough understanding of its interaction with the circadian rhythm.

Calorie Restriction (CR) – Eating approximately 25 to 40 percent fewer calories than recommended for your age and gender.
Intermittent Fasting (IF) – A water-only fast of 24 hours or more. Typically one to three days in length.
Time Restricted Eating (TRE) – Eating only during a limited period of time, typically a window of 12 hours or less each day.

Circadian Secrets: WHEN We Eat, May be More Important Than WHAT We Eat

So much of the body's 24-hour energy cycle is dependent on metabolism. Consider the three main goals of a healthy body:

- Nutritious eating
- Restorative sleep
- Appropriate physical activity

We want to rise in the morning feeling well rested, light, and with maximal energy for the new day. This requires having gone through a fast of at least ten to twelve hours or more. We do not want to feel like we are carrying undigested food in our stomachs. Throughout the day we want to be productive, focused, and make time for physical activity that we enjoy. Ideally, we should stop eating three to four hours before bed so, as evening approaches, we feel tired and fall asleep fast. If we go to bed with a full stomach, blood is directed to the GI tract, our core body temperature rises, and deep restful sleep becomes more challenging. Clearly, there is a rhythm that matters deeply to health and longevity.

It can be hard to appreciate all that your internal "body clock" helps manage and control. You can get a clear picture of it by looking at the health risks of night-shift workers who regularly experience disruption of their circadian rhythms. Studies show that they have increased rates of disease for many conditions including obesity, diabetes, infections, and certain cancers. Night-shift work is such an assault to the circadian rhythm that the World Health Organization has declared night-shift work to be "Potentially Carcinogenic."[21-24] Clearly, circadian rhythm disruptions increase our chances of getting sick. Additionally, mice that have mutations in circadian clock genes experience diseases of metabolism and develop Type 2 diabetes, atherosclerosis, and fatty deposits in their livers.[25,26]

We have nearly a billion people worldwide struggling with obesity, diabetes, and other metabolic diseases. Yet, the conventional medical approach for those patients almost never considers these circadian influences.

Our circadian rhythms run much deeper than we ever imagined. Consider a few more findings regarding the tie between circadian rhythm and metabolism. Healthy adults who eat *identical* meals at breakfast, lunch, and dinner experience the smallest increase in blood sugar after breakfast and the largest increase after dinner. Healthy adults given a constant IV infusion of glucose for 24 hours will have the highest levels of glucose at night with levels falling around dawn.[27,28] This is referred to as "Evening Diabetes". Our bodies are designed to process more food earlier in the day and steadily head toward a fasting state in the evening.

I have repeatedly hinted at the countless circadian rhythms found in the human body that direct so much of human physiology. Every one of the body's 40 trillion cells has a "clock" function that plays a role in the sleep-wake cycle, hormonal cycles, repair physiology, and even what time of day organs function best and when they rest. For example, a healthy body experiences its deepest sleep at 2:00 a.m. and is most alert at 10:00 a.m. Muscles react the fastest at 3:30 p.m. Blood pressure usually peaks at 6:30 p.m.[29-31] Metabolism is also deeply intertwined with circadian rhythms.

The ringleader of all the individual cell and organ clocks has one remarkable name: the *suprachiasmatic nucleus* (SN). It's found in the hypothalamus in the brain, very close to the eyes, and it influences melatonin secretion by the pineal gland. The SN is the master regulator of all the circadian rhythms. It takes in cues from the environment, such as light, and conveys this knowledge to all the body's cells. In fact, our circadian rhythms control about 15 percent of all our genes—**and half of the genes controlled by our circadian rhythm are involved in metabolism**.[32]

Circadian rhythm genes regulate so much more than just the sleep wake cycle. They are key regulators of metabolism and involve many of the genes we use to process sugar, fat, and cholesterol. Circadian rhythm genes also influence the timing of our cellular repair mechanisms. These genes have specific windows of operation—meaning when they are "On" and "Active" and times when they are in "Decline" and "Inactive".[33,34]

A small but growing group of practitioners and researchers are calling more attention to the connection between circadian rhythm and metabolic health. In this community, there is a growing use of language regarding "First Light" and "First Food". First Light simply refers to the time of day when our body experiences light exposure, whether we become fully conscious at that moment or not. First Food refers to the time of day when we take in our first food or drink other than water. These moments of First Light and First Food immediately turn on certain metabolic processes in the body and are the starting point for a limited metabolic window each day.

New research is finding that First Light and First Food determine how our body clocks work. For example, the "liver clock" comprises close to 5000 genes that are activated at different times of the day or night. Experiments clearly show us that the time we eat tells our liver clock to turn certain metabolic genes on. Your First Food at 7:00 a.m. immediately turns on genes that help you process sugar. At that point the metabolic clock is ticking, and it is inherently set by hard-wired circadian rhythms to turn off 12 hours later at 7:00 p.m.[35,36] If you then eat a big meal at 10:00 p.m., the metabolic processes needed to digest it correctly are mostly "off" at that point. Your body will not process that meal intelligently. This means your insulin response will be slow and inefficient, your blood sugar will elevate, nutrient absorption and digestion will be delayed, inflammation will occur, and sleep quality will be poor. TRE can help us get back to our primordial and circadian physiology—the way we were intended to eat.

I realize that the last thing America needs is another diet book. However, we desperately need a new and better approach to disease reversal, wellness, and peak performance. Any discussion on diet needs to begin by appreciating that most Americans eat in a 15-hour window or more, "grazing" on multiple small meals. I know of no benefit from this as a long-term strategy for most people, and it can be quite detrimental over time.

I encourage all my clients to adopt a TRE practice as a foundational, daily, whole-health strategy. TRE can restore circadian balance, reset metabolic health, and even help us make better food choices. When we eat within a narrower window, we have less time to get optimal nutrition to fuel our bodies—our food choices matter more.

TRE and Metabolic Effects

A Landmark Animal Study

In a 2016 study published in *Cell Metabolism*, researchers established two identical groups of mice. Both groups were fed an **unhealthy high fat diet**. The only difference between the groups was that one had access to the unhealthy food *ad libitum* (eating whenever they wanted to). The other group ate the same amount and type of food, but did so in a restricted 12-hour period of time each day.[37] The mice that ate in a time-restricted manner experienced the following benefits:

- Reduction in fat mass
- Increase in lean muscle mass
- Reduced inflammation
- Improved heart function
- Increased mitochondrial volume
- Improved cellular repair
- Improved aerobic endurance in animals that had a TRE window of 9 hours

Again, incredibly, these results were obtained by feeding the TRE mice a high fat diet that was equal in calories to the *ad libitum* fed mice. The TRE mice showed an increase in muscle mass despite restricting their eating. Remember that 15 percent of our entire genome is controlled by our circadian rhythm, and half of those genes control our metabolism—how we process sugar, protein, and fat.[38] Mammalian bodies process food differently when we eat in a time-restricted manner, and these metabolic differences can mean the difference between health and disease.

Think about all the diet books out there and all that has been tried to control weight. In this animal study, unhealthy high-fat food was given in an amount that typically makes the animals fat. However, simply restricting the eating window resulted in dramatic metabolic improvements.

There is no calorie-counting required for these benefits. No portioning of any kind. The benefits stem from the fact that the human body simply wasn't designed to experience *ad libitum* eating. How many of us might be able to get control of our weight management goals by simply eating in a time-restricted manner? The effects on weight management are multiplied exponentially when we eat in a time-restricted fashion AND make more intelligent eating choices. So, no, I'm not endorsing that people utilize TRE only while eating low-quality food. All the health benefits are magnified when TRE is combined with healthy eating and the other therapies presented in this book.

TRE and Immunity: Normalizing Immune Function

At the beginning of this chapter, I mentioned a study regarding the connection between illness behaviors and the ability to fight infection. That remarkable study was published in *Cell* in 2016. In it, mice were infected with a non-lethal bacterial infection—something mice can normally fight off easily. One group of mice was allowed to self-treat, to fast if they wished to. Two other groups of mice had their glucose levels brought up to normal, either through force-feeding or through intravenous infusion of glucose. Amazingly, simply increasing glucose levels to **normal**, was enough to turn the non-lethal bacterial infection into a lethal one. We are learning that fasting and other illness behaviors represent an evolved strategy to support host recovery from infection.[39]

Fasting is way more powerful than most of us appreciate. Not only does it appear to help turn on certain reparative and immune system activities, it also causes stress for unhealthy cells.[40] This has implications in the presence of one of the most significant immune system challenges: cancer.

Fasting cycles have been reported to be as effective as chemotherapy against certain tumors in mice. Another set of laboratory studies combined fasting with chemotherapy and resulted in significantly enhanced healthy cell survival. By contrast, a control group in one study demonstrated a 100 percent death rate when the animal subjects were administered chemotherapy alone.[41-44]

TRE is showing powerful success reducing cancer recurrences in both animal and human studies. A 2016 study analyzed 2,500 breast cancer survivors followed for 7.5 years. Those who practiced TRE, and had a nine-hour eating window or less, reduced their recurrence rate significantly compared to those who did not practice TRE.[45]

TRE's Additional Benefits

Anti-aging Effects – TRE's ability to enhance longevity and healthy aging, likely stems from the way fasting can upregulate autophagy,[46] that system by which the body's cells recycle old or damaged cellular componentry and turn them back into usable material. This is at the heart of cellular repair. It's well accepted that aging results from a breakdown of the body's structure combined with a failure to properly repair itself. Autophagy is an evolutionary conserved process that is consistently and robustly upregulated during periods of fasting. Up-regulating autophagy ultimately helps individual cells remain in a younger-looking profile for a longer time.[47,48]

Probiotic Health: The *microbiome* refers to all the different bacteria species in the intestinal tract and in many other locations inside and on the surface of the human body. Collectively, intestinal microbes play roles in metabolic function, immune function, and vitamin production,[49] and may even affect brain health.[50] A diverse microbiome is fundamental to whole-body health, and TRE has been found to promote microbiome diversity. It seems that a fasting state encourages the growth of specific microbial strains.[51,52] Eating supports another group of microbes. It would appear that the microbiome optimally follows and prefers an eating-fasting circadian rhythm like all our cells and organs.

Other Digestive Challenges – Viewed collectively, heartburn, acid reflux, and irritable bowel affect millions of Americans. Case stories and preliminary studies have shown that TRE can improve acid-related symptoms and reduce the severity of irritable bowel conditions.[53] This is currently unpublished data, but it makes intuitive sense. Such conditions would improve as microbiome diversity increases and the patient reduces late night eating. As noted earlier, TRE supports a normalized metabolism and a healthy circadian rhythm, both of which are intertwined with digestion.

Improved Sleep and Enhanced Energy – Significant human data has demonstrated improvements in sleep and more reported energy in those who practice TRE with an eating window of twelve hours or less.[54]

Improved Heart Rate Variability (HRV) – TRE in animal models shows improvements in Heart Rate Variability (HRV).[55] HRV is a measure of overall heart health, as discussed in Chapter 2.

Meet the Patients Who Have Benefitted

Fasting is the hormetic therapy that is the easiest to incorporate into daily life. The actual impact of TRE and IF can be hard to comprehend until you learn how these simple practices have worked in real life challenges. These two individuals provide vivid portraits of the dramatic improvement triggered by relatively simple lifestyle choices.

Case Story #1
54-year-old Female with Diabetes

Mary is a 54-year-old Type 2 diabetic whom I met at one of our Vitality Health Challenge resort weekend experiences. Over the previous decade fighting her disease, she had gained weight, developed arthritis, cut back on playing tennis because of pain, and needed to increase her oral diabetic medications. When we met, she informed me that her doctor's and nutritionist's advice to eat multiple small carbohydrate containing meals was helpful to maintain her blood sugar and prevent falls in her glucose level. I challenged her on that point extensively as we had touched on this concept during the weekend's workshops.

"Knowing all that you know now, does that make sense to you?" I asked. "How can elevating your blood sugar many times throughout the day help restore your insulin sensitivity? Isn't this part of the problem in the first place?"

"Well, it prevents my blood sugar from getting too low," she insisted.

I acknowledged that was true, but low blood sugar wasn't her underlying problem. Her *reduced insulin sensitivity* was the real challenge. If she could improve her insulin sensitivity, her body would regulate blood sugar better and reduce the times when it over- or under-corrected. "A better goal would be to eat in a fashion that keeps your insulin levels low," I said. "Practice TRE, and work toward narrowing the TRE window as a hormetic challenge. That can help repair many of the underlying problems you're facing." I upped the challenge and said that I was sure we could improve things in six to eight weeks or less.

She was skeptical but definitely intrigued. "Why is this information not out there?" she asked. "What if I get into trouble with low blood sugars?"

I explained how our modern medical system isn't designed to optimally manage metabolic conditions. "You are a powerful example of this," I said. "Your disease has progressed, and you're on more pharmaceutical medications. I promise, you'll know quickly if we're making progress with these suggestions."

Those comments reached her. She wanted to learn what to do next on a practical level.

First, we needed to shift her eating style, away from the high carbohydrate foods she believed that she needed to maintain steady blood sugar levels. I wanted her to incorporate more raw and fermented foods since they are so nutrient dense and tax the digestive system the least. I educated Mary that cooking our food by any means destroys enzymes and other nutrients present. Raw foods and plant-based foods can help diabetics maintain more constant blood sugar readings over time.[56] I promised her that, at any time, if she felt dizzy, lightheaded, or had signs that she was experiencing low blood sugar, she could rescue herself with whatever she typically used—candy, juice, etc.

Mary started incorporating raw, plant-based, protein smoothies consisting of mostly nuts, seeds, berries, and greens. These replaced her carb heavy oatmeal and juice breakfasts. She added in more healthy salads, vegetables, and organic eggs and meats to replace her typical sandwiches, pastas, and snacks. I taught her how to make a raw, grain-free, granola using a low temperature food dehydrator. I wanted her to see that she could maintain stable blood sugar without the need for refined carbohydrates.

Within one month, Mary had adjusted well to this healthier foundational nutrition. She'd also had no signs or symptoms of low blood sugar.

Our next goal was to reduce Mary's typical daily number of meals from six to three.[57] This was a challenge because of how accustomed she was to eating anytime she wanted. I did limit her physical activity for the first two weeks, as I wanted her system to have some time to adjust to the new dietary plan with limited external stress. We discussed the goal of shifting from burning a constant supply of carbohydrates to accessing the better energy source: her body's stored fat. Again, within two weeks of reducing her number of meals, she was surprised that she never needed to "rescue herself" from low blood sugars, her energy was more stable, and she was sleeping better than she had in years.

Now that Mary was down to three meals a day, we focused on trying to have her eat most of her food at breakfast and lunch. We made those meals much bigger and reduced the size of her dinners. She also resumed her exercise program. She felt stronger and noted better energy later in the day, which was quite new for her.

The next phase was to begin a strict twelve-hour TRE window with the goal of reducing it down to under ten. This was a big psychological challenge. Mary took six weeks to get to a true twelve-hour window. Ultimately, she discovered that eating nothing was actually easier for her system to manage than eating a little. This is something I hear from almost everyone who begins TRE or fasting. *It is easier to eat nothing than to eat a little.* This is because even small meals elevate blood sugar, cause an insulin response (and trigger other hormones), and either start or continue our organ clocks. Eating nothing promotes all the metabolic changes outlined in this chapter, including helping us burn body fat, reduce blood sugar, and increase insulin sensitivity.

In addition to the dietary modifications, Mary also benefitted from other therapies aimed at targeting her inflammation and training her exercise/recovery physiology, along with trying certain oxygen therapies. She was ultimately able to reduce her diabetic medication for the first time in a decade and hopes to wean off it eventually.

Case Story #2

37-year-old Nurse with Frequent Cravings While at Work

Sean is a 37-year-old nurse who had worked with me in the past to treat an underactive thyroid condition that was not well managed previously. After we addressed that concern, he asked if I had anything to offer regarding his constant cravings during busy workdays. He reported feeling hungry at 10:30 or 11:00 a.m. and having trouble thinking about anything other than food if he did not eat by 11:30.

This occurred regularly, despite a big breakfast that he ate at 6:00 a.m. just before leaving from home. I asked if he was hungry at 6:00, and he said, "No, but isn't breakfast the most important meal of the day?"

I knew I had a solution when he said that.

Sean was eating in a 15-hour window. I gave him a target of an eight to ten-hour window to help meet some of his other health goals. I suggested that he take his breakfast to work and eat it when he first noticed he was hungry. Then he could try waiting an additional 30 minutes to one hour to eat his breakfast the next day. This was a hard change, as he was so accustomed to always having food in him prior to work.

Initially, the first step of bringing his breakfast to work wasn't too difficult. But as the window narrowed, and breakfast was delayed more, Sean described feeling intense hunger initially. He said he ate quickly and ate more food than typically needed, as soon as his TRE window opened. But then he noted that those sensations passed in a few days. After just a few days, Sean could treat the process like yoga or an athletic challenge. That meant he could begin eating his first meal of the day, when his TRE window opened, with a sense of control and relaxation. His experience is similar to what I see in many clients—the sense that TRE is so hard to begin and then so easy and natural once they've practiced it for a week or two.

Sean experienced the full benefits of what TRE has to offer. He told me that after practicing TRE for a month, his "craving problem" was solved. He could concentrate at work and stay focused even if he did not eat until much later in the day. He no longer had to go to lunch first. Even his co-workers noted the difference in his behavior. Sean also noted better sleep and more energy. I explained to him that he had succeeded in changing his metabolism from burning carbohydrates to burning predominantly fat. And when we are predominantly burning fat, it is much easier to maintain constant energy without blood sugar fluctuations.

Vitality Health Challenge TRE Testimonials

"My weight is down nine pounds rather effortlessly. I love the no-diet feeling. No counting calories. No worry about fat grams. No macros. No pressure. I have been dieting for most of my adult life and this does not feel like a diet at all. It is more like a lifestyle change… I satiate faster and longer, and for the first time hunger is not controlling me. When my TRE window closes, it is quite freeing—the eating is done and the fasting begins. I like the cycles."

—Betty; 57-year-old long distance runner who made a single regimen change: A six to eight-hour TRE window for three months

"I am not missing out on any particular type of food. This is such a sustainable way to live. There is nothing about TRE that I do not like."

—Carly; 37-year-old nurse who practiced TRE and made no other changes

"Scales are the devil so I can't quantify weight, but I take a naked selfie every year on my birthday and this one was the best ever."

—Rene; 38-year-old female who tried TRE out of an interest in anti-aging medicine to look youthful

"For the first time in my adult life I don't feel hungry all the time. I also like that I can adjust the window to accommodate a late dinner on vacation or over a weekend."

—Sam; 50-year-old who incorporated TRE and oxygen therapies for treatment of fatigue

Try It! Incorporating Appropriate Fasting Practices into YOUR Life

The easiest at-home hormetic therapy

I individualize my clients' diets. This is because nutrient needs change over time, our activities and goals change, and different diets can support different medical conditions. It's best to begin a fasting protocol with an initial consultation with an integrative physician. But if you have already worked with a professional to develop a healthy eating plan, it's easy to incorporate TRE into your lifestyle. Then meet with your practitioner to discuss occasionally utilizing IF for specific health goals.

There are some common diet and fasting guidelines that I stress to all of my clients:

1. Eat raw and cultured (fermented) foods daily.
2. Eat organic as much as possible. Always buy organic versions of the foods listed in the Environmental Working Group's "Dirty Dozen." (www.ewg.org)
3. Limit animal protein if diabetic, overweight, or if you have heart disease.
4. Eat in a TRE fashion, with an eating window no greater than twelve hours and preferably closer to ten hours.
5. Most importantly, eat in a fashion that keeps your insulin levels low. This is a proven anti-aging strategy. This means

no refined foods and no all-carbohydrate meals. Significantly increase your intake of nutrient-rich cruciferous veggies (broccoli, cauliflower, brussels sprouts) and dark greens. Meanwhile lessen your intake of carb-rich white potatoes, corn, and lima beans. The underlying goal is to burn your stored fat, which is your body's preferred fuel source. Remember, the presence of any carbohydrates in your system halts your body's process for burning stored fat. That is why grazing is such a bad behavior. It essentially guarantees that we will have carbohydrates in our systems all the time and ends any chance of burning stored body fat.

Practical Tips for Starting the TRE Practice

We are all different, and each of us adjust to changes on our own time frame. The first goal is to figure out approximately what your current window of eating is and what your new goal will be.

1. **Identify Your Current Eating Window.** If you're like most Americans, you eat anytime you wish from a quick on-the-run breakfast at 7:00 a.m. until a late-night snack at 10:00 or 11:00 p.m. That's a fifteen to sixteen-hour window.

2. **Set a Goal for a New Window.** I personally like to practice TRE with an eating window of eight to nine hours every day. You can pick the eating window that works best for your schedule and lifestyle, but remember that you want to end the window at least two to three hours before bedtime. You may adjust your window as needed. A good starting point may be a twelve-hour window that opens at 7:00 a.m. and ends at 7:00 p.m. If you wanted a nine-hour window, you might start at 10:00 a.m. and end at 7:00 p.m.

You may find it's easiest to set the goal of a twelve-hour window, but work up to that in stages over several days. **A one-hour shift each day is good progress.** Initially, you might wait an extra 30 to 60 minutes to have your breakfast—without greatly impacting a busy morning routine. Instead of eating shortly after rising, you'll begin extending your usual breakfast time out—one hour at a time. Notice how you feel. Take the time you need for your body to adjust. It will vary for everyone. Many people enjoy the great energy and concentration, without blood sugar swings, that occur in this extended fat-burning phase in the early morning. Essentially, you're increasing your insulin sensitivity and your ability to burn stored body fat as you persist in this early morning fasting state. Once you've shifted your mornings, you might take a week to work on your evening routine, working up to a goal of fasting for at least three hours before bedtime.

3. Minimize grazing and pay attention to what works best for you as your First Food. As you limit your time frame for eating, you'll notice you become more selective about what you eat. Do you prefer a raw, plant-based smoothie or scrambled eggs in the morning? Which lasts longer for you energy-wise as your First Food? Which works best for your digestive system?

4. Be diligent about water-only outside your TRE window. There is significant misinformation claiming that it is acceptable to have coffee or tea outside of the TRE window. Recall that anything other than water will start your body's metabolic and organ clocks. So, avoiding coffee and tea outside the TRE window is best. If you absolutely must get your morning caffeine fix before your TRE window starts, black coffee is better than coffee with cream, milk, or sugar added. Even that small amount of dairy or sugar provides enough protein or carbs to trigger your body's metabolic clock. It acts as your First Food for the day.

5. Track the physical effects. Keep a notebook or computer document tracking the effects you've noticed as you shift your eating window. Note the date along with any fatigue, strengthening, or any changes to sleep patterns, mood, energy, and medical conditions. Use these notes to discuss your TRE practice with your integrative practitioner.

6. Once your TRE rhythm is set and comfortable, consider adding new challenges. I like to view TRE like physical activity; variation and challenges can offer enhanced benefits. I'll occasionally adjust my eating window, reducing it further for an extra challenge. Sometimes I'll eat only one meal a day. I do this to help reset after a trip or holiday.

You can give yourself another four to five hours of fat burning if you wait to eat until noon or 1:00 p.m. to eat your First Food. It is still crucial to finish eating at least three hours before bedtime. Like an intense workout, these additional challenges can be stressful. But remember that our genes evolved to expect stress. These occasional stressors are key to triggering hormesis and its powerful evolutionarily conserved physiology. Our systems suffer without these challenges. Pushing the TRE window definitely qualifies as a hormetic therapy.

A few times per year, I also practice IF—a true multi-day water-only fast. While these fasts should only be implemented under professional guidance, let's take a closer look at the IF protocol, its cautions, and some questions you can ask your integrative practitioner.

Practical Tips for Extended Fasting (IF)

We do not want fasting to ever turn into starvation and threaten organ function and muscle mass. Typically, that process would take weeks. Anyone implementing a short one- or two-day fast would not need to be concerned about that. Nevertheless, each of us should consider how often and for how long we fast beyond 24 hours. I work with my clients to individualize this work. Here are some general guidelines that you can discuss with your own practitioner:

- **Know your body well—this is Priority #1.** Know what your body's indicators are that you've crossed the line between hormetic challenge and damaging stressor. Hormesis has limits—we want challenge, not damage.

- **Get comfortable with TRE and TRE challenge goals.** Before you try a 24-hour fast, try narrowing your TRE window from ten or twelve hours down to a five- or six-hour window. Practice this narrow TRE window for at least five to ten consecutive days before you attempt your first 24-hour fast.

- **Drink water!** Plan to drink purified, high quality water to ensure full hydration. This may mean roughly six to eight eight-ounce glasses per day.

- **Be gentle with yourself on your first fast.** Do not set expectations on your performance. Schedule your first extended fast for a weekend. Pay close attention to your body during the fast. Be flexible. If you transition from hormetic challenge to damaging fatigue, stop the fast. Have food at the ready to address this possibility.

- **Respect your body's limits, and keep in mind the science of fasting.** Once your glycogen supply is exhausted and you are in the fat-burning zone, you may feel great. Still plan to end your first extended fast at 24 hours.

Signs to Pay Attention to While Fasting
If any of these persist and worsen, it is likely a sign you've left the hormetic zone and may be causing damaging stress to your body.

- Headaches
- Feeling Dizzy or Lightheaded
- Weakness
- Dehydration
- Excessive hunger pains

Respect these indicators. When they occur, it's time to end the fast.

Fasting and TRE

HEALTH GOALS TRIAD

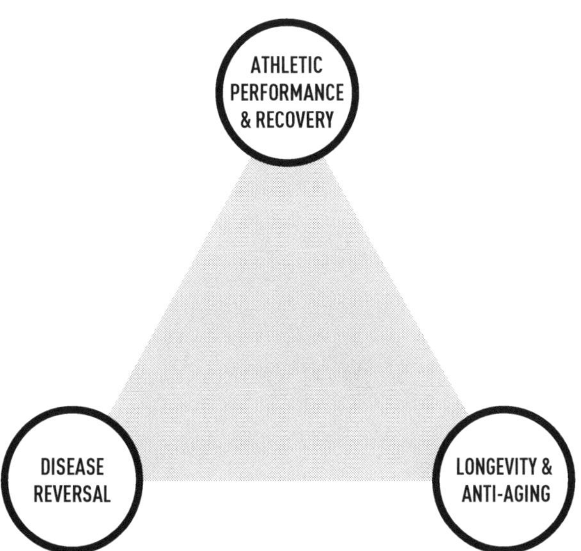

DISEASE REVERSAL Appropriate fasting practices can have far reaching metabolic effects. Time Restricted Eating (TRE) accesses an up-regulated metabolism that helps prevent or treat cardiovascular challenges and diabetes. TRE and Intermittent Fasting (IF) can also enhance immune function. TRE, IF, and ketogenic diets are often recommended in integrative oncology.

LONGEVITY & ANTI-AGING Animal studies show a connection between IF and longevity. That's likely due to an up regulated metabolism and heightened autophagy (cellular repair). As we age, autophagy is compromised, which leads to the symptoms of aging. IF can heighten autophagy, which encourages youthful cellular function. TRE also normalizes circadian rhythm, which results in better sleep and daytime energy.

ATHLETIC PERFORMANCE & RECOVERY Even pro athletes can experience slumps if they don't cleanse the toxins generated during intense workouts. Fasting practices boost autophagy and detoxification. Athletes need to "train" sleep and cellular repair cycles just like they train for performance, and TRE does just that. Exercise within the fasting window provides additional hormetic challenge. Athletes who fast appropriately report improved sleep, energy, and HRV.

WHEN YOU EAT MAY BE MORE IMPORTANT THAN WHAT YOU EAT

Further Science

Read the Research for Yourself

The following provides just a few highlighted studies that can help you expand your understanding of the material in this chapter. Comprehensive chapter References & Notes are found at the end of the book. To read more about these studies, search for "PubMed" online, the world's largest medical library. Reach PubMed directly at: https://www.ncbi.nlm.nih.gov/pubmed/

1.

Panda S. "Circadian physiology of metabolism." *Science.* 2016 Nov 25; 354(6315): 1008-1015.

If you want to review only one article on this subject, Dr. Panda's article is the ideal choice. He is the leading authority on how circadian rhythms influence metabolism. Figure 3 of his article is fascinating as it shows how circadian rhythm disruptions lead to pathological conditions, and how TRE promotes health across a wide array of parameters including weight management, insulin levels, the microbiome, inflammation levels, cancer risk, and sleep patterns. This article should be required reading for everyone.

2.

Kahleova H, et al. "Eating two larger meals a day (breakfast and lunch) is more effective than six smaller meals in a reduced energy regimen for patients with type 2 diabetes: a randomized crossover study." *Diabetologia.* 2014: 57(8): 1552-1560.

As mentioned in Mary's case story, the common advice for diabetic patients to eat many small meals throughout the day does not make metabolic sense. The researchers who published this study certainly found that to be the case. They compared two groups of diabetic patients who consumed the same amount and types of food. The only difference is that one group ate two meals per day (breakfast and lunch), and the other group consumed six smaller meals throughout the day. The two-meal-per-day diabetic group experienced reduced weight, lowered fasting glucose levels, less inflammation, and improved insulin sensitivity. The other group did not.

3.

Maroon J, Bost J, Amos A, Zuccoli G. "Restricted calorie ketogenic diet for the treatment of glioblastoma multiforme." *Journal of Child Neurology.* 28(8) 1002-1008.

This article illustrates how far reaching a calorie-restricted ketogenic diet can be. Glioblastoma multiforme, the most common malignant primary brain tumor in adults, is almost universally fatal. Surgery, chemotherapy, radiation, and steroids can only extend survival periods in adults from six months without therapy, to twelve to eighteen months with therapy. The researchers note that cancer cells have a high demand for glucose as energy. A ketogenic diet avoids glucose and all carbohydrate sources. This leads to the production of ketone bodies from fat sources as an alternative energy source for normal cells, while it starves cancer cells of their required fuel (glucose). Reducing calorie intake, combined with a ketogenic diet, further increases the production of ketone bodies and augments autophagy. Exploiting the metabolic differences of cancer cells by these dietary practices offers a new therapeutic approach to target aggressive cancers. This article summarizes the potential benefits of such a strategy and the current protocols to date, exploring restricted calorie ketogenic diets to treat aggressive cancer.

Chapter 6
Cold Exposure and Autonomic Integration

We have the power to consciously alter immune and hormonal response

If you live in the northern hemisphere, at some point you've likely laughed at a mid-winter news report about a local community group organizing a Polar Plunge. Maybe you've even participated in one. Whatever the case, it's a familiar sight. A group of brave and crazy individuals set a date to break open the ice on a frozen lake and jump into the water together. The scene is always characterized by screaming, crazed laughter, the chaotic jump itself, and a wild scramble for towels and blankets to warm up immediately thereafter. For those watching the report from the warmth of their living rooms, it's worth a headshake and a good laugh.

Try envisioning a completely different scene, involving the same icy water. You're taking a wintertime walk along a frozen river. Suddenly you notice someone a little farther along the shoreline. The man calmly strips down to swim trunks, puts on water shoes, and walks to the edge of a large hole in the ice. Then, with equal calm, he drops himself into the water and swims for a few minutes. Still calm and, astoundingly, not shivering, he walks to his clothes and towel, calmly dries off, drapes the towel loosely around his shoulders, and then carries his clothes up a hill to his house.

The man not only wasn't panicked about the situation, he was completely focused and controlled. He didn't just dip his feet in the water and not wince, he submerged and swam for a few minutes, then walked home as if he'd just taken a refreshing morning dip in the heat of late July.

If you saw such a thing, you'd be justifiably perplexed. Believe it or not, that second scene is just as feasible as the news feed about a local Polar Plunge. There are people who practice cold exposure as a scientifically proven way to access and alter their own autonomic nervous systems. This practice was a stretch for me, but today I'm that man who swims in the river near my home year-round, even when it's ten degrees.

Comfortable? Definitely not at first. It's an athletic and therapeutic practice after all; one that requires pre-conditioning and incremental stages. But today I can ice water swim with calm control. The question is, "Why would I want to do that?"

There are good, and now scientifically proven, reasons for practicing controlled cold exposure. Through unusual activated forms of meditation and breathing, paired with strategic cold exposure challenges, you can affect your own neurology. This is the heart of what I refer to as *Autonomic Integration*—the use of breathing techniques and physical challenges to access and consciously influence autonomic systems. Those are the body systems that are not typically under conscious control, including immune activation, stress and hormonal responses, heart rate, and breathing. True Autonomic Integration is the result of practices that empower people to have a level of willful influence over their autonomic systems. I'm not interested in ice water swimming as a brag or as an extreme athletic accomplishment. I'm interested in how it can completely alter immune and metabolic health.

Why Would Anyone Want to Feel Cold?

Of all the hormetic therapies, cold exposure is the least attractive. Many of my clients would rather complete a 24-hour fast than take an ice bath—and that says a lot! It takes time and learning to break down the walls and misconceptions regarding cold exposure. Starting out, it helps to recognize that we've all used cold exposure medically at some point in our lives.

It's the first home remedy for a sprained ankle or a sore back: the ice pack. At some point, we've all been told to put ice on an injury to promote tissue healing and reduce pain and swelling. When we look at the zone-specific effects of an ice pack applied to soft tissue injury, we can begin to appreciate why whole-body cold exposure is so powerful. When an ice pack is applied, it's immediately anti-inflammatory. Tissue and blood vessels constrict; swelling and pain are reduced. We learn to ice injuries at a young age, and that familiarity and understanding stays with us throughout life.

Cryotherapy is defined as the use of extreme cold for medical or therapeutic benefit. Humankind has recognized the medical value of cold therapies for millennia. The Egyptians used cold to treat injuries and inflammation as early as 2500 BCE. In the time of Napoleon, military surgeons used cold therapy to facilitate amputations. Cryosurgery, the use of the cold to facilitate removal of skin lesions, was introduced in the late 1800s. More recently, whole-body cryotherapy, introduced in the 1980s, is now widely used to treat inflammation, pain, swelling, and to enhance athletic recovery. Whole-body cryotherapy involves exposing the entire body, except the head and neck, to liquid nitrogen gas at freezing temperatures in the range of -200 to -300 Fahrenheit, for up to three minutes.[1]

From ice packs to cryotherapy, it's not such a big leap to recognize the benefit of ice baths for elite athletes—a common practice for tennis stars, World Cup soccer players, and NFL football players after their most grueling games. The ice bath causes immediate constriction of blood vessels and muscle tissue, causing expulsion of built up lactic acid, metabolic byproducts (toxins), and inflammatory mediators. It results in much faster recovery, reduced next-day soreness, and more efficient repair of minor ligament or tendon strains.[2]

It's just like ice packing a sprained ankle, but these athletes are harnessing the cold as a **whole-body anti-inflammatory**. They're using cold exposure as preventive medicine.

I was already aware of athletic applications of ice baths when I first heard about a more refined application of cold exposure. I understood the need for hormetic therapies in all immune and metabolic health goals. I was already educating my clients about the value of enhancing cardio health through cyclic exercise, oxygen therapies, and enhancing metabolism through fasting practices. In all these practices, I'd noticed that common thread of re-awakening and triggering hormesis—all those body systems that are wired for living well in the face of extreme challenge.

We are Well-tuned for Surviving and Thriving in the Cold

Remember how the person who sits in a temperature-controlled office cubicle all day still has a body that's highly adapted for physical struggle? We have deeply wired, remarkable abilities to go without food, to manage sudden bursts of athletic activity, and also to survive temperature extremes. Just as controlled fasting can unlock key aspects of our evolutionary metabolic physiology, exposing ourselves to the cold can unlock other metabolic, vascular, and immune system adaptations that can't be accessed any other way. As I've mentioned before, our bodies need these stressors in order to turn on some of our most vital metabolic functions and immune system activities.

Some of the benefits of cold exposure are still at the edge of published research, but the known benefits of cold exposure are broad.

Those benefits don't stop at the "whole-body anti-inflammatory effect" that elite athletes glean from their ice baths:

- **General Wellness:** Cold therapies are well-known for promoting athletic recovery, reducing inflammation, and supporting tissue healing. Cold exposure facilitates the removal of lactic acid and other toxins trapped in muscles.[3,4]
- **Vitality**: Cold exposure increases general well-being and enhances energy levels.[5]
- **Vascular Tone**: All our blood vessels are lined by tiny muscles. Those muscles are only worked through cold-induced constriction.[6] If we never practice cold training, the muscles in our vasculature are never worked.[7]
- **Metabolic Effects**: Cold exposure can increase metabolic rate, often more so than exercise.[8]
- **Weight Loss**: Regular cold exposure can significantly benefit people with major weight loss goals, especially those who have trouble exercising. Cold exposure can increase "brown fat" production, which can also aid weight loss.[9]
- **Immune Response:** Cold exposure modulates immune response by both reducing inflammatory proteins and heightening white blood cell counts. Even a single cold shower will cause an increase in white blood cell (WBC) count.[10]
- **Mood and Energy:** After cold exposure, people experience a heightened metabolism and an endorphin rush, both of which can be energizing and rejuvenating.[11]
- **Hormesis:** In general, appropriate cold exposure is a powerful hormetic stimulus that benefits overall stress response, adaptability, and resilience.[12]

That last benefit is really at the core of all the other effects of cold therapy. Once again, this is another hormetic therapy with powerful multi-system effects. People who practice cold exposure on a regular basis report an interesting side benefit that's clearly hormetic in nature. The practice seems to re-wire their brains to confront other challenges with greater calm and clarity. The whole body tends to respond better to other stressors in life. By practicing a calm, confident attitude as they enter cold water or a cold room, these clients become healthier in their response to other stress in their day-to-day lives. They're calm in the face of an aggressive work deadline or surprisingly clear-headed when a loved one experiences a major medical crisis. Heart rate, metabolism, and immune response become more dynamic, finely tuned, and responsive.[13] Not only do they feel better mentally in the presence of life stress, they stay healthier too.

It makes sense when you think about it. Someone whose body cells are trained to flex, adapt, and thrive in the face of challenge, should be more capable and effective in managing any of life's stresses than someone whose body only expects constant comfort. When we constantly avoid cold exposure, and other hormetic therapies, we never work these innate systems. This isn't about how awesome and extreme you are for submerging yourself in cold water. It's about the medical benefits and how we can make those benefits accessible to everyone.

We'll explore all of the benefits more in-depth within the Protocol Description section of this chapter. We'll also unpack the specific techniques of the Wim Hof Method (WHM) and how I've adapted the cold exposure activities to make them more accessible. (No, you don't have to take daily ice swims in the wintertime to access the basic benefits of cold exposure.) But before we get to all that, I should let you know what it was like to meet the cold exposure king, Wim Hof.

Meeting Wim Hof

Beyond the Extreme Athlete Persona

As I grew my practice focusing on hormetic principles, I was on several mailing lists that notified me of new studies. One of those news feeds shared an article about a Dutch man named Wim Hof. This man was known as an extreme athlete who specialized in cold exposure feats. He wore summer clothing while hiking up snowy mountains. He held multiple world records for incredible feats in the ice including the longest recorded ice bath, and running a marathon in subzero temperatures wearing only shorts and sneakers. He broke multiple records for the longest swim in ice water.[14] When submerged in ice water, undercooling typically begins at three minutes, and hypothermia-induced death can occur after one hour of exposure. However, Hof defied medical logic when he was able to remain in ice water for 80 minutes without showing signs of undercooling.[15]

That alone piqued my curiosity. But as an integrative physician, what caught my eye was the latest study on Hof's immune system. Hof had developed a meditation and breathing method that he combined with his cold exposure challenges. When he did these practices, he was able to alter his immune response in a profound manner. His white blood cell count increased, and he had a dramatically modulated immune response in the presence of a potential infection.[16]

More importantly, he was able to train other healthy adults in his method, and these individuals demonstrated the same immune system shifts in their lab results.[17] Hof isn't a freak of nature. He'd developed a solid method that is teachable. Other people can use his techniques to alter their own metabolisms and immune systems.

Now that was interesting. I wanted to know how this man had hacked his Autonomic Nervous System (ANS) and how people with everyday health goals might benefit from cold exposure practices. Did it really require regular ice water swimming? Or might there be some cold therapies that were a bit more accessible for the average person? And most importantly, how could these therapies advance my integrative medical model?

I continually research health and wellness, constantly seeking out the best and most effective modalities to incorporate into my practice. I am quite selective. Any new therapy must be natural, scientifically proven, and efficacious. I was immediately drawn to the science of Hof's work and cold training in particular.

Quick Review: The Autonomic Nervous System (ANS)

The **ANS** controls vital subconscious functions such as breathing, blood pressure, temperature, digestion, waste processing, cellular repair, immune response, and all other systems that generally function without conscious control. It is comprised of:

The Sympathetic Nervous System – The fight or flight response system. It prepares the body for action, makes the heart beat faster and stronger, opens airways, and inhibits digestion.

The Parasympathetic System – The rest and repair system. It lowers heart rate, calms breathing, encourages cellular repair, and promotes digestion.

For those of you who haven't heard of Wim Hof, I should mention that he is a daredevil and his extreme athlete platform isn't for everyone. That reality aside, Hof has been able to use his persona to bring attention and scientific validation to new paradigm-shifting findings about the ANS. Hof's feats have shown us that we can influence aspects of our physiology long believed to be outside of conscious control. His work is part of my medical model and worthy of exploration.

I remain amazed by so much about Wim Hof—his incredible feats in the ice, his furthering of our knowledge about the ANS, and his scientific understanding of body systems despite a lack of any formal medical training. A few years ago, I traveled to Brooklyn, New York to attend one of his one-day educational events. I recall arriving early, heading inside the venue, and seeing Hof walking around barefoot in a pair of shorts and a tee shirt. He was so approachable and excited to meet and greet people.

I was equally impressed by Hof's passion, desire to teach, and his determination to improve people's lives. He described his record-breaking ice exposure feats and how they brought him media attention and international recognition. But it became clear that, at this point, furthering the science of his discoveries was his primary motivation. "What I am capable of, anyone can learn," he said. He was obviously willing to put in the effort to teach his cold exposure techniques to any willing student. I could tell this was truly his mission.

I also remember Hof commenting on a more philosophical nuance, saying, "The ice is a mirror." I have spent a lot of time considering that statement and now view the cold as a constant force that simply reflects back to us where we are, what we are feeling, what we believe in the moment, and what we think we are capable of. My capability and resolve in the face of any cold exposure is often directly linked to my current mindset or outlook on life. When I approach a cold exposure with confidence and resolve, I am much more likely to have success. However, if I am distracted or upset about something, cold exposure will be much more challenging, if not impossible.

Hof's team was equally impressive--open, committed, and informative. I spoke to one of his instructors during the one-day event and asked about making my own ice water tank at home. The instructor was generous with tips and instructions. Shortly after that event, I transformed an upright chest-style freezer into an ice bath in my garage. Once I had access to my own ice bath, I had all that I needed to practice this hormetic therapy anytime I desired. I also committed to swimming in the river near my home at least once a month for the next twelve months and began to exercise in my outdoor workout area four times per week all winter, without normal winter clothing. Interestingly, I never caught a cold that winter despite my usual exposure to sick clients.

In addition to the one-day workshop in the U.S., I also attended a week-long intensive experience with Hof and his team the following December in the wintery mountains of Poland. That experience was also transformative. There were sixteen different countries represented in my small group of twenty. We trained for close to twelve hours per day practicing Wim's methods which consisted of breathing exercises, mindset practices, and many different cold exposures. These included hiking in the cold with limited clothing, exposure to active waterfalls with water much colder than 32 degrees, and learning how to actively re-warm our bodies after cold exposure.

I came away from that time with a refined understanding of cold exposure, its whole health benefit, and how to utilize it for myself and for my clients. More than that, I felt I had insights that could expand the Wim Hof Method (WHM) and apply it within a greater context of multiple hormetic therapies. I knew that my integrative medical knowledge could also allow me to reach those who either viewed Hof as too extreme, wanted to more thoroughly understand the science, or needed to address certain medical conditions before undertaking cold training. And since I medically assess each client, I could design hormetic challenges that were safe and customized to the individual.

Let's take a detailed look at the WHM to better understand how it works. Then we'll take a look at how it fits into a much larger context with therapies that complement and balance its effects.

Trained Versus Untrained Cold Exposure

Using the WHM to Befriend the Cold

Cold therapy does have incredible benefits, but it remains a highly under-utilized therapy simply because most people hate feeling cold! I've heard all the typical resistance: *Being cold is dangerous. I will get sick from cold exposure. Are you crazy?!* However, once clients open the door to this therapy, I've seen them go through total transformations both in their health and in their relationship with the cold. Through training and incremental practice, it's possible to alter the physical sensation of the cold and make it more tolerable. Wim's method (WHM) allows for even more benefits than typical cold exposures offer. These include a deeper access to the ANS and the ability to direct and influence immune and hormonal systems.

Untrained exposure to cold differs dramatically from trained exposure. Let's compare that first-time polar plunger to someone trained in cold exposure. The untrained polar plunge participant has a sense of panic. Heart rate increases dramatically. The ice water often feels like it's burning. Muscles tense. Breathing temporarily stops or becomes very shallow. The mind doesn't think clearly.

In trained cold exposure, breathing is controlled. The mind is completely focused. The body performs intelligently. Blood vessels in the extremities vasoconstrict (tighten) as blood is directed to the core, maintaining perfusion to all the vital organs. The metabolic rate increases significantly. Core body temperature remains at safe levels for several minutes.

The Wim Hof Method (WHM) makes it possible to access that calm and focused state during cold exposure. The method is based on three components:

1. Breathing
2. Mindset/Focus
3. Cold Exposure

Active Breathing. The breathing associated with the WHM is much more active than normal breathing. The goal is, essentially, an active hyperventilation—rapid, deep, full inhalations followed by normal exhalations. This creates a powerful effect on your physiology. You'll take in maximal levels of oxygen, lower your CO_2 levels, and alkalinize your cellular pH. This active state engages the sympathetic system and increases cortisol levels.[18] These changes allow the body to generate a stress response that can be "steered" or directed. The body is now prepped for major exertion, and that preparation can be targeted.

Think about exercise for a moment. This type of breathing (rapid deep inhalations and shorter exhalations) is the way you breathe after exercising hard. When you intentionally choose to breathe this way without exercising, in a sense you have "fooled" your body into thinking that it was just exercising. **But, instead of using the enhanced oxygen levels for muscular exercise and to remove lactic acid muscular waste, the body is simply in an active and energized state.** This energized state can now be focused on a demanding task of our choosing, such as tolerating the cold or influencing our hormonal or immune systems.

When most people think of mindful breathing, they're thinking of meditative Recovery Breathing. This is a good and highly beneficial technique for rest and relaxation. But the health of the human body depends on cycles and rhythms. Meditative breathing allows for recovery, while Active Breathing weaponizes the nervous system and activates it—for healing an injury, combatting a disease, or taking on a physical challenge.[19] This breathing technique brings strength and power to the equation. A healthy life requires both parasympathetic calming practices and sympathetic activating practices.

Active Breathing for Peak Performance

You can use Active Breathing to prep yourself for exertion, too. When exercising, we naturally engage our muscles and need more oxygen to meet the enhanced demand. Breathing and heart rate increase to meet these demands for more oxygen. Normally, we are always playing catch-up when we exercise. Our bodies don't know we need more oxygen until we exert ourselves and exhaust our existing supplies. Then we must play catch-up to get more oxygen to the muscles as quickly as we can. Hence that fast-paced breathing with an emphasis on inhalation.

Imagine what a competitive advantage it could be to engage in Active Breathing a few minutes **before** exercising strenuously. Doesn't that make intuitive sense? You're about to tax your system, and that tax is paid with oxygen. Your body doesn't know it needs more oxygen until you develop an oxygen debt. But if you pre-loaded extra oxygen into your system, you could potentially perform differently because you wouldn't develop an oxygen debt as quickly. This is, in fact, a training tool that many of my peak performance clients use whenever they're about to exercise.

Mindset/Focus. A strong mindset is crucial to achieve one's greatest potential. Mindset training differs significantly from typical meditation. It involves regular reflection and active thoughts about positive affirmations, as opposed to emptying thoughts. We'll look at the specific affirmations you can use in the Try It section. For now, realize that mindset and focus are key. They're not aspects of the WHM that can be disregarded. Significant concentration is required to tolerate cold therapies. You'll need a mindset that allows you to enter the cold calmly and with focus as opposed to a state of panic. In fact, you can't get into ice water at all without this factor in place. Applying this degree of focus can produce major health and wellness benefits in itself, as well as help you achieve more in your work and personal life.

Gradual Cold Exposure. Cold exposure practices can be as simple and everyday as a cold shower, or as involved as building your own ice bath tank. Whatever the practice, we start small with brief cold exposure therapies. We have reviewed the significant benefits of cold exposure. But there are additional benefits when cold exposure is combined with the WHM breathing and mindset techniques. To begin with, it's much easier to tolerate a cold exposure after practicing the other two WHM techniques. Researchers have found that the immune and metabolic effects are also enhanced, as we'll see in the science summaries next.

Differences Between WHM and Typical Meditation[20]

Typical meditation techniques involve relaxed breathing, heart rate reduction, clearing of thoughts, an increase in parasympathetic tone, and lowering of stress response and cortisol levels. **In contrast, the WHM is an active process.** The sympathetic nervous system is activated, and that response can be steered or directed in the body.

	WHM	Typical Meditation
Breathing	Active Hyperventilation	Relaxed
Heart Rate	Increases	Decreases
Mindset	Focused	Clearing of Thoughts
Autonomics	Mostly Sympathetic Stimulation	Mostly Parasympathetic
Stress Response	Activated, Targeted	Decreased
Cortisol Levels	Elevated	Reduced

As we will explore, both techniques are needed for optimal health. We need to be able to access and utilize both meditative Recovery Breathing and Active Breathing. Training yourself to access both of these states willfully and with a sense of control is empowering. This is a key paradigm shift towards what I call *Autonomic Integration*, and it equips us to target crucial components of our physiology long believed to be outside of conscious control.

Wim Hof's Contributions to Science

Evidence of the Ability to Influence the ANS, the Hormonal System, and the Immune System

In 2012, Hof claimed that he could influence his ANS. This led to an investigation led by researchers and clinicians at Radboud University in the Netherlands. This was an elaborate study that involved invasive monitoring in an intensive care unit (ICU). The findings were published that year in *Psychosomatic Medicine*, in an article titled "The Influence of Concentration/Meditation on Autonomic Nervous System Activity and the Innate Immune Response: A Case Study."[21]

In the context of this study, Hof practiced his three-part technique and then subjected himself to an endotoxin injection. This sounds severe, but is actually a fairly controlled lab method for triggering an immune response. The endotoxin used was comprised of the outer cell walls of a pathogenic bacteria. The bacteria itself was dead, but the cell walls can temporarily fool the immune system into thinking there is a substantial threat present. Normally, this causes inflammatory responses similar to the flu: Fever, chills, malaise, fatigue, headache, and muscle cramps. When used for research purposes, doses can be standardized and provide a way to study immune and inflammatory responses without causing actual infection.

Hof's response was compared to 112 others that had previously been exposed to the same dose of endotoxin at the University. Because of his breathing, meditation, and cold exposure practices, Hof's blood levels of cortisol were higher than anyone else who received the endotoxin; and his clinical symptoms and inflammation markers were lower. A spike in cortisol can transiently suppress inflammation.

That effect translated into dramatic immunomodulation in Hof's body. He got a mild headache from the injection, but was otherwise unaffected. His method had, effectively, hacked his immune response. The conclusion from the researchers was that the WHM caused:

- a controlled stress response
- sympathetic nervous system activation
- increased cortisol
- and a reduced inflammatory response

Hof was proven correct; he can influence his ANS.

What happened next essentially put Hof, an individual with no medical training, on the world map and corrected our medical knowledge base regarding the ability to influence the ANS. Having proved that Hof could influence his own ANS, the next phase of research was to determine if he could teach other people to do the same.

A follow-up experiment was planned to test the endotoxin results on two different groups. One was a control group of normal subjects. The second was a group of individuals who received WHM training for two weeks. Remarkably, individuals in that second WHM-trained group had results similar to Hof's. They too experienced only mild flu-like symptoms from the endotoxin and recovered quickly. They also successfully influenced their ANS activities, and directed the stress response in their bodies. In contrast, the untrained group struggled with more intense and prolonged flu-like symptoms and a slower recovery.

The authors of that research summed it up best in an article published by the *Proceedings of the National Academy of Sciences* in 2014:

> "The present study demonstrates that, through practicing techniques learned in a short-term training program, the sympathetic nervous system and immune system can indeed

> be voluntarily influenced. Healthy volunteers practicing the learned techniques exhibited profound increases in the release of epinephrine, which in turn led to increased production of anti-inflammatory mediators and subsequent dampening of the pro-inflammatory cytokine response elicited by intravenous administration of bacterial endotoxin."[22]

The researchers concluded that there were "important implications for the treatment of a variety of conditions associated with excessive or persistent inflammation." This is of definite interest to anyone dealing with autoimmune conditions. The WHM can successfully reduce levels of pro-inflammatory cytokines, while still encouraging a healthy white blood cell count.[23] In essence, it *modulates* the immune response. It doesn't suppress it in a blanket fashion. It appears to encourage the immune system to work in a more balanced and focused fashion.

Further Metabolic Effects of Cold Exposure Practices

Brown Fat Activation and Heat Production

Cold exposure can increase and activate our body's production of "brown fat", a type of fat that contains high concentrations of mitochondria. Brown fat is unique because it can be burned for heat production instead of generating ATP for energy. Babies are born with high levels of brown fat and use it to help maintain their body temperatures, which can easily be lost after birth.[24] We used to think that adults have little-to-no brown fat, but recent research has proven that brown fat can be activated and retained by cold exposure training, regardless of age.[25, 26]

When brown fat is burned, body temperature is increased without shivering.[27] This is one reason why, when I do cold trainings, I encourage clients to try *not* to shiver. Shivering is not actually an efficient mechanism to conserve or generate heat. It is much more effective to encourage our bodies to increase their availability of brown fat.

The research on brown fat activation has powerful implications. Cold exposure increases the body's metabolic rate significantly—as much as doubling or even tripling typical levels. This metabolic effect is tied to brown fat activation, which is now emerging as a possible method to fight obesity and other metabolic conditions. For instance, sometimes an obese person is not able to exert intensely. But such a person could, conceivably, increase cardio output up to 300 percent with cold exposure.[28]

On a personal note, when I increased my cold exposure challenges on my Poland winter trip, I could not take in enough calories. I recall remarking to others that I was not able to practice my typical intermittent fasting during that week, and I needed to eat significantly more calories just to maintain my weight and tolerate the increased number of cold trainings. This effect is explained by brown fat activation and recruitment. This profoundly heightened metabolism can occur over a short period of cold exposure practice. To dive deeper into this topic, refer to the second article in the Further Science Section exploring brown fat, cold exposure, and improvements for Type 2 Diabetes.

Only One Half of the Equation

From WHM to Complete Autonomic Integration

As we have explored, the WHM practices are powerful and create a highly activated state in the body. But this active state is only one part of the Autonomic Integration Cycle; **a counterbalance is needed.** When describing the Active Breathing method to my clients, I mention how we need both Active Breathing and Recovery Breathing practices. These two practices balance each other. Recovery

Breathing practices enhance parasympathetic tone and increase Heart Rate Variability, (HRV).[29] Practicing both of these methods can help us achieve complete autonomic integration.

Remember from Chapter 2, that HRV is a measure of the time between successive heartbeats. Your 70 beats per minute (BPM) average may include moments of 64 BPM and 78 BPM during that minute. In fact, in a healthy human, that resting heart rate should vary by several beats per minute—higher on inhalation and lower on exhalation.

We used to think of the heart rate as static and predictable when at rest. The medical establishment used to think all biological systems were fairly static when at rest, predictably plugging along at a set pace. We now know that the heart rate and all ANS-controlled biological systems and organs are constantly making significant adjustments,[30] varying their function from moment to moment. That variability is a good thing. Variability, in heart rate or other systems, can be viewed as a measure of the body's adaptability to stress.[31]

As mentioned in Chapter 2, HRV is such a vital indicator of health, it is closely monitored during child birth. Reductions in HRV typically predict fetal distress even before changes in overall heart rate. In adult humans, a decline in HRV is often associated with, or precedes, a number of disease states. Reductions in HRV can precede a condition called "autonomic neuropathy" in which the autonomic nerves that control important organs and their function are damaged.[32] This can result in bowel, bladder, digestive, and blood pressure problems. Reduced HRV is also observed in patients with anxiety, depression,[33] and asthma,[34] and it's associated with sudden infant death.[35] Reduced HRV correlates with disease and generally reflects a reduced ability to respond to challenges and stressors.

As mentioned previously, I regard HRV as invaluable health data, often more informative than conventional blood work. The good news is that it is entirely possible to access and influence HRV through mindful breathing exercises, similar to those found in Chapter 2.

This kind of Recovery Breathing is an essential counter-balance to the highly activating effects associated with WHM breathing. If you begin to incorporate Active Breathing and cold therapies into your life, it's crucial that you begin a Recovery Breathing practice as well. You can find both Active Breathing and Recovery Breathing exercises in the Try It section of this chapter.

The Effects of Influencing HRV through Recovery Breathing

My Recovery Breathing exercise is inspired by the work and protocols of the Heart Math Institute. This group has fostered research and grown the knowledge base regarding the heart-brain connection. Through their efforts, it has been established that not only is there two-way ANS communication between the heart and brain, but the heart actually sends more information to the brain than the brain sends to the heart. We used to believe that, primarily, the brain told the heart what to do. In fact, the reverse is true. The heart and its rhythms greatly influence how we think, feel, and reason in any given moment.[36,37]

Working on HRV through Recovery Breathing isn't just about taking a relaxing break from a stressful day. That's certainly a benefit. But ultimately, learning to consciously influence your heart rate and variability can have ramifications for mood stability, as well as your ability to solve problems, think creatively, remember details, and generally access higher cognitive function.[38]

Heart Math researchers have noted that, not only is HRV important, so is the *pattern* of how those varied rates are reached. A person might have decent HRV, but during a stressful day, that varied heart rate might jump around a great deal from beat to beat. If you charted the resting rate between each of the beats in a minute, it might jump back and forth in a fairly disorganized fashion: 68, 74, 65, 71, 77, and so forth. In a truly healthy state, you might see similar rates, but with more of an order to them, a gentle increasing and decreasing wave: 65, 68, 69, 71, 74, 72, 70, 68, 66, and so on. (See the Heart Rhythm Chart). That wave would also move in time with the person's breath, increasing on inhale and decreasing on exhale. Researchers refer to this state as *psychophysiological coherence.*[39]

Heart Rhythm Chart

Heart rhythm in a state of psychophysiological coherence.

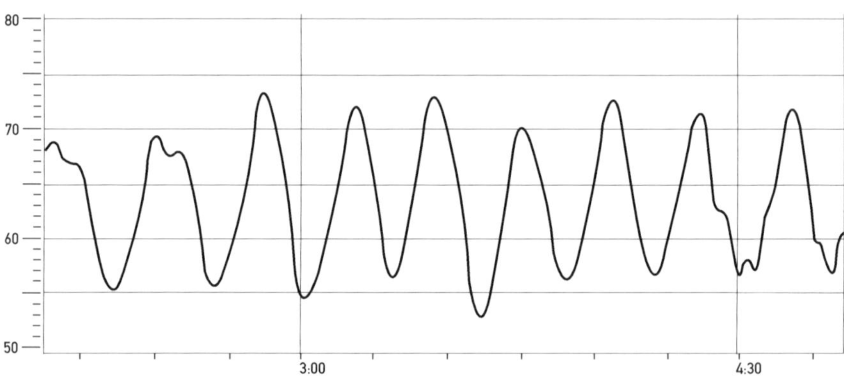

Chart Source: Author's files.

This state of smooth HRV *coherence* indicates that the client not only has a healthy HRV, he also accesses that variable range with a sense of focus and calm. The body is ready for anything, calm and responsive as opposed to panicked and jumpy. To efficiently achieve and practice this coherence state, Heart Math researchers recommend pairing recovery style breathing techniques with guiding your mind to focus on a positive emotion and vivid memory associated with that emotion.[40] You can learn more about their specific techniques in the Resources section.

Pairing mindful Recovery Breathing with WHM is a lot like incorporating Cyclic Exercise into an endurance exercise routine. You're training for both sides of the equation: Performance and Recovery, Activation and Coherence. In both cases, you're setting the stage for greater health across broad body parameters, you're training every cell in your body to be more flexible and adaptable to any challenge that life brings your way. **I cannot overstate how important these counter-balances are.** Given that the ANS controls and influences every body system from digesting and detoxing, to immune response and energy levels; it's vital that we train for both *activation* and *coherence* when exploring Autonomic Integration practices.

Autonomic Disrepair

What Happens When We Don't Bother with ANS Practices

The aging process is associated with a reduction in HRV.[41] That's a reflection of what's happening in the body as a whole: inflexibility, loss of range of motion, and flattening of function. As ANS adaptability declines, the body becomes more and more delicate, less able to handle major change. Ultimately, the next time the body is presented with a significant stressor (perhaps a bacterial infection, major life change, or significant loss), the body may not have the flexibility to adapt and respond in an effective fashion. That's why we often hear of older adults who survive a fall and resulting broken bone, but then acquire a fatal case of pneumonia shortly thereafter. The shock of the fall completely taxed their limited autonomic resources. There was nothing left to address the additional immune challenge.

In short, flattening HRV indicates compromised flexibility in the ANS. When autonomic function is compromised, it translates into a reduced ability to respond effectively to life's challenges.[42] Many of us lose health and eventually die because, on a cellular level, we've become brittle. Declining HRV is commonly associated with the normal aging process. Yet in my practice, people who maintain healthy HRV tend to experience a higher quality of life into their mature adult years.

On one end of the spectrum of ANS dysfunction, you see this flattening of HRV, essentially a lack of autonomic range. But there's another direction that ANS dysfunction can take. It's called *Autonomic Conflict*. To understand that concept, let's take a metaphorical dive back into cold water. One of the worst outcomes occurs when an unprepared, untrained individual unexpectedly experiences a lethal cold exposure.

Over the years, there have been numerous reports of cold-water exposure incidents that result in sudden death. Most of these reports involve boating accidents at sea, but a few involve people who dove into cold water as a dare or, tragically, for ice bucket fundraising events.[43] What's strange in these deaths is that it's not possible that they occurred from hypothermia or inability to swim. Consider:

1. Many deaths in cold water sea accidents occur in the first two minutes, but hypothermia takes much longer to occur, about 30 to 60 minutes.
2. Over 65 percent of drowning victims are good swimmers.
3. Over 50 percent of these victims die within 10 feet of safety.[44]

The authors of the book, *Essentials of Sea Survival*, Michael Tipton and Frank Golden, have noted the likely cause. It involves two autonomic reflexes in the human body, which are triggered as soon as a person is suddenly and unexpectedly submerged in cold water.[45]

Cold Shock Reflex: This is mediated by receptors found on the skin, all over the body. This reflex causes hyperventilation, an increase in heart rate and blood pressure, and a decrease in blood flow to the arteries that supply blood to the heart muscle.

Dive Reflex: This is activated if the face is fully or partially submerged. The involved receptors are found around the eyes, nose, and mouth. Humans share this reflex with other mammals, and it serves to conserve oxygen when we are submerged. It causes breath holding, lowering of the heart rate, and peripheral vasoconstriction, all designed to increase our time underwater.

If both of these reflexes are triggered simultaneously, the ANS is basically short circuiting—telling the body to both increase breathing and slow it down, to increase heart rate and lower it. The electrical signals are jagged and fully conflicting. Many researchers have described it as trying to drive while pressing both the brake and the accelerator pedal. The result is a dramatic Autonomic Conflict that is so severe it can cause a fatal arrhythmia leading to death within seconds. It's actually been known for several decades that, even if boating accident survivors are wearing life preservers in the high seas, the continual cold waves splashing in their faces can induce fatal Autonomic Conflict long before hypothermia sets in.[46]

Tipton and Golden reported that the intensity of cold water-induced Autonomic Conflict could probably be minimized through training in advance of potential exposure. In one study, participants spent 40 minutes in cool water for eight consecutive days. On day seven, hyperventilation was less than a third of its original value on day one, and participants experienced far less distress on immersion. The principles outlined in Tipton and Golden's book are so reliable that they've influenced the British Royal Navy's sea survival training and protective gear.[47]

This is all good reason to begin practicing cold therapies **solely** in an incremental fashion and to **never** dive headfirst into ice water no matter how trained you are! Of course, few of us will ever fully submerge in ice water and even fewer will be at risk of dying during an accident on the high seas. So what does Autonomic Conflict have to do with the rest of us? Actually, quite a bit.

I believe that many of us cope with far lower intensity, but still real, Autonomic Conflicts. Think about all of life's chronic stresses. How many times do you find yourself trying to relax, but suddenly think of something that makes you feel upset or angry? How many times do you wind up in a taxing or stressful situation, but you're too fatigued to respond at your best? How often have you felt physically exhausted at night, but too mentally alert to fall asleep? I believe these common modern experiences have all the hallmarks of minor Autonomic Conflict. This state is not immediately fatal, but these stress-exhaustion combinations do compromise health and ANS responsiveness over the long term. Embracing some degree of Autonomic Integration practice can go far to help restore ANS balance, as well as provide a level of reflex acclimation.[48]

The long-standing science of Hormesis is clear. These therapies enhance your physiology by training your systems to be flexible, responsive, and adaptable. The more hormetic therapies you train in, from cyclic exercise to cold exposure, the more adaptable your body will be when confronted with the stresses of daily life. Your body will be able to effectively adjust its own autonomic balance and fine-tune its stress response systems. This has powerful real world consequences, transitioning you from disease to vitality.

We each must find our individualized hormetic zones where we are pushed, but not damaged. Using environmental challenges that illicit an autonomic response is part of this process. Pairing controlled cold exposure with Recovery Breathing practices can help us achieve Autonomic Integration. I believe that these training combinations represent one of the most powerful practices for promoting whole health and quality of life at any age—and also when dealing with major health challenges.

Meet the Patients Who Have Benefitted

Though my clients are sometimes more opposed to cold therapy than fasting, most find that cold exposure is easier to do and even more immediately beneficial. It can integrate smoothly into an existing exercise program and noticeably assists with exercise recovery. In certain disease states, cold therapy conveys powerful benefits that are hard to acquire any other way. These two stories reflect the full spectrum of benefits gleaned from wisely implemented cold therapies.

Case Story #1
42-year-old Male with MS

Gary is a 42-year-old kitchen designer recently diagnosed with multiple sclerosis (MS), an autoimmune condition. Gary presented with intermittent symptoms that involved lower extremity muscle weakness, mild coordination impairment, stiffness, and generalized fatigue. He was prescribed steroid and immunotherapy medications by his other specialists. He did not tolerate these medications well and was seeking alternative therapies from me.

We met and talked about several potential strategies that included oxygen, intravenous ozone therapies, nutrient therapies, exercise therapies, and Wim Hof Method strategies. (I always make a point to introduce WHM to my Clients, and especially those with autoimmune conditions, since it has demonstrated such great evidence for influencing the autonomic and immune systems.) I recall Gary's comment when I told him about Wim's method and what was involved. He said that he was not interested in the cold, and that he would prefer to stay in his comfort zone.

That led to a much more involved discussion about the problems of continuous 24-hour comfort. That got his attention.

Since he was not experiencing an MS flare-up at that time, I suggested he try a few of the breathing sessions, and follow that with some stretching and yoga. He agreed, and was shocked that, after doing the breathing exercises for the first time, he was able to complete 30 breath-hold pushups after one of the cycles. (See the Variation to Breathing Exercise 1 at end of this chapter.) This was something that he never would have been able to even imagine. This result, combined with my reinforcement that autoimmune conditions may benefit the most from this type of work, encouraged him to do more. Gary also made equally surprising flexibility gains. It is a major accomplishment to make flexibility gains in an MS patient with something so simple, easy, and non-invasive. In fact, Active Breathing, by oxygen loading and reducing acid waste (C02), has provided energy and flexibility gains for everyone I know who has tried it. Gary was no exception.

These gains made Gary more confident about trying cold therapies. We started slowly with warm showers, then introduced a minute of cold, with warm recovery, then progressed to ending a shower with a minute of cold. He did not like it, but his symptoms responded well. I had him spend more time outside in the cold with limited clothing. Gary had less stiffness, and his fatigue diminished significantly. He built on these gains and became stronger and healthier. He got to the point where cold was no longer the enemy. This was real progress. In fact, he came to almost embrace the cold. He was able to reduce his medications initially, and in a few months, got to the point where he only needed his medications for symptom flares.

Over time, I introduced many more therapies to Gary including cyclic exercise, intravenous ozone therapy, and a host of dietary changes. He has not had a flare of his condition in several months and is as active as he was before his diagnosis. Gary continues his regular practice of the breathing and cold therapies. He sums it up best in his own words: "This work has given me many things back that I thought I had lost. I can fight back. My condition is not gone, but now I am in control of it."

Case Story #2

32-year-old Female Feeling Limited in Hot Yoga Practice

Becky is a 32-year-old female working on improving her performance with her hot yoga practice: a 90-minute class completed in a room with high humidity and heated to 105 degrees. I serve as the Medical Director for a yoga teacher's training, and practice this yoga myself. I was familiar with its unique challenges.

Becky's was having trouble tolerating the heat, felt dependent on drinking water throughout the workout, and found it difficult to keep her breathing calm during strenuous parts of the class. Drinking water during the class is problematic because it depletes energy as the body diverts blood flow to the GI tract and must then bring the cold water up to body temperature.

Becky's first task was to perform a few classes using a heart rate monitor, so I could get a sense of what was happening for her and to track when she felt the most challenged or out of breath. What we learned with that monitoring is that there were a few places when Becky's heart rate spiked to 90 percent of her maximum, and remained elevated for several minutes. This occurred in both the first half of the class, which is all standing poses, as well as the second half of the class, which is all floor postures. Also, at these times, she was not able to control her breathing.

Ideally, once accustomed to this yoga, the goal is to be able to breathe calmly and maintain a heart rate well below maximum. If there are brief HR elevations, a secondary goal is to be able to rapidly recover both heart rate and breathing closer to baseline levels.

First, I made sure that Becky did not have any adrenal or thyroid issues via salivary and blood analysis. Then we focused on working with her ANS with three types of breathing exercises.

The first was **WHM type Active Breathing** with three cycles of maximal, hyperventilation inhales for 30 breaths followed by breath holding for as long as possible. (See Breathing Exercise 1 in the Try It section). Her breath holds improved quickly and dramatically. Her baseline breath hold was only around 30 seconds. With this type of breathing she was able to expand her breath holds, ranging from 45 to 50 seconds on cycle one, 60 seconds on cycle two, and 90 seconds on cycle three after about two weeks. By the end of a month, her final breath hold on cycle three was around two minutes.

Next I taught Becky about basic **Recovery Breathing** utilized during cyclic exercise (Chapter 2). Specifically, I told her to complete four brief exercise cycles, each elevating her heart rate to 90 percent of maximum for 30 to 40 seconds, then to stop exercising, sit down, and focus on Recovery Breathing. Her goal was to actively train recovery, by taking slow deep inhales and exhales, and to reduce her elevated heart rate and rapid breathing as fast as possible. She focused on Recovery Breathing until her heart rate returned to within ten points of her baseline. Then her next exertion would begin. I had her complete this exercise a few times while breathing high flow oxygen, which greatly augments recovery. After the four exercise cycles, I instructed Becky on the more focused **Recovery Breathing** in Breathing Exercise 2 (see Try It section).

Both Recovery Breathing methods are HRV exercises, and I was very interested in seeing improved HR differences. At first, Becky only experienced a few points difference, with an inhaling HR of 74 and an exhaling HR of 70. But after one month of these exercises at least twice per week, she was able to achieve HR differences of up to eight points without the oxygen assist.

Becky's return to the hot yoga room was remarkable. Her heart rate pattern never exceeded 90 percent of her maximum. She felt more in control of her breathing, even though it still became rapid at times. We trained her to learn to judge her HR accurately, without electronic monitoring, and to better control her breathing. I instructed her to sit and recover if needed during class, to prevent her breathing from becoming rapid and uncontrolled.

I also suggested some cold therapies to further help with autonomic control. Becky began taking full cold showers after her hot yoga sessions. This was a good inroad for her. Her progress in the yoga room mirrored her progress with the cold. As Becky became more aware of her breathing during cold exposure, she was able to control her breathing better in the hot room. She is now able to make it through the entire class without drinking water or taking breaks, and while also keeping her HR and breathing controlled.

Vitality Health Challenge Cold Exposure Testimonials

"After my diagnosis, most doctors only told me what was no longer possible for me. Now I feel stronger, more refreshed, more flexible, and most importantly, more hopeful. (Cold exposure) is now part of my daily routine."

—Pat, 62-year-old male with Rheumatoid Arthritis (RA)

"I have not done yoga headstands in over ten years. However, after this breathing work, I felt like I had the power to do them

again. On my second attempt, I did a headstand again for the first time in years, and it felt great."
—Sam, 50-year-old male

"The mix of cold therapy and specialized breathing exercises leaves me feeling very recharged—like I plug myself in for an energy boost. It also makes me feel happy and grounded."
Samantha, 47-year-old female

"I became a friend of the cold. Working to control my autonomic nervous system is perhaps an ancient skill we have all forgotten how to use."
—Jeff, 36-year-old male

Try It! Incorporating Autonomic Integration Practices into YOUR Life
The most natural at-home hormetic therapy

Each of us has an edge that defines where our body and mind meet. That edge is not fixed in stone. It moves with training, and breathing is the entry point into influencing our autonomic nervous system. The first two exercises below simply bring intentional balance to your breathing cycles and the intertwined stress response. From that foundation, we can begin a successful cold exposure practice.

Breathing Exercise 1

Caution: This exercise can have powerful influences on your physiology. It should only be attempted in a safe space and never in water or while driving. Initial Active Breathing (hyperventilation) can result in dizziness, tingling of hands, cold extremities, and cramps. These result from either excess oxygen and/or reductions in CO_2 levels. The symptoms often improve over time. If they don't, you may want to consult an integrative physician or someone experienced in breath work.

1. Sit or lie down in a comfortable position.
2. Begin Active Breathing: Take a full, deep, and rapid inhalation followed by a normal exhalation. Repeat. The breathing rate is quite rapid, around 30 breaths per minute.
3. Count your breaths. After you inhale on breath number 30, instead of a de-emphasized exhalation, you'll deliberately exhale fully. Then, with your lungs empty, hold your breath as long as possible. Time this breath-hold, and log that time.
4. When you need to breathe, take a deep inhale and hold that breath in for ten seconds. Then breathe normally for 1-2 minutes. This completes one cycle.
5. Complete three of these cycles. You will note that your breath-hold duration will increase significantly with each successive breath-hold in the series. The third breath-hold will far exceed the first one.

This is a great first encounter exploring your edge. Breath-holding is usually a reality that is under autonomic control. You can't consciously control when your body decides you absolutely must breathe again, right? Except, after completing this exercise you just did precisely that. You lightly altered a function of your ANS.

Variation: The day before you try Breathing Exercise 1, take a moment to do as many strong push-ups as you can in a single set. Stop when you cannot complete another push-up with steady strength. The next day, complete the three cycles of Active Breathing outlined above. Then complete a fourth cycle of breathing and, after inhale number 30, again fully exhale and hold your breath. During this breath-hold begin a series of push-ups. Go as fast as you can until you either need to stop or breathe. Remarkably, your number of breath-holding pushups will far exceed the number you can do while breathing normally. This is hard to imagine, but your system is so well oxygenated and your CO_2 so low that you have much more reserve than your brain realizes.

Breathing Exercise 2

Breathing Exercise 1 is quite active and predominantly stimulates sympathetic activity. In contrast, I often use Breathing Exercise 2 to increase parasympathetic activity and to increase heart rate variability. I almost always use this exercise after exertion. Remember, we need to practice both forms of breathing—Active and Recovery. To fully complete this exercise, you will need a heart rate monitor that transmits via Bluetooth to a smart phone or video screen.

1. Sit or lie down in a comfortable position.
2. Take a slow, deep inhalation that lasts at least 4 to 5 seconds.
3. Pause at full inhalation for 1 to 2 seconds.
4. Exhale slowly and completely over 5 to 6 seconds.
5. Pause at full exhalation for 1 to 2 seconds.
6. Begin with another slow, deep inhalation.
7. You will take only 5 to 7 breaths per minute. It may take time to get your breathing rate that slow but it will improve over time.
8. Let your mind relax. Focus on your breathing and relaxation. While Recovery Breathing, keep eyes relaxed or closed. Only open your eyes gently for a split second to see your heart rate at full inhalation and exhalation.

The goal is to see your heart rate rise and fall 8 to 10 beats (or more) with each inhale and exhale. Heart rate will increase with inhalation and will fall with exhalation. For example, at the end of each inhale your heart rate may be 68. By the end of exhalation your heart rate may be 58. This is the ultimate heart rate variability (HRV) breathing exercise. I often instruct clients to do this while breathing high concentrations of oxygen after workouts for an even deeper recovery.

Mindset Exercises

My Vitality Health Challenge work has exposed me, and my peak performance clients, to extensive physical training associated with all the hormetic therapies covered in this book. Mindset is key to all this work. I will detail the most challenging workout I personally do in the Synergy Chapter, but for now imagine a 20-minute, maximum intensity, interval training workout, performed in a fasted state, while breathing low levels of oxygen. This is an advanced and aggressive workout to be done rarely and only by those working on peak performance. Such workouts absolutely require intentional mindset training

Recently, while performing this workout, I recall telling myself at minute 17, "My brain knows I am recovering before my body." In that moment, I was fully exerting physically and had low levels of oxygen. It could have been a moment to easily panic, lose concentration, or give up due to fatigue. Instead, I knew my limits, my training, the physiology, and believed in myself under these stresses. I knew recovery was coming soon and continued to perform until my body experienced actual recovery.

Mindset can make or break us. When under physical stress, the body can fatigue and the brain can easily follow. The converse is also true. When under emotional stress, mindset can fatigue and the body can easily follow. In my own training and with my clients, I've repeatedly seen that lack of mindset training can perpetuate and magnify a loop of negative effects in the body leading to unintended sympathetic stimulation and:

- Increased heart rate

- Increased blood pressure
- Chronically increased cortisol
- Anxiety
- Tightness
- Muscular fatigue
- Worsening performance

Increasing heart rate and cortisol in a transient fashion can be good, when it's associated with healthy burst-type activity. Remember from Chapter 2 that we're wired for sudden bursts of physical activity. The increased heart and breathing rates we experience from Cyclic Exercise are beneficial. But we're meant to cycle through and to come back down to a restful state. In contrast, the chronically elevated cortisol and heart rates in a constant high stress lifestyle are not beneficial. The key difference is that concept of heightening our stress markers and then dropping back down to homeostasis.

Successful Mindset training helps with managing both the transient stressors of exercise and cold exposure, as well as the effects of ongoing lifestyle stress. Mindset training acknowledges and intelligently monitors physical stress and automatically relays conscious and unconscious messages like:

- I am fit
- I am healthy
- I can stick with this
- I can stay focused
- I can peak perform
- My body is growing stronger from this challenge
- Rest and recovery are coming

Your affirmations should be customized to your situation. Always phrase them in positive form ("I will finish strong" works better than "I won't give up.") Repeat such affirmations to yourself at least five times. Reciting them quietly in your mind is fine, though speaking them aloud whenever possible is even more powerful. You can work on mindset training at any time, including while driving, during workouts, and when you feel stressed. Reciting affirmations prior to cold exposure may be the most reinforcing on a subconscious (ANS) level. When you say aloud, "I can experience the cold with calm resolve," and then you do just that, it serves as powerful re-training for the brain's panic and stress responses. Cold exposure requires complete focus and provides an immediate mindset challenge.

Cold Exposure Exercises

I need to stress that no one can outlast or beat the cold. We all have our limits, and it is important to monitor ourselves intelligently during any type of cold exposure. Listen to your body and respond wisely to its unique limits. Do not ever dive into cold water as this can cause a rapid drop in heart rate and blood pressure and possibly lead to passing out, even if you are well trained.

That said, there are many different types of cold exposure practices to choose from. Most are completely accessible and not too far-fetched, as you can see below:

- Turning down the heat a little
- Placing just hands or feet in cold water
- Showering using alternating one-minute cycles of hot and cold water
- Taking a cold shower
- Standing in the snow barefoot
- Cold exposure with limited clothing
- Hiking in winter terrain with limited clothing
- Lying bare-chested in the snow
- Wading in ice-cold water
- Complete submersion in ice water

- Swimming in ice water
- Regular use of an ice tank/bath

Pick one from near the top of this list to begin with, and start slowly. Do not do any full body, cold water immersion attempts alone until you are quite experienced with more basic exposures. It is important to appreciate that we will achieve less in colder and colder water. For example, last year I submerged myself in the river near my home all winter. It was refreshing in September and October, and I could easily swim. By November, swimming was more limited, and I did not venture out too far. In December and January, I did not move far from my pier and did not swim. You get the idea.

The most common initial cold exposure protocol is the cold shower. Whatever practice you chose, you might first take one small pre-conditioning step towards it:

1. If you plan to take regular cold showers as your main practice, you could start by taking a shower that's cooler than normal, or you could simply soak your feet in cold water.
2. Go slow. Begin with a round of Breathing Exercise 1 before attempting any cold exposure.
3. Focus your mind fully on the task at hand and begin the cold exposure. Time how long you're able to tolerate the experience without shivering or panicking.
4. The next time you try this practice, make the shower or foot-bath slightly colder, and stay in it longer.
5. Get to the point where you can take a full five-minute cold shower before progressing to any other cold exposure attempts.

Variation: If you are working up to a cold shower, try cycling from cold to hot and not vice versa. Starting with hot water is much easier than starting with cold, since pre-warming your core will make it easier to tolerate the cold. But a hormetic therapy needs to *challenge* your body to produce a beneficial effect. Try starting with cold, and then transition to warm water toward the end of your shower. Or start with cold, cycle to warm, then back to cold and end the shower cold. This is a greater challenge, as it commands your body to warm itself more. **The ability to adapt autonomic function to the context you are in is a crucial health marker.**

Cautions on Re-Warming

Some caution must be taken with re-warming for anyone practicing more prolonged cold exposures including cold air hiking or climbing with limited clothing. As mentioned previously, blood flow re-directs from the periphery (arms and legs) to the core to ensure adequate blood flow to vital organs. However, when the cold exposure session ends, and you begin to recover in a warm environment, warmer blood will enter colder extremities and may drop your core temperature too fast. Also, re-established blood flow to the extremities can wash muscle waste products back into circulation. This combination can leave you feeling uncomfortable, nauseous, and disoriented. And it can be dangerous depending on how long you were exposed to the cold and how rapidly you warmed back up, as well as your baseline conditioning and training.

It's vital to build your cold exposure time slowly for any practice, but especially cold air hiking and climbing. There is no substitute for training and knowing your limitations. When you are done with a cold exposure, continue to hike or walk and **put on additional clothing while you're still in the cold**. This allows for a staged re-warming. Take several minutes with this, and only then seek shelter and warmth. It is important to re-warm slowly.

Because we lose body temperature so much faster in cold water than in cold air, ice-bath times will be a small fraction of what you can do with cold air exposure. Nevertheless, until you fully appreciate your body's abilities, always be aware of re-warming potentials from any cold exposure.

Other Special Situations

We must always remember that every hormetic therapy offers us that fine line between a beneficial optimizing stressor and damage. In addition to proceeding slowly with any cold challenges, it is especially important to work with an integrative physician or someone experienced in these types of therapies if you have any medical condition. The concept of Autonomic Conflict reminds us of the potential ramifications of untrained, aggressive, full body cold exposures. Though research has found that the cold shock response reduces steadily over time with proper training.

That said, those with any cardiac condition (arrhythmia, coronary artery disease, congestive heart failure, etc.) need to be carefully evaluated medically to make sure their conditions are optimized and to ensure these therapies make sense for them. Limited and slow exposure with cardiac monitoring can be useful.

It is also important that anyone with known adrenal fatigue or untreated hypothyroidism address these conditions first and foremost. A four-point salivary cortisol test can help identify the type of adrenal fatigue one may be experiencing and determine the best options for therapy such as adrenal supplements or adrenal hormone. Blood testing for levels of TSH, as well as free and total T3 and T4, can help identify thyroid imbalances. Most patients who need correcting of thyroid deficiencies do best with combination therapy involving replacement of both T3 and T4. Adrenal or thyroid imbalances should be successfully addressed before beginning cold therapies.

Cold Exposure & Autonomic Integration

HEALTH GOALS TRIAD

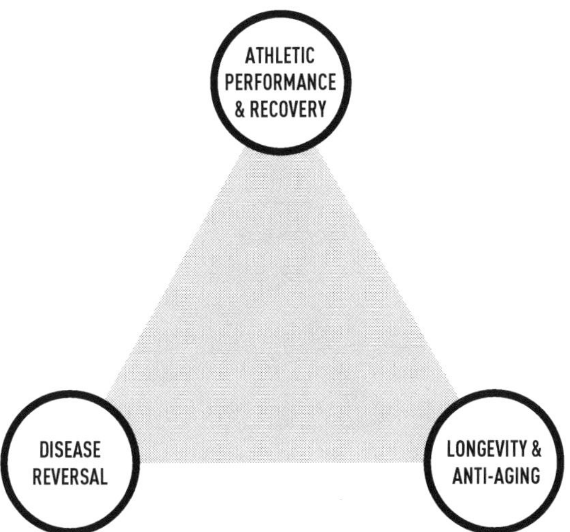

DISEASE REVERSAL Cold exposure's anti-inflammatory effects are beneficial for arthritis and chronic re-injury states. With the guidance of a skillful integrative practitioner, the immune modulation effects can be beneficial for autoimmune conditions such as MS and rheumatoid arthritis. The metabolic enhancement is also valuable for weight management, diabetes, and cardiovascular issues.

LONGEVITY & ANTI-AGING Well-practiced cold exposure can enhance mood and energy, as well as overall response to daily stress. Metabolic gains can enhance longevity by addressing cardio and weight loss goals. Ultimately, cold exposure is an invaluable addition to any plan that enhances HRV—a key indicator of whole body wellness.

ATHLETIC PERFORMANCE & RECOVERY Countless elite athletes already benefit from regular ice baths. The anti-inflammatory and detoxing effects are fantastic to encourage a short and smooth recovery from peak performance. The metabolic and HRV benefits are less well-known but equally valuable for any athlete.

DISCOVER THE POWER TO CONSCIOUSLY ALTER IMMUNE AND HORMONAL RESPONSE

Further Science
Read the Research for Yourself

The following provides just a few highlighted studies that can help you expand your understanding of the material in this chapter. Comprehensive chapter References & Notes are found at the end of the book. To read more about these studies, search for "PubMed" online, the world's largest medical library. Reach PubMed directly at: https://www.ncbi.nlm.nih.gov/pubmed/

1.
Hanssen MJ, et. al. "**Short-term cold acclimation recruits brown adipose tissue in obese humans.**" *Diabetes.* 2016 May; 65(5): 1179-89.

We have discussed how cold exposure can help recruit and maintain brown fat. This has been proven in young, lean, and healthy subjects. More recently, brown fat recruitment by cold exposure has become a hot topic as a possible mechanism to help counteract obesity, diabetes, and other metabolic conditions. The term *adaptive thermogenesis* is now used to describe an increased capacity to burn fat for heat production following cold exposure. This is the first study demonstrating that obese subjects can achieve these results in a relative short period: Ten days sitting in a cold room at 15 degrees Celsius (59 Fahrenheit) for 4 to 6 hours per day. It is likely that significant results would also be obtained with more intense cold therapies used for a shorter period of time.

2.
Hanssen MJ, et al. "**Short-term cold acclimation improves insulin sensitivity in patients with Type 2 diabetes mellitus.**" *Nature Medicine.* 2015 Aug:21(8):863-5

Similar to study number 1 above, this article shows the effectiveness of cold exposure and brown fat recruitment for Type II Diabetes patients. Simply sitting in a cold room for ten days increased insulin sensitivity by 43 percent. This is a remarkable result, and can offer a new inroad to anyone seeking to enhance insulin sensitivity. Cold exposure offers significant metabolic benefits.

3.

Kox M, et al. "**Voluntary activation of the sympathetic nervous system and attenuation of the innate immune response in humans**." *Proceedings of the National Academy of Science*, 2014 May 20; 111(20): 7379-7384.

This is the landmark study that showed, after a brief training in the WHM, it was possible for a group of previously untrained individuals to influence their autonomic, immune, and hormonal systems, following a controlled exposure of endotoxin. An ICU setting, invasive monitoring, and blood gas analysis were used to capture this remarkable data. The authors concluded that this type of cold-exposure and breathing practice could have powerful influences on conditions characterized by excess inflammation and autoimmune challenges.

CHAPTER 7
Synergy

Combining multiple natural therapies for exponential gains

I wish I could pick one of these therapies, and guarantee that it alone would singularly change your life. But I'd be lying. The reality is, if you're dealing with chronic pain or one of countless degenerative disease states, it took multiple factors over several years to bring you to your present challenge. It will take multiple therapies, along with dietary and lifestyle changes, to bring you to a higher level of health and performance. Even if you're an athlete in good health, your performance goals are influenced by multiple dietary and environmental factors that limit all people today. Right now, our bodies are under greater stress, with fewer tools to meet those demands. Reaching your next level will likely require several interdependent changes and therapies.

You've probably noticed that, in all my case stories, the clients wound up using multiple therapies to foster their health transformation. Often, they started with a turnkey therapy that changed the tide and caused the first tangible effects. But ultimately, it was the synergy of a full complement of therapies that made complete transformation possible.

I often say, "You are only as healthy as your weakest link." This means that overlooking any one determinant of health can have powerful effects that keep you from achieving your greatest potential.

You could purchase an HBOT unit and have it installed in your house and use it diligently every day. But if you continue to eat poorly and fail to address other crucial factors, the HBOT effects will be limited. Natural therapies work in synergy with each other. The more natural healing inputs we embrace, the greater the likelihood of reaching our medical and athletic goals.

To adopt a holistic and synergistic approach, we must first shed the old "single-symptom-single-pill" mindset. As discussed in Chapter 1, that pharmaceutical mindset worked well in the age of eradicating *infectious* diseases, but it doesn't serve in this era of *degenerative* disease. Today's degenerative and metabolic diseases involve every system in the body. Instead of popping a chemical pill to manage each symptom, we need to look for multiple natural therapies to fully remedy root causes. We need to treat and empower the whole person.

I look at every spoke in the wheel of my client's life. One by one, I address each of my Vitality Health Challenge therapeutic assessments. Multiple factors set the stage for pain, limitation, or metabolic disease. Multiple modalities will be needed to reverse that state and restore health. Let's take a look at how these whole-life consultations work.

How All My Client Evaluations Begin

Inside a Vitality Health Challenge Consultation

As a physician who continues to practice both conventional and alternative disciplines, I appreciate all that modern medicine has to offer. However, I strongly prefer designing multi-therapy integrative regimens for my clients. While each chapter of this book has focused on a different natural and hormetic therapy, the reality is that I always use combinations of multiple therapies to solve medical conditions or help a client reach peak performance.

I initially called my clinic Vitality7. The name was derived from seven major determinants of health and wellness (below). Its name today, Vitality Health Challenge, better embodies our values and more quickly communicates what we're about. But the seven major health determinants are the same. We provide over 40 integrative medical therapies specifically designed for each client. By focusing on root causes, Vitality Health Challenge can provide specific solutions to help reverse and prevent many chronic conditions, or help athletes perform at peak levels.

Vitality Health Challenge evaluates every patient through the lens of the core Seven Determinants:

- Natural Hormone Restoration
- Nutrition and IV Therapies
- Detoxification Therapies
- Oxygen Therapies
- Ozone Therapies
- Core Strength, Flexibility, Athletic Recovery
- Stress Reduction Therapies

With every client, I begin by ordering far more comprehensive lab tests (see the Crucial Lab Tests after this chapter) than most conventional general practitioners. Focusing on the first three of the Seven Determinants, I use the client's lab results to develop supportive care and establish personalized foundational hormonal, dietary, and detox therapies. Then, I begin looking at the next four of the Seven Determinants, the possible hormetic therapies that could help the client gain serious ground.

Even though many clients cannot begin exercise therapies right away, they can initially consider low effort hormetic therapies such as ozone therapies or Time Restricted Eating (TRE). There may be a need for a pre-conditioning program before starting a hormetic challenge. I walk with my clients through the pre-conditioning efforts and lifestyle changes. I'm there with them during their first hormetic therapy experiences and design the programs that they can implement in the clinic and at home. Ultimately, restoring and maintaining health literally requires leaving one's comfort zone. Combining hormetic therapies with the Vitality Health Challenge approach sets the stage for real transformation.

Another hallmark of my clinic is that it does not look like a typical medical office. I wanted the space to embody the idea of whole-person care. So the Vitality Health Challenge space combines elements of a medical clinic, a spa, a gym, an education center, and a teaching kitchen. It houses many different therapies under a single roof. Clients come on a regular basis and participate in many different strategies to continue their journeys from disease to vitality.

Vitality Health Challenge Philosophy: Health is Adaptation

To increase health and wellness, build your body's ability to adapt

At the core of all the human-made metabolic diseases, you'll find an imbalance between the human body's evolved systems for confronting physical and environmental challenge and the lack of challenge in our current lifestyles. This is that loss of *adaptive homeostasis,* or *hormesis*, which we've defined and explored all throughout this book.[1] We're too comfortable in our daily lives, and we're paying the price. Hormetic therapies—from exercise to ozone, from intermittent fasting to cold therapies—restore balance, build resistance, and strengthen the stress response. They bring physical and cellular challenge back into the picture and trigger the body to employ its powerful innate systems for maintenance and repair.

That strange word, *hormesis*, has been a major focus in these pages, and it's the over-arching theme in the restorative health programs I design for my clients. When we really grasp this concept, we appreciate how finely adapted the body is for confronting and benefitting from physical and environmental challenge. This knowledge base allows us to redefine our perspective on health and wellness.

What really is health?

Is it the absence of disease, or is it the presence of something greater? Perhaps it's optimal energy production by all our body's cells. Maybe it's feeling and living at your very best. There are many different definitions of health, but the one I use in my practice is:

> "One's ability to adapt to multiple and varied physical and environmental challenges."

This definition is a paradigm-shift for many of my clients. Think about what that implies. We don't increase health by taking a pill to cover up an annoying symptom. **We increase health by giving our bodies new and appropriate challenges to adapt to.** Those challenges kick our immune, metabolic, cardiovascular, and many other systems into a higher, restorative gear. Our bodies are awakened, repair functions are activated, and our resiliency is enhanced.[2,3,4]

This definition hints at the cause of aging and poor health: The loss of *adaptive range*. We all age, and the aging process is defined by a loss of adaptive range and by a vulnerability to disease.[5] It is as if all our cells become rigid and brittle, unable to flex in response to challenge. How do we maintain adaptive range? The answer involves the whole-body Vitality Health Challenge approach paired with the hormetic therapies that I use with my clients. Let's look at some common therapy sets I use to treat well-known conditions and achieve health goals.

Powerful "Synergy Sets" that Break Disease Cycles

Natural Therapy Combinations I Use for Common Health Challenges

There is no magic bullet. But there are some common therapy combinations that show up repeatedly in my practice. In all my initial consultations, I first look for the therapy that might yield the most tangible effects the fastest, to restore the client's sense of hope. As you read about these synergy sets, ask yourself which therapies you gravitate toward. Make note of that and share it with your integrative physician. Use this section as a discussion guide when working with your own doctor.

A. Chronic Pain and Inflammation

We develop chronic pain when the cells in a certain region are no longer optimally producing energy.[6] Remember the concept of anaerobic versus aerobic metabolism (Chapter 3). That anaerobic state, characterized by severely low cellular energy, is at the core of chronic pain.[7] The first priority is to enhance blood flow (nutrient and oxygen delivery) to these poorly functioning cells. **Oxygen** and **Ozone therapies,** such as Prolozone, are very effective.[8,9] Prolozone provides highly active oxygen plus healing nutrients. It's also one of the few hormetic therapies you can start right away, without pre-conditioning.

I evaluate chronic pain clients for hormonal imbalance since it can predispose the body to a catabolic state—breaking down tissues faster than the body can re-build them.[10] On the nutrition side, it is crucial to detect and remedy all nutrient deficiencies, especially B vitamins. I run a complete nutrient profile and provide both custom IV infusions and supplements as needed. Dietary recommendations often include avoiding pro-inflammatory foods, eating more antioxidant-rich greens, and **TRE** (Time Restricted Eating). As soon as the pain is controlled enough that clients can exercise, I get them started with pre-conditioning care to heal injuries, begin sweating, increase flexibility, and build strength. Then we work towards introducing **cyclic exercise** and Exercise with Oxygen Therapies (**EWOT**).[11] Eventually, we also work on any fear factor regarding **cold therapies**. Over the long term, these are some of the most powerful strategies for overall health, immune enhancement, recovery, and preventing pain recurrence.

B. Metabolic Challenges

Whether clients are dealing with diabetes, heart disease, obesity, or all of the above, I listen first to everything they've already tried. I get a sense of their overall health, current strategies, and any physical limitations. I carefully review their pharmaceutical lists and the possible side effect profiles of their medications. Then I start looking for gaps in the clients' past and current care, as well as what may motivate them the most to move forward.

I often begin with a hormone testing series that looks at anabolic/catabolic balance as well as complete thyroid and adrenal function, since these often influence metabolic problems.[12] Then, I look for evidence of any toxicity and nutrient deficiencies that often aggravate metabolic conditions. The body will often deplete nutrient reserves and maintain a higher weight to manage a toxic state.[13] Toxicity states must be addressed gently, but thoroughly, to avoid further setbacks. Additionally, people who are overweight are often malnourished! Nutrient deficiency can cause excessive craving and over-eating as the body continues to try to acquire real nutrition.[14] Once deficiencies and insufficiencies are addressed, it's time for dietary overhaul. Education is crucial to this work. I teach my clients how to eat to keep insulin levels low. We also explore the benefits of raw and cultured foods, and the power of **fasting** and **TRE**.[15]

Next, we determine the best therapies to naturally boost the clients' metabolism, which will help even further with sweating out toxins and burning fat. What pre-conditioning do they need? If heart or weight issues are so severe that movement is limited, I'll recommend using an **ozone sauna** and gentle stretching along with supplemental **oxygen**. The goal is to work up to **cyclic**

exercise and **EWOT**,[16] eventually trying **interval training** to promote natural growth hormone release[17] and further heighten metabolism. When clients are ready, I strongly recommend **cold therapies** too, with all their benefits for brown fat activation and improved insulin sensitivity.[18]

C. Fatigue and Sleep

Fatigue is the number one presenting symptom among people seeking medical attention.[19] It's also the least understood and probably the most poorly treated. Fatigue is often tangled in with sleep issues, and both often resolve as the Vitality Health Challenge pillars are brought back into balance. I'm not at all daunted by treating fatigue. I've noticed I can essentially start anywhere in the Vitality Health Challenge model and see significant improvements.

The first step is to determine the severity of the fatigue. Is the client functional to some degree or fully impaired by exhaustion? If they're so fatigued they can barely manage life, I start them on a passive **oxygen therapy** immediately, usually **HBOT**, simply to restore cellular oxygen levels and resulting cellular energy production.[20] This is often life-changing for the client. If the client is able to function but simply has low quality of life due to poor energy, I will often begin with **EWOT** instead. They'll benefit from the detoxification and endorphin release, as well as get more oxygen into their systems.[21]

I always look closely for the root cause. This requires complex assessments. We need to address toxicity, nutrient deficiencies, dietary habits, chronic pain states, exercise routines, oxygen levels, and hormonal imbalances—all of these can contribute to the causes of fatigue. It's crucial to evaluate the client's stress response system, too. That brings in **HRV work** and **Autonomic Integration**. Often, there are multiple reasons to explain the fatigue, with many corresponding natural therapies that can restore health.

D. Immune Dysfunction: Chronic Infection, Cancer, and Autoimmune Conditions

Both chronic infection and cancer are immune *deficiency* states. On the flip side, autoimmune conditions are characterized by an *over-responsive* immune system that targets the body's own tissues. Ironically, conventional treatments for all three often have immune destructive effects. Invasive surgery, chemotherapy, radiation, biologics, powerful antibiotics, and other pharmaceuticals all cause extreme stress on immune cells. An integrative method takes a more natural approach with three primary goals: Support immune cell function, reduce inflammation, and combat oxidative stress.

Ozone and other hormetic therapies accomplish all three goals and more.[22] **MAH** (Major Auto Hemotherapy, Chapter 4) and **UBI** (Ultraviolet Blood Irradiation, Chapter 4) are especially effective for addressing low-grade chronic infection, boosting immune cell activity, and reducing inflammation[23]—all root cause factors involved in both under-active and over-active immune states.

Other Vitality Health Challenge therapies are valuable depending on the precise nature of the immune imbalance. **HBOT** is effective for resolving chronic or resistant infections.[24] Cancer responds best to comprehensive whole-person therapies including: **Oxygen** and **ozone** therapies,[25] major dietary change,[26] **fasting** and **TRE**,[27] detoxification, stress reduction through lifestyle change**, HRV work,**[28] and **hormetic exercise.**[29]

Autoimmune challenges also require multiple synergistic inputs and are often responsive to: Wim Hof Method breath work and cold exposure **(WHM) Autonomic Integration, HRV** work,[30] and **cyclic exercise** or **interval training,**[31] when supported by appropriate rehab and pre-conditioning measures. Of course, like any new client, all my immune health clients are also screened for hormonal imbalance, nutrient deficiencies, and toxicity to ensure we establish that basic health foundation.

E. New Injury and Past Injury – Loss of Range of Motion

This is a favorite aspect of my practice: Helping people recover from injury and return to full function—or become even more fit and capable than before the injury. Often, conventional medicine struggles to return us to complete function and full range of motion. Its treatments include pain medication, complex and invasive surgical procedures, and limited physical therapy strategies. Many clients come to me after surgery leaves them worse off.

My approach to injury is radically different. Whether it's a new injury or an old injury that healed poorly, the first priority is to bring more **oxygen** to the injured tissues (muscle, tendon, ligament, or cartilage). When these tissues are well-oxygenated, they can relax their protective reflexes.[32] Enhancing oxygen levels lead to flexibility and enhanced healing, with tissue fibers that can flex, bend, and twist with no pain or reinjury. Mending any injury can only occur in the presence of ample oxygen. In addition to oxygen, **Prolozone** offers tremendous regenerative healing.[33] Another advanced therapy that can offer significant regenerative changes involves an ozone-activated growth factor injection[34] (see Case Story 3 in this chapter) using the body's own stem cells and growth factors.

Once movement becomes possible, many injuries respond well to what I refer to as "Synergy Workout Cycles." These are a combination of therapies completed one right after the other, then cycled through again two or three times. I combine mild **exercise** with breathing high-flow **oxygen**, massage, stretching, and pulsed electromagnetic field therapy (PEMF). An example is covered in more detail in Case Story 3 in this chapter.

My post-injury clients also benefit from an integrative approach that includes all my foundational Vitality Health Challenge therapies: Optimized nutrition, oxygenation, immune enhancement, and detoxification therapies. Ensuring hormonal balance is also crucial as the tissues need to be in a healthy anabolic state to heal.[35] Finally, it's crucial to include range of motion exercises to keep the injured tissues pliable as they're healing, and a strength-building protocol for the muscles above and below the original injury to prevent re-injury.

F. Vitality and Peak Performance

It is always special when clients come to me solely to support vitality and peak performance. Rather than dealing with a health problem, they're seeking to build on an already healthy state or improve athletic performance. I wish more people viewed health with such proactive motivation. Thankfully, many clients who initially come to Vitality Health Challenge with a medical issue, eventually enjoy their transformation so much that they naturally grow into a "vitality mindset". As with all clients, I begin vitality consults with my comprehensive assessment. Often, hormone balance is my first focus since by age 50, we have half the normal levels of hormones that we had in our twenties.[36,37] Those hormones are needed not only for optimal energy levels and sexual health, but also for long-term protection of bone, heart, and brain function.[38] I routinely test these clients for free T3, free T4, TSH, growth hormone, salivary four-point cortisol, DHEA, testosterone for men, and progesterone and estrogen with metabolites for women (see the Crucial Lab Tests list following this chapter).

Once hormone levels are in balance, I teach these clients more about nutrition and how to best meet their nutritional goals. I have designed programs for: Building muscle, burning fat, reducing carbohydrate intake, increasing raw and fermented foods, incorporating juicing, and more. I personalize nutritional plans for each client, and these plans change and evolve over time. All clients are educated about the hormetic benefits of **TRE** and occasional longer **fasts**. Athletes with peak performance goals are encouraged to occasionally train in a fasted state.

The right diet helps the body detox appropriately, which is vital since toxin buildup compromises energy levels and performance. Additional detox therapies include: **Ozone sauna** or *far infrared* sauna (a special low-temperature sauna for detox),[39] monthly IV nutrient infusions, and access to specialized drinking water that includes reverse osmosis, remineralization, ionization, and alkalization.

My vitality clients also regularly complete **EWOT with hormetic challenges.** They understand that all cellular functions depend on ample supplies of oxygen. Additionally, exercise provides all its other synergistic benefits including detoxification, improved lymphatic flow, and better mood and energy.[40,41] Lastly, these clients learn about the benefits of **cold exposure**, **recovery breathing,** and **HRV**. True wellness and optimized athletic performance absolutely depend on some level of **Autonomic Integration**.

Some Thoughts About "Treatment Overwhelm"

The past few pages have certainly communicated that total health transformation stems from multiple therapies and lifestyle choices implemented simultaneously. That's what synergy is all about. But the thought of so many major changes all at once can feel over-whelming. I get that. I want to encourage and assure you that major synergistic treatment plans can be manageable. Most of my clients grow into their plans. They don't do everything all at once. I'm always sensitive to the realities that my clients are juggling too: stressful work, busy families, financial strain, and possibly several major health challenges.

I never want to leave any client feeling like his treatment plan is just one more stress. My goal is to structure for success.

I always look for the initial therapies that are easiest and will yield an immediately useful benefit—especially reduced pain and greater energy. A therapy that reduces pain and leaves you feeling clear-headed and energized is a game changer. Often this is all that's needed to feel charged and inspired about the rest of the treatment plan. These initial therapies also put you in a better space for dealing with the other stresses in your life. It's crucial to partner with a practitioner who can similarly help you determine the most impactful stepping stone therapies for you.

As you take those initial steps into a treatment plan, also keep in mind how much effort you've been putting into managing the stress of your health challenges. **Yes, it's work to get healthy, but I've often found that it takes way more effort to stay sick.** As you begin to experience more release from your symptoms, you will organically have more energy to put toward other health-building therapies. My clients who have truly committed to health transformation come back to me months and years later saying that they are happier and healthier in every way imaginable. That success is within your reach too!

Meet the Patients Who Have Benefitted

From reversing serious disease states to enhancing athletic performance, I hope you notice the diversity of these client stories and the versatility of the Vitality Health Challenge approach. I hope you recognize yourself in one of these stories and you begin to see a path for yourself—from where you are right now to enjoying life at your very best. The concept of "therapy synergies" can be hard to grasp; there are so many moving parts. But these case stories show concrete examples of how integrative multiple-therapy programs work to restore health, promote longevity, and enhance athletic performance.

Case Story #1

37-year-old Female with Chronic Fatigue, Multiple Food Allergies, and Leaky Gut

When I met Sherry, she was intense, tearful, and justifiably angry. She had an incredibly low quality of life due to chronic fatigue and multiple food allergies. She literally struggled to make it from one day to the next, unable to remain awake and functional beyond 7:30 p.m. on most days. Her work was taxing, and she had little to offer her husband and pets. Sherry's diet was extremely limited; she was only able to eat beef, fish, chicken, nuts, and eggs. She could not tolerate dairy, grains of any kind, and most vegetables. She also informed me that she needed to exercise for her mental health even though she recognized that it further exhausted her.

Perhaps the most important symptom Sherry relayed to me was her inability to get a full night of restful sleep. She suffered from insomnia and was only sleeping four to five hours a night. She typically went to bed around 9:00 or 9:30 p.m., but would usually wake around 2:00 to 3:00 a.m. and was unable to fall back to sleep even with prescription sleep medication. She knew this only aggravated all her other problems and that it played a key role in her constant sense of frustration and exhaustion. She spoke with anger about modern medical doctors who had attempted to treat her but were unsuccessful. She was also deeply disappointed with several other alternative providers who failed her as well. Sherry had been barely managing for some time and had no reserves left. She could not withstand another setback from a practitioner who could not help her. Clearly I needed to go slowly with her. She was hanging on by a small thread!

I explained my approach and was clear that, realistically, she would have to work at re-establishing her health for more than a year. This timeline hit her hard. I appreciated how dysfunctional many of her systems had become, and I knew how much work it would take to transition her from disease to vitality. I told her that I do not promise results but I do not set any limits on progress either. I want my clients to appreciate that they can make choices and work to change their health. I told Sherry what I tell every new client, "Resiliency is the greatest asset of the human body." Her body was in trouble, but she could help it return to greater health.

I explained the pillars of my Vitality Health Challenge practice and the seven major determinants of health and wellness that need to be in balance. We would look at how each of these pillars could be addressed for her personally, since treatment is different for every individual. So far, the philosophy rang true for her and she was open to learning more.

Based on her symptoms alone, I was sure that Sherry had significant hormonal imbalances, toxicity states, and nutrient deficiencies. My suspicions were confirmed by her initial lab work. One of the tests I ordered was a 24-hour urine collection that analyzes all the steroid hormones and their metabolites. This test provides the ratio of the amount of overall hormones involved in growth and repair (anabolic function) and the amount of overall hormones involved in wear and tear (catabolic function). We need a balance of both of these functions in the body. Sherry's test revealed a very low ratio of anabolic to catabolic hormones, a hallmark of the excess tissue breakdown often seen with aging, insomnia, chronic stress, and chronic illness.[42] This was a worrisome finding in a 37-year-old woman. She definitely had adrenal fatigue, and testing also indicated low thyroid levels, too.

The first step for Sherry was to address these hormonal imbalances, beginning with her adrenal fatigue and then focusing on her low thyroid state. I also suggested she stop exercising for now, but she refused, claiming it was a "must" to be able to work at all. We reached the understanding that she would reduce her work hours, rest more, and simply limit her exercise. She agreed to exchange her 45-minute elliptical or stair master workout for a 20-minute cyclic exercise or interval training routine.

It took six weeks to determine the right combination of adrenal support needed to restore her energy levels some, while not compromising her already poor sleep. After some work, we established an adrenal support regimen that was helpful, and then we added in low-dose, combined T3 and T4 thyroid hormone.

Now it was time to address her sleep, which was limited in both duration and quality. Sherry had tried many different remedies, but we hit a home run when she spent some time in my Hyperbaric Oxygen Therapy (HBOT) chamber and felt noticeably different after a single session. "It felt like being in the womb," she said. "I actually feel rested and alert right now." This was quite a rare response, as most clients do not experience such dramatic effects with a first treatment. Sherry was quite intuitive and knew she needed more of this therapy daily.

We discussed why HBOT was such a good fit for her. I explained how oxygen is the currency of life in the body's cells. Her cellular oxygen levels were undoubtedly low because of the host of medical issues she was facing. When we provided excess oxygen, her body was finally able to thoroughly accomplish many basic tasks. These tasks included detoxification, elimination, immune enhancement, hormone production, healing in general, stress response modulation, and more restful sleep.[43] I told her about my habit of sleeping for an hour or two in my HBOT chamber after a busy all-night hospital call, and how that hour of oxygenated sleep lets me stay functional all day until a normal bedtime. Both her initial experience and my explanation of HBOT science convinced her to commit to this powerful therapy.

I installed a portable HBOT unit in her home and trained her how to use it. I also installed an oxygen concentrator to help Sherry breathe higher concentrations of oxygen while in the unit. As she put it, "HBOT was the single greatest thing for my condition ever." Once she understood how to best use the unit, we settled on the following plan. When she wakes in the night, she heads into the chamber and stays there at least until 6:00 a.m. She does not have to sleep in the HBOT unit, but has to do her best to rest and relax. No work, no computers, no reading. She uses HBOT every night religiously.

Once I'd earned Sherry's trust, we introduced multiple stress reduction therapies. I educated her on Recovery Breathing techniques, massage, and yoga. I also had her try sensory deprivation flotation—another stress reduction therapy I use in my practice. After three more months of combined therapies, Sherry was noticeably more functional throughout each day, and her energy was better without crashing in the early evening. She was no longer stressed about her insomnia, as the HBOT time left her recharged and more energized than she had felt in years. This was a major turning point in her life and in overcoming her medical conditions.

It was time to address Sherry's multiple food allergies. She had leaky gut, a condition that allows intestinal food material to leak across the gut lining and enter the blood stream. Once in the blood stream, her body viewed this material as a foreign invader and generated an immune response. Because of leaky gut, essentially almost anything she ate could make her allergic.[44] We addressed this by increasing her beneficial bacterial in her colon with raw fermented foods and eliminating some items that were further stressing her such as soy milk products and other processed foods. I started her on supplements designed to help heal gaps in the tight junctions that lined her digestive track. She was also immediately drawn to the TRE style of eating.

This further helped her energy and stamina as we worked toward reducing her eating window to eight or nine hours. I am convinced that more restful sleep and extra oxygen from her HBOT sessions provided additional support to help heal her gut lining.

We worked closely together over a 16-month period. Sherry now has better health than ever and enjoys excellent quality of life. She sleeps much better naturally and still uses her HBOT unit every night. Her devastating fatigue is long gone. She is able to eat more foods, including many vegetables, though she continues to prefer a mostly Paleo (grain free) approach. She continues TRE and maintains an ideal weight. Her work feels rewarding now, and she has become a leader in her field.

Sherry's Core Vitality Health Challenge Therapies
Hormone restoration, adrenal support, cyclic exercise, HBOT, recovery breathing, massage, yoga, sensory deprivation flotation, dietary changes, fermented foods, gut healing supplements, TRE

Case Story #2
60-year-old Male with Severe Toxicity, Bladder Cancer, and Sedentary Lifestyle

Jack came to see me after recently being diagnosed with bladder cancer and undergoing a urologic procedure to remove a tumor. His major lifestyle risk factors included a 30-year smoking history, though he'd quit by the time we met. There was also evidence of possible heavy metal toxicity, and he had a reduced capacity for exercise of any kind. He knew that he was in serious trouble when he came to see me. He was shocked that the medical establishment had no further program or recommendations to offer him aside from a repeat cystoscopy to re-image his bladder in one year.

Jack's three big questions were: Why do you think I got this cancer? How can I avoid its recurrence? And why haven't my doctors addressed these issues with me?

I told him that in the integrative oncology world, many practitioners believe that cancer results from a combination of toxicity, nutrient deficiency, and poor cellular energy production. We went over the Disease Progression Model (Chapter 1). I also told him that I believe that chronic inflammation and continuous 24-hour comfort significantly contribute to disease. We spent the majority of our first visit discussing that spiral of disease characterized by acidosis, degeneration, and low levels of oxygen in the body's cells. "It's this combination of multiple factors that predisposed you to your cancer," I said. We all are only as healthy as our weakest link. For Jack, it made the most sense to pursue an integrative plan that restored balance to all the determinants of health.

Just looking at him, I could see the effects of chronic low levels of oxygen in his tissues. He had deep wrinkles and a slightly bluish tinge to his face. There was also extra tissue fluid (edema) in his face, and the whites of his eyes were not clear. These observations, combined with his extensive smoking history, influenced my decision to begin with a toxicity and nutrition analysis. The initial results indicated heavy metal toxicity. I had Jack complete a heavy metal "challenge test" that involved taking a one-time dose of an oral chelator and then completing a six-hour urinary collection test. The chelator serves to provoke heavy metals out of the body as they are stored deeper in the tissues and may be missed on non-provoked testing.

His results were off the charts—extremely high—for many heavy metals. He was both shocked and relieved that we had possibly found a contributing factor for his cancer.[45] He began a series of several intravenous chelation therapies, each separated by one week. These were designed to bind the heavy metals and encourage their excretion in the urine gently over time. I also administered customized nutrients and vitamins in the IV after the chelator was infused.

Once the initial set of treatments were complete, we did repeat testing that showed improvement. Jack elected to use continued chelation therapy in the form of a rectal suppository. The entire chelation process took several months and was combined with multiple repeat testing to ensure the metals were mostly removed. He felt noticeably stronger as this work progressed. He noted being able to walk longer before feeling winded. I noticed less facial swelling and improved coloration.

Because Jack's bladder tumor was localized, his conventional physicians had no adjunct therapies to offer him. They never explored any of the nutrient testing or toxicity issues we addressed. Yet I knew there was much more to do to establish greater health and discourage recurrence. I suggested a series of ozone and UBI therapies (Chapter 4) to support additional detoxification and immune enhancement,[46] since cancer (and his surgery) further reduce immune function. We started with minimal doses of ozone to ensure that his systems would respond in a positive hormetic fashion. My hope was that this combination therapy would inactivate any of the low level infections that are common in many cancer patients.[47,48] Jack experienced good energy and improved sleep for several days after these therapies. He was beginning to make important inroads back to health.

Jack fully embraced the Vitality Health Challenge integrative model and wanted to learn and incorporate as much as he could. We initiated a plan to restore his ability to exercise. To pre-condition for that process, he spent time in a far infrared sauna to start sweating again. He began a series of physical therapy sessions for one month to loosen his muscles and build flexibility. Then, I introduced cyclic exercise paired with oxygen and recovery breathing. Jack felt more youthful than he had in years. We had successfully re-introduced exercise and all of its benefits back into his life!

I spent a lot of time educating him about diet strategies for wellness and cancer prevention. Cancer cells are characterized by a high metabolic rate. They need a source of glucose (sugar). Jack needed to eat in a fashion that kept his insulin levels and blood sugar levels low.[49] I instructed him to restrict all refined carbohydrates, limit animal protein, and to begin TRE with an eating window that was less than ten hours each day. I also introduced many raw and cultured foods into his diet.

Through all these therapies and major lifestyle changes, Jack progressed from disease to vitality. His improved quality of life was evident to everyone around him. His wife and kids noted his improved appearance, better energy, weight loss, and more positive mood. He took a real interest in learning as much as he could about health and wellness.

Jack is now one of my long-term clients and considers himself healthier than ever. He's transitioned from a focus on disease reversal to giving himself peak performance goals. He regularly utilizes EWOT, and we build hormetic challenges into his workouts. This is a huge accomplishment as he was barely able to exercise at all when we met. Lastly, and perhaps most importantly, all of Jack's repeat cystoscopies continue to show no evidence of any cancer recurrence. He successfully learned how to take his health into his own hands.

Jack's Core Vitality Health Challenge Therapies

IV chelation, IV nutrients, Ozone-UBI therapy, infrared sauna, PT, cyclic exercise, oxygen therapies, recovery breathing, low/no-carb diet, TRE, EWOT

Case Story #3
49-year-old Male with Recent Knee Injury

Kent came to me with knee pain and muscle tightness that kept him from exercising. His knee pain was at a level 6 out of 10 with walking, but increased to an 8 or 9 when heading down stairs or trying to stand after sitting. He had undergone an arthroscopy two years before and was told that he would need a joint replacement down the road. His cartilage was mostly gone, and there were regions in the joint space where he was close to experiencing a bone-on-bone situation. We talked for a while about how little blood flow reaches our joints typically, and this reduced blood flow, combined with inflammation, is a set up for joint pain. We discussed the Vitality Health Challenge approach and several therapies aimed at addressing the root causes of the problem.

Kent first underwent a series of three Prolozone injections containing a mixture of oxygen and ozone plus nutrients into his right knee.[50] These were administered once a week over the next three weeks. I also had him ice and elevate the knee while sleeping for the first month and apply a compression wrap during the day. He was amazed that after a single Prolozone injection his pain was 50 percent improved while walking and essentially gone after his second treatment. I explained that we were off to a good start, but there was much more to be done if he wanted to restore his ability to exercise and rebuild the health of his knee.

Now that Kent was out of pain most of the time, we began focused rehabilitative therapies for the knee and began work in preparation for weight-bearing exercise. The goals were to strengthen the muscles above and below the knee, increase his flexibility, and reduce inflammation. He came to the center twice a week for the next month to complete what I call "Synergy Workout Cycles". These are combination of hormetic therapies, structural therapies, and physical therapy exercises. I customize these cycles to meet the specific needs of each client. Components include, but aren't limited to: Healing therapies focused on injury care, strength training, oxygen and ozone therapies, exercise therapies, massage, and chiropractic care. For Kent, I designed the following series of treatments for every visit:

- **PEMF.** This stands for Pulsed Electromagnetic Field Therapy, a non-invasive method of providing pulsed magnetic energy to a localized area of the body. When we experience pain, those cells are not producing energy optimally, and the cells' overall voltage is low. PEMF serves to jump start these low-energy-producing cells. PEMF is proven to reduce pain, swelling, bruising, muscle spasm, and inflammation. It also stimulates stem cells, wound repair, tissue regeneration, and bone healing.[51,52] A PEMF treatment typically lasts eight minutes, and Kent completed two cycles each visit.
- **Ozone Sauna with Supplemental Oxygen.** This is the detoxification device described in Chapter 4. The pod encloses the entire person except the head, then fills with steam and ozone, which diffuses into the skin (see Chapter 4). This powerful oxygenation and detoxification therapy can be combined with additional oxygen administered through a nasal cannula. This is very effective for removing toxins as well as promoting athletic recovery.[53,54] In Kent's case, we capitalized on all three major benefits: Sweating, detoxification, and oxygenation.
- **Foam Roller.** Basic PT work with a firm foam roller helped to break up minor adhesions and relax the muscles.
- **Mild Rehab Training.** Kent began a series of exercises, in clinic and at home, which were designed to help strengthen and stabilize his knee. These exercises were initially performed using only his body weight as resistance. As he gained strength, we added in light

ankle weights. The PT exercises included: Straight leg raises, hamstring curls, prone straight leg raises, wall squats, calf raises, and step-ups.

- **Soft Tissue and Structural Care**. Kent also received massage and chiropractic care throughout his restorative program.

Kent got stronger and his knee pain remained minimal. After three months, I adjusted his Synergy Workout Cycles. It was time to begin cyclic exercise followed by recovery breathing. The goal was to get his heart rate up to 80 to 85 percent of his max for 45 seconds and then stop, sit, relax, and concentrate on breathing to get his heart rate back down to his baseline. Then, he would begin the next cycle. He was to complete four of these cycles three times per week. After the set of four cycles, he was to work on recovery breathing techniques designed to enhance his HRV.

In the third phase of Kent's recovery, while still working on his own home exercise and PT program, he also came to the clinic once a week to complete an intensive Synergy Workout Cycle. This began with EWOT and cyclic exercise for one to two minutes of exertion then complete recovery. Then, while still breathing high-flow oxygen, he would begin stretching, undergo a PEMF treatment, and work with the firm foam roller. Kent completed three or four of these cycles with each clinic visit. These combinations worked powerfully together to help circulate blood and oxygen deep throughout the body and to all joint spaces. They also help remove lactic acid and other toxins from the muscles.

Kent was finally able to do more with his body than he had done in years. He had a solid game plan. He was back to exercising and feeling strong and confident with his knee. His exercise capacity grew dramatically. I continued to work with him for another two months and got him interested in cold exposure training as another modality to provide healing and synergistic input for his knee.

Finally, Kent and I discussed other options we could use if there was ever a setback or major pain recurrence. I educated him about a specialized therapy that I offer: ozone-activated growth factor injection, which is similar to Platelet Rich Plasma (PRP, Chapter 4). In this regenerative stem cell therapy a small amount of the patient's blood is drawn and placed in a gradient centrifuge to concentrate the growth factor and stem cell components. These stem cells and growth factors are then activated with ozone and injected into the injured joint. These activated components have special regenerative abilities including: Reducing inflammation, inducing bone growth, repairing soft tissue (cartilage and muscle), and promoting wound healing.[55] Kent continues to do well at present, but is grateful that there are even more alternatives to surgery should he ever deal with knee pain again.

Kent's Core Vitality Health Challenge Therapies

Prolozone injections, PEMF, ozone sauna, supplemental oxygen, PT exercises, massage, chiropractic care, cyclic exercise, recovery breathing, HRV training, in-clinic multi-therapy exercise sessions, cold exposure

Case Story #4

50-Year-Old Male with Goals for High Altitude Athletic Performance

I don't want to end this book without letting readers know that I fully embrace this work for my own health too. This case story is MY story of how I came to develop my most challenging workout and solved a problem with high altitude symptoms.

I love to snowboard and go out west once a season. A few years back, I first experienced very mild altitude symptoms. I didn't want them to hold me back from enjoying a favorite sport. When I got home—on the East Coast—I decided to design a high-altitude training method that I could use at sea level to enhance all of my athletic activities and also solve the altitude sensitivity that I recently experienced. I wound up combining EWOT, low-oxygen altitude training, and other hormetic therapies to enhance the challenge.

It took me about one year to get to the level that I am at now with this workout. This is an extreme activity that requires vigilance and use of heart rate and oxygen monitoring. I reserve this for athletic peak performance clients only.

There are a few components of the workout, which I continue to use today:

- **Phil Campbell's Peak 8 Maximal Intensity Interval Training.** This workout consists of eight 30-second intervals (see Chapter 2). Each interval is separated by 90 seconds of recovery at 50 percent effort. This is a very challenging workout in itself; most people need weeks to months to be able to perform each of the eight intervals at maximal effort. The entire exercise takes twenty minutes, including a three-minute warm up and a 2.5-minute cool down.[56]
- **EWOT.** I use a special EWOT device attached to a large oxygen reservoir, anesthesia tubing, and a facemask. There is also a smaller, separate reserve of LOW oxygen air that contains **half** the normal amount of oxygen. A switch allows me to change instantly between the two reserves as desired. This design offers me the ability to engage in high altitude equivalent training any time I want, anywhere I want. I am re-creating the challenge of high altitude by breathing a reduced amount of oxygen.

> When breathing from the low oxygen reserve, it is equivalent to breathing at 10,000 feet of elevation. There is also additional challenge from breathing resistance through the use of a face mask and anesthesia tubing.

For additional hormetic challenge, I complete this workout in a fasted state, typically having gone without eating for more than twelve hours. Initially, I started this customized workout using low oxygen during the first fifteen seconds of each interval before switching back to high oxygen.

This is something I often recommend for many performance athlete clients as it offers an immediate altitude challenge. The work of breathing increases. Heart rate increases. We are intensely challenged.

After this brief challenge, I typically switch back to the EXTRA oxygen setting. Now, as my heart and lungs are working intensely, they begin to circulate large volumes of high-speed fully-oxygenated blood all throughout my body. Powerful changes occur and result from the synergy of increased respiration, elevated heart rate, and pure oxygen.

To focus my work on the altitude training element, I modified this workout over time. I continually increased my low-oxygen time by five seconds for each week that I completed the workout. Over the past year, I have worked up to the point where I am now using the low oxygen setting for almost the entire duration of the workout—all but nine seconds following each interval.

Here is what it looks like today:

- Low oxygen warm-up for three minutes
- Low oxygen for first 30-second interval
- Nine-second high oxygen recovery
- 81-second low oxygen recovery
- Low oxygen for second 30-second interval

- Nine-second high oxygen recovery
- 81-second low oxygen recovery

And so forth. This process continues until I complete the eighth interval on low oxygen at 17:30, and then enter a prolonged recovery on full high oxygen.

This is extremely challenging. I am making a maximal effort for each of the eight intervals and consuming low oxygen for all but 63 seconds total in the 17.5 minute workout. This requires significant focus, mindset, concentration, and training. It is a huge challenge, and it pushes me. It is my most intense workout. It's worth it!

There are countless benefits. One of the most important occurs at minute 17:30 as I am fully taxed, my heart rate is above 95 percent of my maximum, my body is fatigued, and oxygen reserves are fully depleted. As I switch to high oxygen, my entire circulatory system pumps high-speed high-velocity blood carrying maximum levels of oxygen deep throughout my body. This is a powerful experience that I palpably feel. At that moment…

- My heart rate is approximately 2.5 times above my normal rate.
- I am breathing five times the amount of oxygen that I normally breathe (20 percent in air vs. 100 percent in the high-oxygen setting).
- So I have 12.5 times the normal amount of oxygen circulating all throughout my body.

This is much more oxygen than most of us ever experience in daily life. Oxygen is the cellular regenerative currency in the body. The more we have, the more we can do at a cellular level: More detoxification, more tissue remodeling, more hormone synthesis, more immunity, more recovery, more healing.[57] More of everything.

I spend the first ten minutes after this workout flooding my system with oxygen and remain on my elliptical trainer exercising at 50 percent effort. After the first ten minutes of recovery, I continue to breathe the high oxygen while stretching for another ten minutes. Then I begin Recovery Breathing and HRV training (see Chapter 6). I know I have recovered fully when I see more than a twelve-point change in my heart rate as I go from one inhalation to my next exhalation. **My most challenging workout is paired with my greatest recovery.**

This workout has changed my life in ways I hadn't expected. I perform better in all the sports that I enjoy. My strength training has improved. I do not fatigue as quickly, and I recover much faster after any high intensity exertion. In day-to-day life I've noticed that I'm better able to manage other stresses that come my way. My immune system seems stronger. Oh, and I no longer experience altitude symptoms when I head to the mountains to snowboard.

Try It! Incorporating a Synergistic Philosophy into YOUR Life

Finding the multiple therapies that will work best for your goals

The specifics of your plan and path toward greater health will depend on countless factors. Not simply your age, sex, weight, and current health issues. An integrative approach looks at your lifestyle, relational support, exercise habits, nutrition, supplement protocols, sleep quality, current and past stressors, injuries, toxin exposures, and so much more. It's tempting to use Dr. Google and treat yourself. Please be cautious about that. Taking a DIY mentality toward your own health can be risky. None of us can see our own blind spots! That's why your first step involves finding the right integrative practitioner to serve as an objective guide.

1. Find a Guide.

The journey ahead of you is long, challenging, and exciting. If you set out on a mountain climbing expedition, you'd hire at least one guide. The climb ahead of you is no less challenging or risky. This work is best done with the aid of a knowledgeable integrative physician and may include a larger team of integrative health providers including: Chiropractors, exercise physiologists, rehab specialists, massage therapists, and IV therapists. You may screen your practitioners using the question list following this chapter. If you have any trouble finding a solid integrative practitioner in your region, know that I, and other Vitality Health Challenge practitioners, are available for in-person and distance consultations.

2. Address Foundational Needs

Work with your integrative practitioner to test for and evaluate hormone balance, micro- and macro-nutrient deficiencies, and detox challenges. Use the Crucial Lab Tests list at the end of this book to guide this process. Begin corrective hormone therapies, nutrient infusions, and detox support as needed.

3. Pre-condition as Needed

Pushing yourself is appropriate only when you're prepared. Work with your practitioners to address any underlying medical problems, chronic pain, and old or recent injuries. Pre-condition as needed with passive hormetic therapies like TRE, ozone therapies, and cold exposure.

4. Begin Utilizing Hormetic Therapies

Select your hormetic therapies wisely. Keep in mind that a fine line exists between beneficial hormetic stressors and causing new damage. Respect the program and limitations that your practitioner develops for you. Monitoring will be crucial.

This can involve specialized devices such as oxygen saturation monitoring and heart rate monitoring. Over time, these hormetic therapies and recovery breathing strategies will build your body's ability to confront and adapt to new stressors.

A Note of Caution: As you do your own research you'll notice that hormesis applies to many more potential practices than those explained in this book. I have intentionally focused on well-researched, proven, and natural medical therapies that are also hormetic. You may find "experts" encouraging the use of radiation, toxins, and other agents as "hormetic" therapies. Be wise! As an integrative physician, I would never recommend those for my clients. Stick with proven, scientifically-validated therapies.

5. Live It!

Integrative health and hormetic therapies aren't meant to be reserved for a three-month or one-year health kick. This is a life-long commitment. If you want to increase your adaptive range even further, layer in multiple hormetic therapies and focus even more on your recovery strategies. This is the kind of work I do for myself and my most motivated clients.

If you resonate with my approach to health, I offer video consulting sessions intended for further education and design on how to begin your own program. I also offer in person and online consultations for those facing complex health problems. You can learn about these initiatives at **www.VitalityHealthChallenge.com.**

You're on the Right Path

I hope reading this book has generated a paradigm shift in your view of health and wellness. Exploring and working with hormetic challenges has changed my life and the lives of my clients. I know it can do the same for you. You've got the tools to take the next steps and begin writing your own chapter in this evolving view of what it means to be healthy.

Health is the ability to adapt to new challenges. I believe that this hormetic principle will become mainstream in the near future. Hormesis is one of the few universal truths that unite us all. We have the power to reclaim our health.

As other physicians begin to enter this new paradigm, they will need to engage in major reprioritization. Physicians will need to lead by example and take steps to improve their own health and wellness. They will need to offer a more integrative approach recommending natural therapies first, or at least in tandem with conventional medicine. New skill sets will be needed to assess and monitor patients differently and to develop customized hormetic challenges for each person. The typical medical office setting will need a major structural overhaul.

These are lofty goals, but I believe that you, the patient, have power to lead that change. I hope you'll keep in touch with me as you look for hormetic therapies in your own region and help educate and inspire your own practitioners. Let me know if there's any way I can help!

Synergy

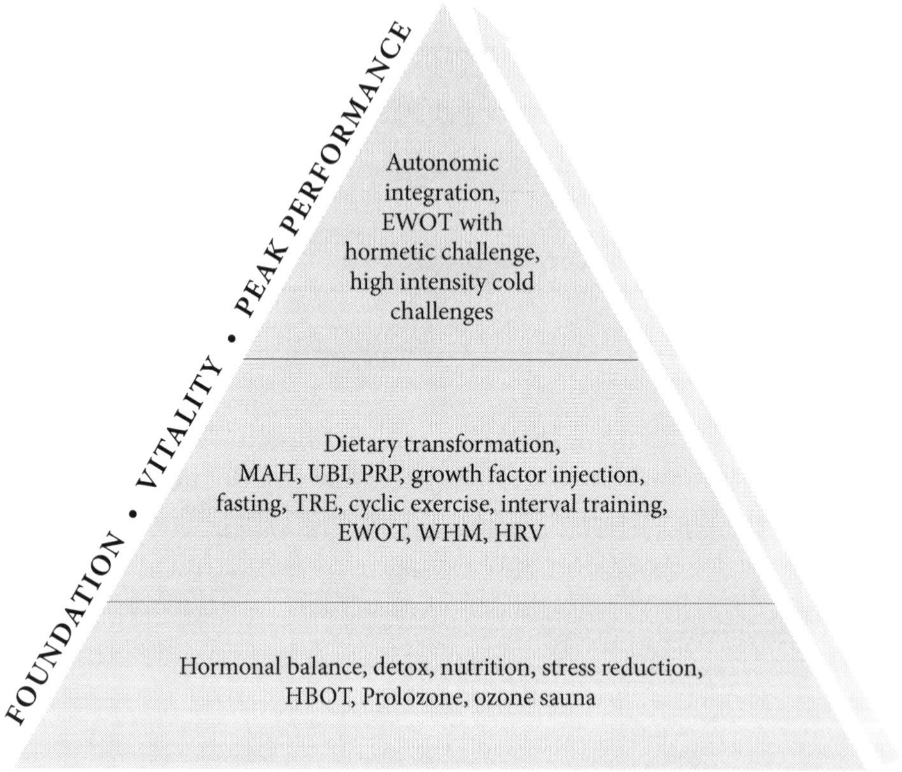

FOUNDATION • VITALITY • PEAK PERFORMANCE

Autonomic integration, EWOT with hormetic challenge, high intensity cold challenges

Dietary transformation, MAH, UBI, PRP, growth factor injection, fasting, TRE, cyclic exercise, interval training, EWOT, WHM, HRV

Hormonal balance, detox, nutrition, stress reduction, HBOT, Prolozone, ozone sauna

Wherever you find yourself in the health journey, remember that the therapeutic principles that promote disease reversal are the same ones that help you reach athletic goals. We only alter intensity and pre-conditioning plans.

SYNERGY: COMBINING MULTIPLE NATURAL THERAPIES FOR EXPONENTIAL GAINS

Further Science

Read the Research for Yourself

Researching whole health synergies is one of modern medicine's biggest challenges. The empirical method is inherently limited in its focus on measuring one-cause, one-effect. The vast majority of medical research is focused on the effect of *one chemical* on *one biological system*, or a single drug's effects related to one measured outcome. But health is way more complicated and layered than that! The medical research community is finally catching on to that, even if general practice often seems light years away.

There is a growing body of research exploring complex hormetic effects in multiple body systems. Meanwhile new population studies are exploring the synergy of multiple health and lifestyle choices—usually combinations of traditional foods and physical activity. This new research focus is small but full of curiosity and fresh thinking. The following provides just a few highlighted studies that can help you expand your understanding of the material in this chapter. Comprehensive chapter References & Notes are found at the end of the book. To read more about these studies, search for "PubMed" online, the world's largest medical library. Reach PubMed directly at: https://www.ncbi.nlm.nih.gov/pubmed/

1.

Leak RK, Calabrese EJ. **"Enhancing and Extending Biological Performance and Resilience."** *Dose Response.* 2018 Jul-Sept; 16(3): 1559325818784501.

This is a current review from an Air Force sponsored event exploring the limits of human performance. The heart of the article focuses on an understanding of conditioning, hormesis, and the stress response. The investigators are most interested in how to best design future research protocols to enhance health and to promote longevity for civilians, soldiers, athletes, and the elderly. There is discussion about combining hormetic therapies such that we can enter an "extended" hormetic zone and achieve biological fitness. The article includes a section titled "How do we define health and can we boost it in both the sick and healthy?" For these authors, health is defined as the ability to adapt. They note that stress adaptation can lead to improved cellular resistance and improved health, as opposed to the reduced adaptive range that is so common in aging and disease

2.

Cook R, Calabrese EJ. **"The Importance of Hormesis to Public Health."** *Environmental Health Perspectives.* 2006 Nov; 114(11): 1631-1635.

This article reinforces the fact that hormesis is found in countless biological models and studied by almost every possible scientific discipline imaginable: Medicine, molecular biology, pharmacology, nutrition, aging, geriatrics, microbiology, immunology, toxicology, exercise physiology, and carcinogenesis. According to these researchers, hormesis is studied "literally across the biological spectrum." Yet, it has not been adequately incorporated into regular practice. This article outlines the known science to date and details the potential improvements to public health that hormesis can offer us.

3.

Chatzianagnostou, et. al. **"The Mediterranean Lifestyle as a Non-Pharmacological and Natural Antioxidant for Healthy Aging."** *Antioxidants (Basel).* 2015 Dec; 4(4): 719–736._

These researchers explore the synergy created by a Mediterranean lifestyle as a model for healthy aging. The article explores the central connection of oxidative stress and aging as well as the appropriate balance needed to achieve homeostasis and hormesis while avoiding cell damage and death. We are reminded how exercise was built into the cycles of feast-or-famine and hunting-or-resting that our ancestors regularly faced.

4.

Scarmeas, et. al. **“Physical Activity, Diet, and Risk of Alzheimer Disease.”** JAMA. 2009;302(6):627-637.

The authors remind us that a low inflammatory Mediterranean type diet as well as increased physical activity are both associated with a reduction in Alzheimer's disease (AD) risk. However, their combined risk reduction potential had not been studied and was the focus of this work. Researchers carefully evaluated both variables using a large sample size over a fourteen-year period. Results showed the greatest AD risk reduction indeed appeared in those who adhered to a low-inflammatory diet and were the most active.

Practitioner Questions

Interview Questions for Evaluating Your Integrative Practitioner Partner

It can be hard to tell if your physician is truly integrative and a good fit for your goals.

Here are some questions you can ask:

1. What is your medical training? (Ideally, having both a conventional medical degree and alternative training can be advantageous.)

2. Do you have an integrative medical approach, or do you exclusively offer natural therapies? Do you provide conventional therapies as well? *(Offering both means the practitioner has a broader base and more options to offer you.)*

3. Are you Board Certified and Fellowship Trained in Anti-Aging and Regenerative Medicine? In Functional or Integrative Medicine?

4. What is your therapeutic model and how did you develop it?

5. What integrative therapies do you offer?

6. Are you familiar with the growing body of hormetic therapy research, and what hormetic therapies do you offer? What is your personal experience with using environmental and physical challenges to enhance health?

7. Are you trained in monitoring and enhancing Heart Rate Variability (HRV) and recovery physiology?

8. Are you trained in ozone and other oxidative therapies? Where did you receive your training?

9. How is your practice set up? Do you have a training facility where I can learn this work?

10. Are there ancillary services and practitioners working within your clinic (exercise physiologists, rehab specialists, chiropractors, etc.)? If not, do you do this work yourself?

11. What is your own knowledge level and training regarding athletic recovery, flexibility, and strength training?

12. Are you comfortable assisting patients with complex, multi-layered medical challenges? What type of situations have you successfully addressed in the past?

13. How has your program benefitted you and your clients?

Crucial Lab Tests We All Need But Rarely Receive

Based on Vitality Health Challenge
Lab Testing and Analysis

Innovative medical programs require access to many different types of laboratory analyses. A basic complete blood count (CBC) and electrolyte test is simply not sufficient to pinpoint the myriad of imbalances that can occur in our bodies. Here is a partial list of some of the testing I routinely order for my clients.

1. **SpectraCell Micronutrient Analysis**. Unlike a simple electrolyte test that looks at levels in the serum (non-cellular portion of blood), this test measures over 30 nutritional components (vitamins, antioxidants, minerals and amino acids) within the white blood cells themselves. This is a better measure of what is—and isn't—inside our cells. Individualized nutritional formulas are designed for each client based on this report.

2. **Four-Point Salivary Cortisol Test.** Salivary cortisol testing is easy to do at home. It measures unbound, biologically active hormone levels. The test assesses the Hypothalamic-Pituitary-Adrenal (HPA) axis using carefully timed samples measured throughout the day.

3. Comprehensive Thyroid Assessment. This test evaluates thyroid hormone metabolism through analyzing serum levels of TSH, free T4, free T3, reverse T3, anti-TG antibodies, and anti-TPO antibodies. This complete panel assesses central and peripheral thyroid function, as well as thyroid autoimmunity. **NOTE**: If you've "had your thyroid levels checked" at a conventional clinic, it was not likely this thorough. Most conventional thyroid tests only measure free T3 level.

4. Complete Hormone Testing. This urinary hormone test assesses parent hormones, their metabolites, and key metabolic pathways. This paints a clearer picture of age-related hormonal shift in men (andropause) and women (menopause). These results influence treatments for weight management, anxiety, fatigue, low sex drive, sleep problems, mood change, and even brain fog.

5. Bone Resorption Assessment. This urinary test provides an accurate assessment of the rate of bone turnover. It identifies clients who are more likely to develop osteoporosis and can be used to monitor bone health protocols.

6. Advanced Cardiovascular Risk Testing. While traditional lipid markers (LDL/HDL and triglycerides) are helpful, they do not fully account for a person's cardiovascular risk. Risk Testing assesses both standard lipid markers and advanced biomarkers. This combined data can be used to promote better treatment for cholesterol metabolism, inflammation, and insulin resistance.

7. Comprehensive Digestive Stool Analysis. This analyzes the overall health of the gastrointestinal tract. It's crucial for clients who struggle with poor digestion, malabsorption, irritable bowel syndrome, and bacterial overgrowth.

8. Comprehensive Urine Toxic Elements Testing. This exposure test measures urinary excretion of 20 toxic metals. It shows if the body struggles with excreting specific toxins. The health ramifications of toxicity are diverse, affecting energy levels, reproductive function, cancer risk, and neurological function.

9. Single Nucleotide Polymorphisms (SNPs or snips) Testing. These common non-fatal genetic variations consist of a single nucleotide substitution in the DNA sequence. Knowing a client's SNPs can help with predicting sensitivities to certain environmental factors (toxins, etc.) and pharmaceutical drugs, as well as risk of developing certain diseases. This knowledge influences preventive health protocols.

10. Essential and Metabolic Fatty Acids Analysis. This test assesses the balance between essential Omega-6 and Omega-3 fatty acids, as well as additional key fatty acids important in metabolism and cellular function. Fatty acid imbalances are often root causes in chronic pain states, depression, heart disease, and obesity.

11. Food Antibody Assessment and Intestinal Permeability Testing. Food sensitivity tests help identify those with true IgE-mediated "immediate" allergies as well as IgG-mediated "delayed" food sensitivities. Permeability testing is a non-invasive method to detect "leaky gut", determining whether an increased number of foreign compounds are crossing the gut lining and entering the bloodstream.

12. Oxidative Stress Analysis. This is a blood test evaluating the body's oxidative stress status and antioxidant reserve capacity. This test helps me gauge which hormetic therapies to offer, as well as when and how much to challenge or support a specific client. Essentially, it helps tell me how much stress the body can tolerate at present.

13. Oxygen Utilization and Exercise Capacity. Before disease states manifest, we can first detect changes in how our cells interact with oxygen. I evaluate HRV, VO_2 Max, maximum oxygen utilization, anaerobic threshold, and maximum energy produced from fat and glucose (Chapter 3). I also evaluate flexibility and core strength. Full evaluation of oxygen utilization and exercise capacity is often more informative than conventional blood work.

Acknowledgements

I have been fortunate to have many great teachers all along my career path. After completing medical school and residency, my first exposure to natural health methods was through The Weston A. Price Foundation, which taught me about the nutrient dense ancestral diets that have the capacity to ensure health and wellness for generations. I remember attending an overseas course on ozone therapies presented by Dr. Adriana Schwartz. That was the first time I heard the word *hormesis*, as Dr. Schwartz explained how ozone worked in the body. I so value her teaching and mentorship. I also want to recognize the important contributions from Dr. Irving Dardik, Dr. Frank Shallenberger, Phil Campbell, and Wim Hof.

I cannot thank Dr. Jeff Muneses enough for fulfilling so many pivotal roles—best friend, colleague, motivator, and guide as I pursued my alternative career. He is the one person who has seen it all and helped me incorporate and assimilate so much diverse knowledge. He has always encouraged me to push forward, even at times that felt impossible.

I want to recognize all my Vitality Health Challenge clients, especially the early ones who put their trust and confidence in me as I began to branch out. Those early successes motivated me to learn more.

This book would not be nearly as impactful without the editorial insight and recommendations provided by Anika Hanisch. She helped shape and transform this book into so much more then I could have ever imagined. Several others helped with revision requests along the way including: Chris Choin, Nicole Cohn, John Hosking, Ramona Mead, Ursula Morell, and Amy L. Pass. Their observations were invaluable for polishing the final manuscript. I want to acknowledge the dedicated work of Leslie Atkinson who kept track of all the deadlines and obligations innate to finishing a book. James Bennett did a superb job interpreting my health concept sketches and rendering them as easy to comprehend graphics.

Thanks to Stan, Harry, Jimmy, Mr. Moose, and Piggles for their support.

Lastly, to my family: Roberta, Alan, Magdalena, Jerry, and Zora. I appreciate all of your efforts in supporting me so well. You were always present, listening and making suggestions, as I devoted so much time and effort figuring out how best to put this all out there. Thank you!

Resources

Books

Adrenal Fatigue by James L. Wilson, ND, DC, PhD (Smarty Publications, 2001)

Alkalize or Die by Dr. Theodore A. Baroody (Holographic Health Press, 1991)

Black Mold by Richard F. Progovitz (The Forager Press, 2003)

The Body Ecology Diet by Donna Gates with Linda Schatz (B.E.D. Publications, 1996)

Bursting With Energy by Frank Shallenberger, MD, HMD (Basic Health Publications, 2007)

Change Your Genetic Destiny by Dr. Peter J. D'Adamo with Catherine Whitney (Broadway Books, 2007)

The China Study by T. Colin Campbell, PhD and Thomas M. Campbell II (Benbella Books, 2019)

The Cholesterol Myths by Uffe Ravnskov, MD, PhD (New Trends Publishing, Inc., 2000)

Cracking the Metabolic Code by James B. LaValle, R.Ph, CCN, ND, with Stacy Lundin Yale, RN, BSN (Basic Health Publications, 2004)

Dangerous Grains by James Brady, MD and Ron Hogan, MA (Avery, 2002)

Detoxify or Die by Sherry A. Rogers, MD (Sand Key Company, 2002)

Flood Your Body with Oxygen by Ed McCabe (Energy Publications, 2003)

From Fatigued to Fantastic by Jacob Teitelbaum, MD (Avery, 2007)

The Healing Power of Light by William Campbell Douglass II, MD (1995)

The Heart Revolution by Kilmer McCully, MD (Harper Collins, 1999)

The Hidden Story of Cancer by Brian Scott Perkins, BSEE and Amid Habib, MD, FAAP, FACE (Pinnacle Press, 2011)

Hormesis in Health and Disease by Suresh I.S. Rattan and Eric Le Bourg (CRC Press, 2014)

Hyperbaric Oxygenation for Cerebral Palsy and the Brain-Injured Child by Richard A. Neubauer, MD (Best Publishing Company, 2002)

Hyperbaric Oxygen Therapy by Richard A. Neubauer, MD and Morton Walker, DPM (Avery, 1998)

Life Without Bread by Christian B. Allan, PhD and Wolfgang Lutz, MD (Keats Publishing, 2000)

The Maker's Diet by Jordan S. Rubin, N.M.D., PhD (Destiny Image, 2013.)

Making Waves by Roger Lewis (Rodale, 2005)

The Miracle of Bio-Identical Hormones by Michael E. Platt, MD, (Clancy Lane Publishing, 2007)

More Natural "Cures" Revealed by Kevin Trudeau (Alliance Publishing Group, Inc., 2006)

Oxygen Healing Therapies by Nathaniel Altman (Healing Arts Press, 1995)

Oxygen Multistep Therapy by Manfred von Ardenne, M.D. (Publishers' Graphics, 1990)

Oxygen to the Rescue by Pavel I. Tutsis, MD (Basic Health Publications, 2003)

Oxygen-Ozone Therapy by Velio Bocci (Springer Netherlands, 2002)

Ozone: A New Medical Drug by Velio Bocci (Springer, 2004)

PEMF-The Fifth Element of Health by Bryant A. Meyers (Balboa Press, 2013)

PEO Solution by Brian Scott Perkins, and Robert Jay Rowen, MD (Pinnacle Press, 2015)

Principles and Applications of Ozone Therapy by Frank Shallenberger, MD, HMD, ABAAM (2011)

Ready, Set, Go! by Phil Campbell, MS, MA, ACSM-CPT, FACHE (Pristine Publishers Inc. USA, 2012)

The Second Brain by Michael D. Gershon, MD, (Harper Perennial, 1998)

The Sinatra Solution by Stephen T. Sinatra, MD, FACC, FACN, CNS (Basic Health Publications, 2005)

Sprint 8 Cardio Protocol by Phil Campbell, MS, MA, FACHE, ACSM-CPT (2016)

Stop Aging or Slow the Process by William Campbell Douglass II, MD (Rhino Publishing, S.A., 2003)

Stop the Clock by P.D. Mangan (Phalanx Press, 2015)

Superfoods by David Wolfe (North Atlantic Books, 2009)

Tired of Being Tired by Jesse Lynn Hanley, MD and Nancy Deville, GP (Putnam's Sons, 2001)

What Doesn't Kill Us by Scott Carney (Rodale, 2017)

Websites

The Andrew Weil Center for Integrative Medicine. https://integrativemedicine.arizona.edu/index.html

American Academy of Ozonotherapy. https://aaot.us/

Institute for Functional Medicine (IFM) physician locator tool. https://www.ifm.org/

Longevity Resources ozone generators. https://www.ozonegenerator.com/

MyZone fitness and HRV monitor. https://www.myzonemoves.com/

National Health Freedom Action (NHFA). www.nationalhealthfreedomaction.org

Phil Campbell's Sprint 8 cardio protocol. https://shop.matrixfitness.com/sprint-8/phil-campbell

Spanish Association of Medical Professionals in Ozone Therapy, *Madrid Declaration on Ozone Therapy*. https://aepromo.org/en/madrid-declaration-on-ozone-therapy/

Vitality Health Challenge Integrative Medicine Institute.
http://www.VitalityHealthChallenge.com/

The Weston A. Price Foundation for Wise Traditions in Food, Farming, and the Healing Arts. https://www.westonaprice.org/

References & Notes

Introduction

1.
Bartels, HA. "Historical Portraits in Dental Culture; Weston Price (1870-1948)." *New York Journal of Dentistry*. 1965 Mar; 35: 97-8.

2.
Smith J. *$29 Billion Reasons to Lie About Cholesterol: Making Profit by Turning Healthy People into Patients*. Kibworth Harcourt, United Kingdom: Matador. 2009.

3.
"The Lipid Research Clinics Coronary Primary Prevention Trial results. I. Reduction in incidence of coronary heart disease." *JAMA*. 1984 Jan 20; 251(3): 351-64.

4.
Ravnskov U. *The Cholesterol Myths, Exposing the fallacy that saturated fat and cholesterol cause heart disease.* Washington, DC: New Trends Publishing, 2000.

Chapter 1

1.
Makary MA, Daniel M. "Medical error—the third leading cause of death in the US." *The BMJ*. 2016 May 3; 353:i2139. doi: 10.1136/bmj.i2139.

2.
Donohoe MT. "Comparing generalist and specialty care: discrepancies, deficiencies, and excesses." *Archives of Internal Medicine*. 1998 Aug 10-24;158(15):1596-608.

3.
Grol R, Grimshaw J. "From best evidence to best practice: effective implementation of change in patients' care." *Lancet.* 2003 Oct 11;362(9391):1225-30.

4.
Smith T. "Not your grandfather's med school: Changes trending in med ed." *Accelerating Change in Medical Education (AMA).* 2017 Feb 7. Accessed December 26, 2018 at: https://www.ama-assn.org/education/accelerating-change-medical-education/not-your-grandfathers-med-school-changes-trending

5.
Peskin BS, Habib A. *The Hidden Story of Cancer.* Houston, Texas: Pinnacle Books, 2008.

6.
Strong, WM. "Is Cancer Mortality Increasing?" The Journal of Cancer Research July 1 1921 (6) (3) 251-256; DOI: 10.1158/jcr.1921.251.

7.
National Cancer Institute. *Cancer Statistics.* United States. Accessed January 9, 2019 at: https://www.cancer.gov/about-cancer/understanding/statistics

8.
Simon S. "Cancer Statistics Report." American Cancer Society. 2016 January 7. Retrieved 29 April 2019 at: https://www.cancer.org/latest-news/cancer-statistics-report-death-rate-down-23-percent-in-21-years.html

9.
Peskin BS, Habib A. *The Hidden Story of Cancer.* Houston: Pinnacle Books, 2008.

10.
CDC Report. *Long-term Trends in Diabetes.* CDC's Division of Diabetes Translation. United States. Accessed December 26, 2018 at:
https://www.cdc.gov/diabetes/statistics/slides/long_term_trends.pdf

11.
Merai R, Siegel C, Rakotz M, Basch P, Wright J, Wong B; DHSc., Thorpe P. CDC Grand Rounds: A Public Health Approach to Detect and Control Hypertension. *MMWR Morbidity and Mortality Weekly Report.* 2016 Nov 18;65(45):1261-1264

12.
Johns Hopkins Monograph: "Cardiovascular Disease Statistics." Accessed November 20, 2018. https://www.hopkinsmedicine.org/healthlibrary/conditions/cardiovascular_diseases/cardiovascular_disease_statistics_85,P00243.

13.
Hales CM, Carroll MD, Fryar CD, Ogden CL. Prevalence of obesity among adults and youth: United States, 2015–2016. NCHS data brief, no 288. Hyattsville, MD: National Center for Health Statistics. 2017.

14.
Dahlhamer J, Lucas J, Zelaya, C, et al. Prevalence of Chronic Pain and High-Impact Chronic Pain Among Adults – United States, 2016. *MMWR Morbidity and Mortality Weekly Report.* 2018;67:1001–1006.

15.
Wide-ranging online data for epidemiologic research (WONDER). Atlanta, GA: CDC. National Center for Health Statistics; 2017. Accessed November 20, 2018 at: https://wonder.cdc.gov/controller/datarequest/D76

16.
Taylor CA, Greenlund SF, McGuire LC, Lu H, Croft JB. Deaths from Alzheimer's Disease — United States, 1999–2014. *MMWR Morbidity and Mortality Weekly Report.* 2017;66:521–526.

17.
CDC Monograph: "Alzheimer's Disease: Promoting Health and Independence for an Aging Population." Updated June 2018. Created from data in Hebert LE, Weuve J, Scherr PA, Evans DA. "Alzheimer disease in the United States (2010–2050)" estimated using the 2010 Census. *Neurology.* 2013;80(19):1778–1783. Accessed December 26, 2018 at: https://www.cdc.gov/chronicdisease/resources/publications/aag/alzheimers.htm

18.
Blaxill MF. "What's going on? The question of time trends in autism." *Public Health Response.* 2004 Nov-Dec; 119(6):536-551.

19.
"CDC increases estimate of autism's prevalence by 15 percent, to 1 in 59 children." Analysis of CDC data by *Autism Speaks.* Analysis retrieved on April 29, 2019 at: https://www.autismspeaks.org/science-news/cdc-increases-estimate-autism's-prevalence-15-percent-1-59-children.
CDC data available at: https://www.cdc.gov/ncbddd/autism/data.html

20.
Global Burden of Disease Health Financing Collaborator Network. "Future and potential spending on health 2015–40: development assistance for health, and government, prepaid private, and out-of-pocket health spending in 184 countries." *The Lancet.* 2017 May 20; 389(10083): 2005–2030.

21.
WHO Report: "The World Health Report 2000 – Health systems: Improving performance." World Health Organization. June 2000; Accessed December 11, 2018: https://www.who.int/whr/2000/media_centre/press_release/en/

22.
Allman MF, Ortiz Arjona MA. "Health promotion or pharmacological treatment for chronic diseases?" Journal of Preventive Medicine and Hygiene. 2013 Mar; 54(1):11-13.

23.
Peskin BS, Habib A. *The Hidden Story of Cancer.* Houston: Pinnacle Books, 2008.

24.
Perdrizet GA. "Chronic Diseases as Barriers to Oxygen Delivery: A Unifying Hypothesis of Tissue Reoxygenation Therapy." *Advances in Experimental Medicine and Biology.* 2017;977:15-20.

25.
Williams ME. "Oxygen and Aging: Is oxygen our friend or our enemy?" *Psychology Today.* 2016 Sep 28. Accessed December 26, 2018 at: https://www.psychologytoday.com/us/blog/the-art-and-science-aging-well/201609/oxygen-and-aging

26 – 27.
Ibid.

28.
Cai D, Liu T. "Hypothalamic inflammation: a double-edged sword to nutritional diseases." Annals of the New York Academy of Sciences. 2011 Dec.; 1243:E1-39.

29.
Picard M, Wallace DC, Burelle Y. "The rise of mitochondria in medicine." Mitochondrion. 2016 Sep;30:105-16. doi: 10.1016/j.mito.2016.07.003. Epub 2016 Jul 14.

30 – 31.
Ibid.

32.
McCabe E. Flood Your Body With Oxygen: Therapy for our Polluted World. Miami Shores, Florida: Energy Publications, 2003. 6th edition.

33.
McCabe E. O_2xygen Therapies: A New Way of Approaching Disease. Morrisville, New York: Energy Publications, 1988.

34.
Warburg O. *The prime cause and prevention of cancer.* Revised lecture at the meeting of the Nobel-Laureates on June 30, 1966; Lindau, Lake Constance, Germany. English Edition by Dean Burk; National Cancer Institute, Bethesda, Maryland, USA.

35.
Peskin BS, Habib A. *The Hidden Story of Cancer.* Houston: Pinnacle Books, 2008.

36.
Ibid.

37.
Webster KA. "Hypoxia: Life on the Edge." Antioxidants & Redox Signaling. 2007 Sep;9(9):1303-7.

38.
Calabrese EJ, Mattson MP. "How does hormesis impact biology, toxicology, and medicine?" *NPJ Aging and Mechanisms of Disease.* 2017 Sep 15;3:13. doi: 10.1038/s41514-017-0013-z. eCollection 2017.

39.
Calabrese EJ, et. al. "What is hormesis and its relevance to healthy aging and longevity?" *Biogerontology.* 2015 Dec; 16(6):693-707.

40.
Panda S. "Circadian physiology of metabolism." *Science.* 2016 Nov 25;354(6315): 1008-1015.

41.
Ji LL, Kang C, Zhang Y. "Exercise-induced hormesis and skeletal muscle health." *Free Radical Biology & Medicine.* 2016 Sep:98:113-122.

42.
Shepherd JT, Rusch NJ, Vanhoutte PM. "Effect of cold on the blood vessel wall." *General Pharmacology*. 1983; 14(1):61-4.

43.
Lewin R. "Making Waves: Tuning biorhythms through cyclic exercise." *Holistic Primary Care*. 2006; 7:1. Accessed December 26, 2018 at: https://holisticprimarycare.net/topics/topics-a-g/cardiovascular-health/325-making-waves-tuning-biorhythms-through-cyclic-exercise.html

44.
Pomatto LCD, Davies KJA. "The role of declining adaptive homeostasis in ageing." *Journal of Physiology*. 2017 Dec 15;595(24):7275-7309. doi: 10.1113/JP275072. Epub 2017 Nov 21.

45. Calabrese EJ, Mattson MP. "How does hormesis impact biology, toxicology, and medicine?" *NPJ Aging and Mechanisms of Disease*. 2017 Sep 15;3:13. doi: 10.1038/s41514-017-0013-z.

46.
Calabrese EJ, et. al. "What is hormesis and its relevance to healthy aging and longevity?" *Biogerontology*. 2015 Dec; 16(6):693-707.

47.
Calabrese EJ, Iavicoli I, Calabrese V. "Hormesis: its impact on medicine and health." *Human & Experimental Toxicology*. 2013 Feb;32(2):120-52.

48.
Baldwin J, Grantham V. "Radiation Hormesis: Historical and current perspectives." *Journal of Nuclear Medicine Technology*. 2015 Dec;43(4):242-6.

49.
Poljsak B. "Strategies for Reducing or Preventing the Generation of Oxidative Stress." *Oxidative Medicine and Cellular Longevity*. 2011 Dec 10; doi: 10.1155/2011/194586.

50.
Zemva J, et. al. "Hormesis enables cells to handle accumulating toxic metabolites during increased energy flux." *Redox Biology*. 2017 Oct; 13: 674-686.

51.
Suresh ISR, et. al. "Heat Stress and Hormetin-Induced Hormesis in Human Cells: Effects on Aging, Wound Healing, Angiogenesis, and Differentiation." *Dose Response.* 2009; 7(1): 90-103.

52.
Wiegant FAC, et. al. "Hormesis and Cellular Quality Control: A Possible Explanation for the Molecular Mechanisms that Underlie the Benefits of Mild Stress." *Dose Response.* 2013; 11(3): 413-430.

53.
Martucci M, et. al. "Mediterranean diet and inflammaging within the hormesis paradigm." *Nutrition Reviews.* 2017 Jun; 75(6): 442-455.

54.
Vaiserman AM. "Hormesis, Adaptive Epigenetic Reorganizaton, and Implications for Human Health and Longevity." *Dose Response.* 2010; (8)1: 16-21.

Chapter 2

1.
MedlinePlus Monograph "Benefits of Exercise." U.S. National Library of Medicine, NIH. Last updated 2017 Aug 30. Accessed December 26, 2018 at: https://medlineplus.gov/benefitsofexercise.html

2.
Lavie CJ, et. al. "Exercise and the Cardiovascular System: Clinical Science and Cardiovascular Outcomes." *Circulation Research.* 2015 Jul 3;117(2):207-219

3.
Booth FW, Roberts CK, Laye MJ. "Lack of exercise is a major cause of chronic diseases." *Comprehensive Physiology.* 2012 Apr; 2(2):1143-1211.

4.
Gomez-Pinilla F, Hillman C. "The Influence of Exercise on Cognitive Abilities." *Comprehensive Physiology.* 2013 Jan; 3(1):403-428.

5.
Clarke SC, et. al. "Cognitive Interpretation Bias: The Effect of a Single Session Moderate Exercise Protocol on Anxiety and Depression." *Frontiers in Psychology.* 2018; 9: 1363. Published online 2018 Aug 8. doi: 10.3389/fpsyg.2018.01363

6.
Raichlen DA, Alexander GE. "Adaptive Capacity: An evolutionary-neuroscience model linking exercise, cognition, and brain health." *Trends in Neurosciences.* 2017 Jul; 40(7): 408-421.

7.
Archer T, Kostrzewa RM. "Physical exercise alleviates ADHD symptoms: regional deficits and development trajectory." *Neurotoxicity Research.* 2012 Feb;21(2):195-209.

8.
MedlinePlus Monograph "Benefits of Exercise." U.S. National Library of Medicine, NIH. Last updated 2017 Aug 30. Accessed December 26, 2018 at: https://medlineplus.gov/benefitsofexercise.html

9.
Lewin R. *Making Waves: Irving Dardik and His Superwave Principle.* New York: Rodale Books (Penguin Random House), 2005.

10.
Havranek RD. "Exercise and Digestive Health." Gastroenterology monograph. Last updated 2017 Sep 11. Accessed December 26, 2018 at: https://russellhavranekmd.com/exercise/

11.
Harding AT, Beck BR. "Exercise, Osteoporosis, and Bone Geometry." *Sports (Basel)* 2017 Jun; 5(2):29. Published online 2017 May 12. doi: 10.3390/sports5020029

12.
Rogers SA. *Detoxify or Die.* Solvay, NY: Prestige Publishing. 2002.

13.
Blackburn EH, Epel ES, Lin J. "Human telomere biology: A contributory and interactive factor in aging, disease risks, and protection." *Science.* 2015 Dec 4;350(6265):1193-8. doi: 10.1126/science.aab3389.

14.
Aubert G, Lansdorp PM. "Telomeres and aging." *Physiological Reviews.* 2008. Apr;88(2):557-79.

15.
Campisi J, Robert L. "Cell senescence: role in aging and age-related diseases." *Interdisciplinary Topics in Gerontology.* 2014;39:45-61.

16.
Diman A, et. al. "Nuclear respiratory factor 1 and endurance exercise promote human telomere transcription." *Science Advances.* 27 Jul 2016:2(7) e1600031. DOI: 10.1126/sciadv.1600031.

17.
Ludlow AT, Roth SM. "Physical Activity and Telomere Biology: Exploring the Link with Aging-Related Disease Prevention." *Journal of Aging Research.* 2011: 790378. Published online 2011 Feb 21.

18.
Arikawa AY, et. al. "Sixteen weeks of exercise reduces C-reactive protein levels in young women." *Medicine and Science in Sports and Exercise.* 2011 Jun;43(6):1002-9.

19.
O'Keefe JH, Lavie CJ, Guazzi M. "Part 1: potential dangers of extreme endurance exercise: how much is too much? Part 2: screening of school-age athletes." *Progress in Cardiovascular Diseases.* 2015 Jan-Feb;57(4):396-405.

20.
Medeiros HB, de Araujo DS, de Araugo CG. "Age-related mobility loss is joint-specific: An analysis from 6,000 Flexitest results." *Age (Dordrecht, Netherlands).* 2013 Dec;35(6):2399-407.

21.
Staehler RA. "Epidural Steroid Injections: Risks and Side Effects." *Spine Health (Veritas Health).* 2007 July 17. Accessed December 26, 2018 at: https://www.spine-health.com/treatment/injections/epidural-steroid-injections-risks-and-side-effects

22.
Coates LC, et. al. "Psoriasis, psoriatic arthritis, and rheumatoid arthritis: Is all inflammation the same?" *Seminars in Arthritis and Rheumatism.* 2016 Dec;46(3):291-304.

23.
Gur A, Okatayoglu P. "Status of immune mediators in fibromyalgia." *Current Pain and Headache Reports.* 2008 Jun;12(3):175-81.

24.
Nimmo MA. "The effect of physical activity on mediators of inflammation." *Diabetes, Obesity & Metabolism.* 2013 Sep;15 Suppl 3:51-60.

25.
Ambrose KR, Golightly YM. "Physical exercise as non-pharmacological treatment of chronic pain: Why and when." *Best Practice & Research: Clinical Rheumatology.* 2015 Feb;29(1):120-30.

26.
Knutson GA, Owens EF. "Active and passive characteristics of muscle tone and their relationship to models of subluxation/joint dysfunction. Part II." *The Journal of the Canadian Chiropractic Association.* 2003 Dec; 47(4): 269-283.

27.
Lewin R. *Making Waves: Irving Dardik and His Superwave Principle.* New York: Rodale Books (Penguin Random House), 2005.

28.
Gross J. "James F. Fixx Dies Jogging; Author on Running was 52." *New York Times.* 22 July 1984. NYT Archive, page 001024.

29.
Lewin R. *Making Waves: Irving Dardik and His Superwave Principle.* New York: Rodale Books (Penguin Random House), 2005.

30.
Lewin R. "Making Waves: Tuning Biorhythms Through Cyclic Exercise." *Holistic Primary Care.* Spring 2006; 7(1). Published online. Accessed December 26, 2018 at https://holisticprimarycare.net/topics/topics-a-g/cardiovascular-health/325-making-waves-tuning-biorhythms-through-cyclic-exercise.html

31.
Lewin R. *Making Waves: Irving Dardik and His Superwave Principle.* New York: Rodale Books (Penguin Random House), 2005.

32.
Calabrese EJ. "Hormesis: a fundamental concept in biology." *Microbial Cell (Graz, Austria).* 2014 Apr 23;1(5):145-149.

33.
Zimmermann A, et. al. "When less is more: hormesis against stress and disease." *Microbial Cell (Graz, Austria).* 2014 May 5;1(5):150-153.

34.
Gamble KL, et. al. "Circadian clock control of endocrine factors." *Nature Reviews: Endocrinology.* 2014 Aug;10(8):466-75.

35.
Portaluppi F, et al. "Circadian rhythms and cardiovascular health." *Sleep Medicine Reviews.* 2012;16:151–166.

36.
Kawano Y. "Diurnal blood pressure variation and related behavioral factors." *Hypertension Research.* 2011 Mar;34(3):281-5.

37.
"Diurnal Cortisol Curves." ZRT Lab monograph. Educational material published by CLIA-certified diagnostic laboratory. Accessed December 26, 2018 at https://www.zrtlab.com/landing-pages/diurnal-cortisol-curves/

38.
Fisk AS, et. al. "Light and Cognition: Roles for Circadian Rhythms, Sleep, and Arousal." *Frontiers in Neurology.* 2018; 9: 56.

39.
Walker HK, Hall WD, Hurst JW; editors. "Chapter 218: Temperature." *Clinical Methods: The History, Physical, and Laboratory Examinations.* Boston: Butterworths (Elsevier). 1990.

40.
McGinnis GR, Young ME. "Circadian regulation of metabolic homeostasis: causes and consequences." *Nature and Science of Sleep.* 2016; 8: 163–180.

41.
Oster H, et. al. "The Functional and Clinical Significance of the 24-Hour Rhythm of Circulating Glucocorticoids." *Endocrine Reviews.* 2017 Feb 1; 38(1): 3–45.

42.
Kolata G. "For Athletes, the Time of an Event Can Affect Performance." *The New York Times.* ePub 2015 January 29. Print version 2015 January 30; A12. Accessed December 26, 2018 at https://well.blogs.nytimes.com/2015/01/29/for-athletes-the-time-of-an-event-can-affect-performance/

43.
Lopez-Messa JB, et. al. "[Circadian rhythm and time variations in out-hospital sudden cardiac arrest]." *Medicina Intensiva.* 2012 Aug-Sep;36(6):402-9.

44.
Elliott WJ. "Circadian variation in the timing of stroke onset: a meta-analysis." *Stroke.* 1998 May;29(5):992-6.

45.
Fox AW, Davis RL. "Migraine chronobiology." *Headache.* 1998 Jun; 38(6):436-41.

46.
Ando N, et. al. "Allergen-specific basophil reactivity exhibits daily variations in seasonal allergic rhinitis." *Allergy.* 2015 Mar; 70(3):319-22.

47.
Cutolo M. "Chronobiology and the treatment of rheumatoid arthritis." *Current Opinion in Rheumatology.* 2012 May;24(3):312-8.

48.
Paganelli R, et. al. "Biological clocks: their relevance to immune-allergic diseases." *Clinical and Molecular Allergy.* 2018; 16: 1.

49.
Touitou Y, et. al. "Alterations in circadian rhythmicity in calcium oxalate renal stone formers." *International Journal of Chronobiology.* 1983; 8(3):175-92.

50.
Rigas B, et. al. "The Circadian Rhythm of Biliary Colic." *Journal of Clinical Gastroenterology.* 1990 Aug;12(4):409-14.

51.
Knutsson A. "Health disorders of shift workers." *Occupational Medicine (London).* 2003 Mar; 53(2):103-8.

52.
Erren TC, Reiter RJ. "Defining chronodisruption." *Journal of Pineal Research.* 2009 Apr; 46(3):245-7.

53.
Schwartz T. "Making Waves: Can Dr. Irv Dardik's Radical Exercise Therapy Really Work Miracles?" *New York Magazine.* 1991 March 18; 24(11):30-39.
54.
Lewin R. "Making Waves: Tuning Biorhythms Through Cyclic Exercise." *Holistic Primary Care.* Spring 2006; 7(1). Published online. Accessed December 26, 2018 at https://holisticprimarycare.net/topics/topics-a-g/cardiovascular-health/325-making-waves-tuning-biorhythms-through-cyclic-exercise.html

55.
Shaffer F, McCraty R, Zerr CL. "A healthy heart is not a metronome: an integrative review of the heart's anatomy and heart rate variability." *Frontiers in Psychology.* 2014 Sep 30;5:1040.

56.
Ibid.

57.
Tsulji H, et. al. "Reduced heart rate variability and mortality risk in an elderly cohort: The Framingham Heart Study." *Circulation.* 1994 Aug;90(2):878-83.

58.
McCraty R, Shaffer F. "Heart Rate Variability: New Perspectives on Physiological Mechanisms, Assessment of Self-regulatory Capacity, and Health Risk." Global Advances in Health and Medicine. 2015 Jan;4(1):46-61.

59.
Shaffer F, McCraty R, Zerr CL. "A healthy heart is not a metronome: an integrative review of the heart's anatomy and heart rate variability." *Frontiers in Psychology.* 2014 Sep 30;5:1040.

60.
Earnest CP, et. al. "Heart Rate Variability Characteristics in Sedentary Postmenopausal Women Following Six Months of Exercise Training: The DREW Study." *PLoS One.* 2008; 3(6): e2288. Published online 2008 Jun 4. doi: 10.1371/journal.pone.0002288

61.
Goldsmith, Rochelle L., et al. "Implementation of a Novel Cyclic Exercise Protocol: Short-Term Impact on Healthy Women." *American Journal of Medicine & Sports.* 2002; 4: 1350141m151.

62.
Wideman L, et. al. "Growth hormone release during acute and chronic aerobic and resistance exercise: recent findings." *Sports Medicine (Auckland, NZ).* 2002;32(15):987-1004.

63.
Rudman D, et. al. "Effects of human growth hormone on body composition in elderly men." *Hormone Research.* 1991;36 Suppl 1:73-81.

64.
Decaroli MC, Rochira V. "Aging and sex hormones in males." *Virulence.* 2017; 8(5): 545–570.

65.
Chertman LS, Merriam GR, Kargi AY. "Growth Hormone in Aging." *Endotext.* De Groot LJ, et. al. (Eds.). 2000. South Dartmouth, MA: MDText.com, Inc. Last updated May 4, 2015. Retrieved from https://www.ncbi.nlm.nih.gov/books/NBK279163/

66.
Colgan M. *Sports Nutrition Guide: Minerals, Vitamins & Antioxidants for Athletes.* 2002. Apple Tree Publishing.

67.
WADA Monograph. "Human Growth Hormone (HGH) Testing." World Anti-doping Agency FAQ on hGH use, effects, and ethics. Retrieved December 26, 2018 at: https://www.wada-ama.org/en/questions-answers/human-growth-hormone-hgh-testing

68.
Campbell P. *Ready, Set, Go! Synergy Fitness.* Nashville: Pristine Publishers Inc. 2nd edition, 2002.

69.
Sesso HD, Paffenbarger RS Jr, Lee IM. "Physical activity and coronary heart disease in men: The Harvard Alumni Health Study." *Circulation.* 2000 Aug 29;102(9):975-80.

70.
Stokes KA, Nevill ME, Hall GM, Lakomy HK. "The time course of the human growth hormone response to a 6s and a 30s cycle ergometer sprint." *Journal of Sports Sciences.* 2002 Jun;20(6):487-94.

71.
Campbell P. *Ready, Set, Go! Synergy Fitness.* Nashville: Pristine Publishers Inc. 2nd edition, 2002.

72.
Ibid.

Chapter 3

1.
McCabe E. *Flood Your Body with Oxygen.* Miami Shores, Florida: Energy Publications: 2003.

2.
Yutsis P. *Oxygen to the Rescue.* Nashville, Tennessee: Basic Health Publications (Turner Publishing), 2003.

3.
Biddlestone J, Bandarra D, Rocha S. "The role of hypoxia in inflammatory disease (Review)." *International Journal of Molecular Medicine.* 2015 Apr; 35(4): 859-869.

4.
Airley RE, et. al. "Hypoxia and disease: opportunities for novel diagnostic and therapeutic prodrug strategies." *The Pharmaceutical Journal.* 2000 Apr 29; 264(7094):666-673.

5.
Kolinko Y, et al "Microcirculation of the brain: morphological assessment in degenerative diseases and restoration processes." *Reviews in the Neurosciences.* 2015; 26(1): 75-93.

6.
Higgins JA, et. al. "Atmospheric composition 1 million years ago from blue ice in the Allan Hills, Antarctica." *PNAS – Proceedings of the National Academy of Sciences (USA).* 2015 June 2. 112(2).6887-6891.

7.
McCabe E. *Flood Your Body with Oxygen.* Miami Shores, Florida: Energy Publications: 2003.

8.
Shallenberger F. *Bursting with Energy: The Breakthrough Method to Renew Youthful Energy and Restore Health.* Laguna Beach, California: Basic Health Publications, Inc., 2007.

9.
Rich PR. "The molecular machinery of Keilin's respiratory chain." *Biochemical Society Transactions.* 2003 Dec: 31(Pt 6): 1095–1105.

10.
Klein DW, Lansing M, Harley J. *Microbiology (6th ed.)* New York: McGraw-Hill, 2006.

11.
Yee AH, Rabinstein AA. "Neurologic presentations of acid-base imbalance, electrolyte abnormalities, and endocrine emergencies." *Neurologic Clinics.* 2010 Feb;28(1):1-16.

12.
Shallenberger F. *Bursting with Energy: The Breakthrough Method to Renew Youthful Energy and Restore Health.* Laguna Beach, California: Basic Health Publications, Inc., 2007.

13.
Schwalfenberg GK. "The Alkaline Diet: Is There Evidence That an Alkaline pH Diet Benefits Health?" *Journal of Environmental Public Health.* 2012; 727630. Published online 2011 Oct 12. doi: 10.1155/2012/727630

14.
McCabe E. *Flood Your Body with Oxygen.* Miami Shores, Florida: Energy Publications: 2003.

15.
Perdrizet GA. "Chronic Diseases as Barriers to Oxygen Delivery: A Unifying Hypothesis of Tissue Reoxygenation Therapy." *Advances in Experimental Medicine and Biology.* 2017;977:15-20.

16.
Taabazuing CY, Hangasky JA, Knapp MJ. "Oxygen Sensing Strategies in Mammals and Bacteria." *Journal of Inorganic Biochemistry.* 2014 Apr; 133:63-72.

17.
McCabe E. *Flood Your Body with Oxygen.* Miami Shores, Florida: Energy Publications: 2003.

18.
Warburg O. *The prime cause and prevention of cancer.* Revised lecture at the meeting of the Nobel-Laureates on June 30, 1966; Lindau, Lake Constance, Germany. English Edition by Dean Burk; National Cancer Institute, Bethesda, Maryland, USA.

19.
Peskin B. *The Hidden Story of Cancer.* Houston, Texas: Pinnacle Press, 2011.

20.
McCabe E. *Flood Your Body with Oxygen.* Miami Shores, Florida: Energy Publications: 2003.

21.
Peskin B. *The Hidden Story of Cancer.* Houston, Texas: Pinnacle Press, 2011.

22.
McCabe E. *Flood Your Body with Oxygen.* Miami Shores, Florida: Energy Publications: 2003.

23.
Klein DW, Lansing M, Harley J. *Microbiology (6th ed.)* New York: McGraw-Hill, 2006.

24.
McCabe E. *Flood Your Body with Oxygen.* Miami Shores, Florida: Energy Publications: 2003.

25.
Eltzschig HK, Carmeliet P. "Hypoxia and Inflammation." *New England Journal of Medicine.* 2011 Feb 17; 364(7):656-665.

26.
Pham-Huy LA, He H, Pham-Huy C. "Free Radicals, Antioxidants in Disease and Health." *International Journal of Biomedical Science.* 2008 Jun; 4(2): 89-96.

27.
McCabe E. *Flood Your Body with Oxygen.* Miami Shores, Florida: Energy Publications: 2003.

28.
Treacher DF, Leach RM. "Oxygen Transport-1. Basic Principles." *BMJ.* 1998 Nov 7; 317(7168): 1302–1306.

29.
Cooper GM. *The Cell: A Molecular Approach.* 2nd *edition.* Sunderland, Massachusetts: Sinauer Associates, 2000.

30.
Shallenberger F. *Bursting with Energy: The Breakthrough Method to Renew Youthful Energy and Restore Health.* Laguna Beach, California: Basic Health Publications, Inc., 2007.

31.
Kahle AC, Cooper JS. *Hyperbaric, Physiological and Pharmacological Effects Gases.* January 2018, StatPearls Publishing LLC. Creative Commons Attribution 4.0 International License. Bookshelf ID: NBK470481. PMID: 29262156

32.
Maltepe E, Saugstad, OD. "Oxygen in Health and Disease: Regulation of Oxygen Homeostasis—Clinical Implications." *Pediatric Research.* 2009 March 01; 65: 261-268

33.
Harch PG, McCullough V. *The Oxygen Revolution: Hyperbaric Oxygen Therapy.* Hobart, New York: Hatherleigh Press (Penguin, Random House), 2010.

34.
Kahle AC, Cooper JS. *Hyperbaric, Physiological and Pharmacological Effects Gases.* January 2018, StatPearls Publishing LLC. Creative Commons Attribution 4.0 International License. Bookshelf ID: NBK470481. PMID: 29262156

35.
Francis A, Baynosa RC. "Hyperbaric Oxygen Therapy for the Compromised Graft or Flap." *Advances in Wound Care (New Rochelle).* 2017 Jan 1;6(1):23-32.

36
Tal S, et.al. "Hyperbaric Oxygen Therapy Can Induce Angiogenesis and Regeneration of Nerve Fibers in Traumatic Brain Injury Patients." *Frontiers in Human Neuroscience.* 2017;11:508. doi: 10.3389/fnhum.2017.00508.

37.
Efrati S, et. al. "Hyperbaric oxygen induces late neuroplasticity in post stroke patients—randomized, prospective trial." *PLoS One.* 2013; 8(1): e53716. Published online 2013 Jan 15.

38.

Wang F, Wang Y, Sun T, Yu HL. "Hyperbaric oxygen therapy for treatment of traumatic brain injury: a meta-analysis." *Neurological Sciences.* 2016 May;37(5):693-701.

39.
Neubauer R, Walker M. *Hyperbaric Oxygen Therapy: Using HBOT to increase circulation, repair damaged tissue, fight infection, save limbs, and relieve pain.* Garden City Park, New York: Avery Publishing Group, Inc., 2001.

40.
Barata P, et. al. "Hyperbaric Oxygen Effects on Sports Injuries." *Therapeutic Advances in Musculoskeletal Diseases.* 2011 Apr; 3(2): 111–121.

41.
Ishii Y, et. al. "Hyperbaric oxygen as an adjuvant for athletes." *Sports Medicine.* 2005;35(9):739-46.

42.
Pittman RN. *Regulation of Tissue Oxygenation.* "Chapter 4: Oxygen Transport." San Rafael, California: Morgan & Claypool Life Sciences, 2011.

43.
Kahle AC, Cooper JS. *Hyperbaric, Physiological and Pharmacological Effects Gases.* January 2018, StatPearls Publishing LLC. Creative Commons Attribution 4.0 International License. Bookshelf ID: NBK470481. PMID: 29262156

44.
Asadamongkol B, Zhang JH. "The Development of Hyperbaric Oxygen Therapy for Skin Rejuvenation and Treatment of Photoaging." *Medical Gas Research.* 2014; 4: 7

45.
Singh S, Gambert SR. "Hyperbaric Oxygen Therapy: A brief history and review of its benefits and indications for the older adult patient." *Annals of Long-Term Care: Clinical Care and Aging.* 2014; 22(7/8):37-42.

46.
Morgan Choffin, "The Cunningham Sanitarium." *Cleveland Historical.* Accessed January 8, 2019 at: https://clevelandhistorical.org/items/show/378.

47.
Mayo Clinic Staff. *Hyperbaric oxygen therapy. Mayo Clinic Tests & Procedures.* Online patient information. Accessed January 5, 2019 at: https://www.mayoclinic.org/tests-procedures/hyperbaric-oxygen-therapy/about/pac-20394380

48.
Weaver LK, ed. *Hyperbaric Oxygen Therapy Indications 13th edition.* The Hyperbaric Oxygen Therapy Committee Report. North Palm Beach, Florida: Best Publishing Company, 2014.

49.
Harch PG, McCullough V. *The Oxygen Revolution: Hyperbaric Oxygen Therapy.* Hobart, New York: Hatherleigh Press (Penguin, Random House), 2010.

50.
Treacher DF, Leach RM. "Oxygen Transport-1. Basic Principles." *BMJ.* 1998 Nov 7; 317(7168): 1302–1306.

51.
Banham ND. "Oxygen Toxicity Seizures: 20 years' Experience From a Single Hyperbaric Unit." *Diving and Hyperbaric Medicine.* 2011 Dec; 41(4): 202-10.

52.
Chawla A, Lavania AK. "Oxygen Toxicity." *Medical Journal Armed Forces India.* 2001 Apr; 57(2):131-133.

53.
McCabe E. *Flood Your Body with Oxygen.* Miami Shores, Florida: Energy Publications: 2003.

54.
Mao L, Franke J. "Hormesis in Aging and Neurodegeneration—A Prodigy Awaiting Dissection." *International Journal of Molecular Sciences.* 2013 Jul; 14(7): 13109–13128.

Chapter 4

1.
Badenhausen K. "Full List: The World's Highest-Paid Athletes 2017." Forbes. ePub Jun 15, 2017. Accessed January 21, 2019 at: https://www.forbes.com/sites/kurtbadenhausen/2017/06/15/full-list-the-worlds-highest-paid-athletes-2017/#3bdca6ed583b

2.

Matallanas JG. "Ozone to recover the best, Christiano Renaldo." (Article in Spanish.) *DefensaCentral.* Accessed January 21, 2019 at: https://www.defensacentral.com/real_madrid/121634

3.

Gleason KL. "Ozone Basics." *NOAA (National Oceanic and Atmospheric Administration). Last updated 2008 March 20. Accessed January 15, 2019 at:* http://www.ozonelayer.noaa.gov/science/basics.htm

4.

Zhang X, et. al. "Ambient volatile organic compounds pollution in China." *Journal of Environmental Sciences (China).* 2017 May;55:69-75.

5.

Shallenberger F. Principles and Applications of Ozone Therapy: A practical guideline for physicians. 1st edition. Carson City, NV: Author; 2011.

6.

Bocci V, et al. "Studies on the biological effects of ozone. 7. Generation of reactive oxygen species (ROS) after exposure of human blood to ozone." *Journal of Biological Regulators & Homeostatic Agents.* 1998;12:67–75.

7.

Klein DW, Lansing M, Harley J. *Microbiology (6th ed.) New York: McGraw-Hill, 2006.*

8.

Manoto SL, Maepa MJ, Motaung SK. "Medical ozone therapy as a potential treatment modality for regeneration of damaged articular cartilage in osteoarthritis." *Saudi Journal of Biological Sciences.* 2018 May;25(4):672-679.

9.

Dyas A, Boughton BJ, Das BC. "Ozone killing action against bacterial and fungal species; microbiological testing of a domestic ozone generator." *Journal of Clinical Pathology.* 1983 Oct; 36(10): 1102–1104.

10.

Shallenberger F. Principles and Applications of Ozone Therapy: A practical guideline for physicians. 1st edition. Carson City, NV: Author; 2011.

11.

Sagai M, Bocci V. "Mechanisms of Action Involved in Ozone Therapy: Is healing induced via a mild oxidative stress?" *Medical Gas Research.* 2011;1:29. Published online 2011 Dec 20. doi: 10.1186/2045-9912-1-29.

12 – 14.
Ibid.
15.
Bocci V, Luzzi E, Corradeschi F, Silvestri S. "Studies on the biological effects of ozone: 6. Production of transforming growth factor 1 by human blood after ozone treatment." *Journal of Biological Regulators and Homeostatic Agents.* 1994 Oct-Dec;8(4):108-12.

16.
Costanzo M, et. al. "Low Ozone Concentrations Stimulate Cytoskeletal Organization, Mitochondrial Activity and Nuclear Transcription." *European Journal of Histochemistry.* 2015 Apr 13; 59(2): 2515.

17.
Bocci V, Luzzi E, Corradeschi F, Silvestri S. "Studies on the biological effects of ozone: 6. Production of transforming growth factor 1 by human blood after ozone treatment." *Journal of Biological Regulators and Homeostatic Agents.* 1994 Oct-Dec;8(4):108-12.

18.
Bocci VA, Zanardi I, Travagli V. "Ozone acting on human blood yields a hormetic does-response relationship." *Journal of Translational Medicine.* 2011; 9:66. Published online 2011 May 17. doi: 10.1186/1479-5876-9-66

19.
Ibid.

20.
Bocci V, Luzzi E, Corradeschi F, Silvestri S. "Studies on the biological effects of ozone: 6. Production of transforming growth factor 1 by human blood after ozone treatment." *Journal of Biological Regulators and Homeostatic Agents.* 1994 Oct-Dec;8(4):108-12.

21.
Shallenberger F. "Prolozone: Regenerating Joints and Eliminating Pain." *Journal of Prolotherapy.* 2011;3(2):630-638.

22.
Crinnion WJ. "Sauna as a valuable clinical tool for cardiovascular, autoimmune, toxicant-induced and other chronic health problems." *Alternative Medicine Review.* 2011 Sep;16(3):215-25.

23.
Shallenberger F. Principles and Applications of Ozone Therapy: A practical guideline for physicians. 1st edition. Carson City, NV: Author; 2011.
24.
Izadi M, et. al. "Health-related quality of life in patients with chronic wounds before and after treatment with medical ozone." *Medicine (Baltimore).* 2018 Nov;97(48):e12505.

25.
Bocci V, Luzzi E, Corradeschi F, Silvestri S. "Studies on the biological effects of ozone: 6. Production of transforming growth factor 1 by human blood after ozone treatment." *Journal of Biological Regulators and Homeostatic Agents.* 1994 Oct-Dec;8(4):108-12.

26.
Bocci VA, Zanardi I, Travagli V. "Ozone acting on human blood yields a hormetic does-response relationship." *Journal of Translational Medicine.* 2011; 9:66. Published online 2011 May 17. doi: 10.1186/1479-5876-9-66.

27.
Douglas WC. *Into the Light: The exciting story of the life-saving breakthrough therapy of the age.* Muskogee, OK: Artisan Publishers. 2003.

28.
Zembower TR. "Epidemiology of infections in cancer patients." *Cancer Treatment and Research.* 2014;161:43-89.

29.
"Infections in People with Cancer." *American Cancer Society.* Accessed January 23, 2019 at: https://www.cancer.org/treatment/treatments-and-side-effects/physical-side-effects/infections.html

30.
"Cancer, Infection and Sepsis Fact Sheet." Center for Disease Control and Prevention (CDC). CS257671B. Accessed January 23, 2019 at: https://www.cdc.gov/sepsis/pdfs/cancer-infection-and-sepsis-fact-sheet.pdf

31.
Douglas WC. *Into the Light: The exciting story of the life-saving breakthrough therapy of the age.* Muskogee, OK: Artisan Publishers. 2003.

32.

Qinghui M, Kirby J, Reilly CM, Luo XM. "Leaky Gut as a Danger Signal for Autoimmune Diseases." *Frontiers in Immunology*. 2017; 8:598. Published online 2017 May 23. doi: 10.3389/fimmu.2017.00598

33.
Srivastava S, Singh D, Patel S, Singh MR. "Role of enzymatic free radical scavengers in management of oxidative stress in autoimmune disorders." *International Journal of Biological Macromolecules*. 2017 Aug;101:502-517.

34.
Ibid.

35.
Scannapieco FA, Cantos A. "Oral inflammation and infection, and chronic medical diseases: implications for the elderly." *Periodontology 2000*. 2016 Oct;72(1):153-75.

36.
Lynch E. *Ozone: The Revolution in Dentistry*. Copenhagen, Quintessence books; 2004

37.
Zembower TR. "Epidemiology of infections in cancer patients." *Cancer Treatment and Research*. 2014;161:43-89.

38.
"Infections in People with Cancer." *American Cancer Society*. Accessed January 23, 2019 at: https://www.cancer.org/treatment/treatments-and-side-effects/physical-side-effects/infections.html

39.
"Cancer, Infection and Sepsis Fact Sheet." Center for Disease Control and Prevention (CDC). CS257671B. Accessed January 23, 2019 at: https://www.cdc.gov/sepsis/pdfs/cancer-infection-and-sepsis-fact-sheet.pdf

40.
Elvis AM, Ekta JS. "Ozone Therapy: A clinical review." *Journal of Natural Science, Biology, and Medicine*. 2011 Jan-Jun; 2(1):66-70.

41 – 42.
Ibid.

43.

McCabe E. *Flood Your Body with Oxygen.* Miami Shores, Florida: Energy Publications: 2003.

44.
Shallenberger F. Principles and Applications of Ozone Therapy: A practical guideline for physicians. 1st edition. Carson City, NV: Author; 2011.

45.
Based on a PubMed search of the term "medical ozone" conducted January 18, 2019.

46.
Elvis AM, Ekta JS. "Ozone Therapy: A clinical review." *Journal of Natural Science, Biology, and Medicine.* 2011 Jan-Jun; 2(1):66-70.

47.
Horowitz R. *How Can I Get Better? An Action Plan for Treating Resistant Lyme and Chronic Disease.* New York: St. Martin's Griffin. 2017.

48.
As noted in the *Prescriber's Digital Reference* database. Accessed January 23, 2019 at: https://www.pdr.net/drug-summary/lipitor?druglabelid=2338

49.
As noted in the *Prescriber's Digital Reference* database. Accessed January 23, 2019 at:
https://www.pdr.net/drug-summary/Premarin-Tablets-conjugated-estrogens-622

50.
ISCO3 Madrid Declaration on Ozone Therapy. International Scientific Committee of Ozone Therapy. 2010. Accessed January 15, 2019 at: https://www.drsozone.com/wp-content/uploads/2014/02/Madrid-Declaration-updated-July-30.pdf

51.
Ibid.

52.
McCabe E. *Flood Your Body with Oxygen.* Miami Shores, Florida: Energy Publications: 2003.

53.

Rice RG, Graham DM. "U.S. FDA Regulatory Approval of Ozone as an Antimicrobial Agent - What Is Allowed and What Needs to Be Understood." White paper distributed by RICE International Consulting Enterprises. Ashton, MD. Accessed January 23, 2019 at: http://www.technozone.in/img/pdf/FDA-e.pdf

Chapter 5

1.
Hart BL. "Biological basis of the behavior of sick animals." *Neuroscience & Biobehavioral Reviews.* 1988 Summer;12(2):123-37.

2.
Longo VD, Panda S. "Fasting, circadian rhythms, and time restricted feeding in healthy lifespan." *Cell Metabolism.* 2016 Jun 14; 23(6):1048-1059.

3.
Peskin BS, Rowen RJ. "Chapter 5: How carbohydrates keep you fat and PEO's keep you skinny." *PEO Solution: Conquering Cancer, Diabetes and Heart Disease with Parent Essential Oils.* Houston, Texas: Pinnacle Press. 2015.

4.
Izumida Y, et. al. "Glycogen shortage during fasting triggers liver-brain-adipose neurocircuitry to facilitate fat utilization." *Nature Communications.* 2013 Aug 13; 4: 2316. Published online 2013 Aug 13. doi: 10.1038/ncomms3316 .

5.
de Cabo R, et. al. "The Search for anti-aging interventions: From elixirs to fasting regimens." *Cell.* 2014 Jun 19; 157(7):1515-1526.

6.
Puchalska P, Crawford PA. "Multi-dimensional roles of ketone bodies in fuel metabolism, signaling, and therapeutics." *Cell Metabolism.* 2017 Feb 7; 25(2): 262-284.

7.
Hale AN, et. al. "Autophagy: Regulation and role in development." *Autophagy.* 2013 Jul 1; 9(7): 951-972.

8.

Raefsky SM, Mattson MP. "Adaptive Responses of Neuronal Mitochondria to Bioenergetic Challenges: Roles in Neuroplasticity and Disease Resistance." *Free Radical Biology & Medicine.* 2017 Jan; 102:203-216.

9.
Yamada Y, et. al. "Long-term calorie restriction decreases metabolic cost of movement and prevents decrease of physical activity during aging in rhesus monkeys." *Experimental Gerontology.* 2013 Nov;48(11):1226-35.

10.
Fontana L, Partridge L, Longo VD. "Extending healthy life span—from yeast to humans." *Science.* 2010 Apr 16;328(5976):321-6.

11.
Suzuki M, Wilcox BJ, Wilcox CD. "Implications from and for food cultures for cardiovascular disease: longevity." *Asia Pacific Journal of Clinical Nutrition.* 2001; 10(2):165-71.

12.
Most J, Tosti V, Redman LM, Fontana L. "Calorie restriction in humans: an update." *Ageing Research Reviews.* 2017 Oct; 39:36-45.

13.
Das SK, et. al. "Body-composition changes in the Comprehensive Assessment of Long-term Effects of Reducing Intake of Energy (CALERIE)-2 study: a 2-y randomized controlled trial of calorie restriction in nonobese humans." *American Journal of Clinical Nutrition.* 2017 Apr; 105(4): 913–927.

14.
Most J, Tosti V, Redman LM, Fontana L. "Calorie restriction in humans: an update." *Ageing Research Reviews.* 2017 Oct; 39:36-45.

15.
Ingram DK, de Cabo R. "Calorie Restriction in Rodents: Caveats to Consider." *Ageing Research Reviews.* 2017 Oct; 39: 15-28.

16.
Longo VD, Panda S. "Fasting, circadian rhythms, and time restricted feeding in healthy lifespan." *Cell Metabolism.* 2016 Jun 14; 23(6):1048-1059.

17.

Chaix A, Zarrinpar A, Miu P, Panda S. "Time-restricted feeding is a preventative and therapeutic intervention against diverse nutritional challenges." *Cell Metabolism.*

18.
Mattson MP, et. al. "Meal frequency and timing in health and disease." *Proceedings of the National Academy of Sciences USA.* 2014 Nov 25; 111(47): 16647–16653.

19.
Horne BD, Muhlestein JB, Anderson JL. "Health effects of intermittent fasting: hormesis or harm? A systematic review." *The American Journal of Clinical Nutrition.* 2015 Aug; 102(2):464-70.

20.
Longo VD, Panda S. "Fasting, circadian rhythms, and time restricted feeding in healthy lifespan." *Cell Metabolism.* 2016 Jun 14; 23(6):1048-1059.

21.
Sun M, et. al. "Meta-analysis on shift work and risks of specific obesity types." *Obesity Reviews.* 2018 Jan;19(1):28-40.

22.
Liu W, et. al. "Sex Differences in the Association between Night Shift Work and the Risk of Cancers: A Meta-Analysis of 57 Articles." *Disease Markers.* 2018 Nov 26;2018:7925219. doi: 10.1155/2018/7925219. eCollection 2018.

23.
Books C, Coody LC, Kauffman R, Abraham S. "Night Shift Work and its Health Effects on Nurses." *Health Care Management.* 2017 Oct/Dec;36(4):347-353.

24.
"Rotating night shift work can be hazardous to your health." Elsevier. *Science Daily.* January 5, 2015. Retrieved online at: https://www.sciencedaily.com/releases/2015/01/150105081757.htm

25.
Turek FW, et. al. "Obesity and Metabolic Syndrome in Circadian Clock Mutant Mice." *Science.* 2005 May 13; 308(5724): 1043-45.

26.

Vitaterna MH, et. al. "Mutagenesis and Mapping of a Mouse Gene, Clock, Essential for Circadian Behavior." *Science.* 1994 Apr 29; 264(5159): 719-725.

27.
Panda S. "Circadian physiology of metabolism." *Science.* 2016 Nov. 25; 354(6315): 1008-1015.

28.
Van Cauter E, Polonsky KS, Scheen AJ. "Roles of circadian rhythmicity and sleep in human glucose regulation." *Endocrine Reviews.* 1997 Oct;18(5):716-38.

29.
Schibler U. "The daily rhythms of genes, cells and organs." *EMBO Reports.* 2005 Jul; 6(Suppl 1): S9–S13.

30.
Gachon F, et. al. "The mammalian circadian timing system: from gene expression to physiology." *Chromosoma.* 2004 Sep; 113(3): 103-112.

31.
Reilly T, et. al. "Diurnal variation in temperature, mental and physical performance, and tasks specifically related to football (soccer)." *Chronobiology International.* 2007;24(3):507-19.

32.
Panda S. "Circadian physiology of metabolism." *Science.* 2016 Nov. 25; 354(6315): 1008-1015.

33.
Sancar A, et. al. "Circadian clock control of the cellular response to DNA damage." *FEBS Letters.* 2010 Jun 18;584(12):2618-25.

34.
Antoch MP, Kondratov RV, Takahashi JS. "Circadian clock genes as modulators of sensitivity to genotoxic stress." *Cell Cycle.* 2005 Jul;4(7):901-7.

35.
Reinke H, Asher G. "Circadian Clock Control of Liver Metabolic Functions." *Gastroenterology.* 2016 Mar;150(3):574-80.

36.

Mauvoisin D, et. al. "Circadian clock-dependent and -independent rhythmic proteomes implement distinct diurnal functions in mouse liver." *PNAS.* 2014 Jan 7; 111(1): 167-172.

37.
Longo VD, Panda S. "Fasting, circadian rhythms, and time restricted feeding in healthy lifespan." *Cell Metabolism.* 2016 Jun 14; 23(6):1048-1059.

38.
"Genetic switch for circadian rhythms discovered." *University of California, Irvine (UCI) News.* December 12, 2007. Accessed online January 24, 2019 at: https://news.uci.edu/2007/12/12/genetic-switch-for-circadian-rhythms-discovered/

39.
Wang A, et. al. "Opposing Effects of Fasting Metabolism on Tissue Tolerance in Bacterial and Viral Inflammation." *Cell.* 2016 Sep 8;166(6):1512-1525.e12. doi: 10.1016/j.cell.2016.07.026.

40.
Patterson RE, et. al. "Intermittent Fasting and Human Metabolic Health." *Journal of the Academy of Nutrition and Dietetics.*" 2015 Aug; 115(8): 1203–1212.

41.
Lee C, et. al. "Fasting Cycles Retard Growth of Tumors and Sensitize a Range of Cancer Cell Types to Chemotherapy." *Science Translational Medicine.* 2012 Mar 7; 4(124): 124ra27.

42.
Raffaghello L, et. al. "Starvation-dependent differential stress resistance protects normal but not cancer cells against high-dose chemotherapy." *Proceedings of the National Academy of Sciences USA.* 2008 Jun 17; 105(24):8215-20.

43.
Lee C, et. al. "Reduced levels of IGF-I mediate differential protection of normal and cancer cells in response to fasting and improve chemotherapeutic index." *Cancer Research.* 2010 Feb 15; 70(4):1564-72.

44.
Safdie FM, et. al. "Fasting and cancer treatment in humans: A case series report." *Aging (Albany, NY).* 2009 Dec 31; 1(12): 988-1007.

45.

Marinac CR, et. al. "Prolonged Nightly Fasting and Breast Cancer Prognosis." *JAMA Oncology*. 2016 Aug 1; 2(8): 1049-1055.

46.
Raefsky SM, Mattson MP. "Adaptive Responses of Neuronal Mitochondria to Bioenergetic Challenges: Roles in Neuroplasticity and Disease Resistance." *Free Radical Biology & Medicine*. 2017 Jan; 102:203-216.

47.
Liu A, et. al. "Young plasma reverses age-dependent alterations in hepatic function through the restoration of autophagy." *Aging Cell*. 2018 Feb; 17(1): e12708. Published online 2017 Dec 5. doi: 10.1111/acel.12708.

48.
Madeo F, et. al. "Can autophagy promote longevity?" *Nature Cell Biology*. 2010 Sep;12(9):842-6.

49.
Markowiak P, Slizewska K. "Effects of Probiotics, Prebiotics, and Synbiotics on Human Health." *Nutrients*. 2017 Sep; 9(9): 1021. Published online 2017 Sep 15. doi: 10.3390/nu9091021

50.
Umbrello G, Esposito S. "Microbiota and neurologic diseases: potential effects of probiotics." *Journal of Translational Medicine*. 2016; 14: 298. Published online 2016 Oct 19. doi: 10.1186/s12967-016-1058-7

51.
Catterson JH, et. al. "Short-Term, Intermittent Fasting Induces Long-Lasting Gut Health and TOR-Independent Lifespan Extension." *Current Biology*. 2018 Jun 4; 28(11): 1714–1724.e4.

52.
Shin SC, et. al. "Drosophila microbiome modulates host developmental and metabolic homeostasis via insulin signaling." *Science*. 2011 Nov 4;334(6056):670-4.

53.
As observed repeatedly in the author's practice and similar clinics.

54.
Longo VD, Panda S. "Fasting, circadian rhythms, and time restricted feeding in healthy lifespan." *Cell Metabolism*. 2016 Jun 14; 23(6):1048-1059.

55.
Wang HB, et. al. "Time-Restricted Feeding Improves Circadian Dysfunction as well as Motor Symptoms in the Q175 Mouse Model of Huntington's Disease." *eNeuro.* 2018 Jan-Feb; 5(1): ENEURO.0431-17.2017.

56.
Tuso PJ. "Nutritional Update for Physicians: Plant-Based Diets." *The Permanente Journal.* 2013 Spring; 17(2): 61-66.
57.
Kahleova H, et. al. "Eating two larger meals a day (breakfast and lunch) is more effective than six smaller meals in a reduced-energy regimen for patients with type 2 diabetes: a randomised crossover study." *Diabetologia.* 2014 Aug;57(8):1552-60.

Chapter 6

1.
Rose C, et. al. "Whole-body Cryotherapy as a Recovery Technique after Exercise: A Review of the Literature." *International Journal of Sports Medicine.* 2017 Dec;38(14):1049-1060.

2 – 3.
Ibid.

4.
Lateef F. "Post exercise ice water immersion: Is it a form of active recovery?" *Journal of Emergencies, Trauma, and Shock.* 2010 Jul-Sep; 3(3): 302. PMCID: PMC2938508. doi: 10.4103/0974-2700.66570.

5.
Shephard RJ. "Fat metabolism, exercise, and the cold." *Canadian Journal of Sport Sciences.* 1992 Jun;17(2):83-90.

6.
Castellani JW, Young AJ. "Human physiological responses to cold exposure: Acute responses and acclimatization to prolonged exposure." *Autonomic Neuroscience.* 2016 Apr;196:63-74.

7.
Carney S. *What Doesn't Kill Us.* Emmaus, PA: Rodale Books. 2017.

8.

McMillian AC, White MD. "Induction of thermogenesis in brown and beige adipose tissues: molecular markers, mild cold exposure and novel therapies." *Current Opinion in Endocrinology, Diabetes, and Obesity.* 2015 Oct;22(5):347-52.

9.
Hanssen MJ, et. al. "Short-term Cold Acclimation Recruits Brown Adipose Tissue in Obese Humans." *Diabetes.* May;65(5):1179-89.

10.
Mooventhan A, Nivethitha L. "Scientific Evidence-Based Effects of Hydrotherapy on Various Systems of the Body." *North American Journal of Medical Sciences.* 2014 May; 6(5): 199–209.

11.
Smith RL, et. al. "Metabolic Flexibility as an Adaptation to Energy Resources and Requirements in Health and Disease." *Endocrine Reviews.* 2018 Aug; 39(4): 489–517.

12.
Shevchuck NA. "Possible use of repeated cold stress for reducing fatigue in chronic fatigue syndrome: A hypothesis." *Behavioral and Brain Functions.* 2007; 3: 55. Published online 2007 Oct 24. doi: 10.1186/1744-9081-3-55.

13.
Leak RK, et. al. "Enhancing and Extending Biological Performance and Resilience." *Dose Response.* 2018 Jul-Sep; 16(3): 1559325818784501. Published online 2018 Aug 15. doi: 10.1177/1559325818784501.

14.
Hof I. *The Wim Hof Method Explained.* White paper distributed by Innerfire. Last updated January 2016.

15.
Kox M, et. al. "The influence of concentration/meditation on autonomic nervous system activity and the innate immune response: A case study." *Psychosomatic Medicine.* 2012 Jun;74(5):489-94.

16 – 17.
Ibid.

18.

Hof I. *The Wim Hof Method Explained.* White paper distributed by Innerfire. Last updated January 2016.

19.
Kox M, et. al. “Voluntary activation of the sympathetic nervous system and attenuation of the innate immune response in humans.” *Proceedings of the National Academy of Sciences USA*. 2014;111(20):7379-84.

20.
Comparative Table based on information found in:
Hof I. *The Wim Hof Method Explained.* White paper distributed by Innerfire. Last updated January 2016.

21.
Kox M, et. al. “The influence of concentration/meditation on autonomic nervous system activity and the innate immune response: A case study.” *Psychosomatic Medicine.* 2012 Jun;74(5):489-94.

22.
Kox M, et. al. “Voluntary activation of the sympathetic nervous system and attenuation of the innate immune response in humans.” *Proceedings of the National Academy of Sciences USA*. 2014;111(20):7379-84.

23.
Ibid.

24.
Sidossis L, Kajimura S. “Brown and beige fat in humans: thermogenic adipocytes that control energy and glucose homeostasis.” *Journal of Clinical Investigation.* 2015 Feb 2; 125(2): 478–486.

25.
Van Marken Lichtenbelt WD, et. al. “Cold-activated brown adipose tissue in healthy men.” *New England Journal of Medicine.* 2009 Apr 9;360(15):1500-8.

26.
Lee P, Swarbrick MM, Zhao JT, Ho KK. “Inducible brown adipogenesis of supraclavicular fat in adult humans.” *Endocrinology.* 2011 Oct;152(10):3597-602.

27.
Marken Lichtenbelt van, W. D., & Schrauwen. (2011). “Implications of nonshivering thermogenesis for energy balance regulation in humans.” *American*

Journal of Physiology, Regulatory, Integrative and Comparative Physiology. 2011 Aug; 301(2): R285-96.

28.
Šrámek P, et. al. "Human physiological responses to immersion into water of different temperatures." *European Journal of Applied Physiology.* 2000 Mar;81(5):436-42.

29.
Steffen PR, et. al. "The Impact of Resonance Frequency Breathing on Measures of Heart Rate Variability, Blood Pressure, and Mood." *Frontiers in Public Health.* 2017; 5: 222. Published online 2017 Aug 25. doi: 10.3389/fpubh.2017.00222

30.
Shaffer F, McCraty R, Zerr CL. "A healthy heart is not a metronome: an integrative review of the heart's anatomy and heart rate variability." *Frontiers in Psychology.* 2014 Sep 30;5:1040.

31.
Pomatto LCD, Davies KJA. "The role of declining adaptive homeostasis in ageing." *The Journal of Physiology.* 2017 Dec 15; 595(24): 7275–7309.

32.
Ibid.

33.
Zou L, et. al. "Effects of Mind–Body Exercises (Tai Chi/Yoga) on Heart Rate Variability Parameters and Perceived Stress: A Systematic Review with Meta-Analysis of Randomized Controlled Trials." *Journal of Clinical Medicine.* 2018 Nov; 7(11): 404.

34.
Lutfi MF. "Autonomic modulations in patients with bronchial asthma based on short-term heart rate variability." *Lung India.* 2012 Jul-Sep; 29(3): 254–258.

35.
Goldstein RD, et. al. "Sudden Unexpected Death in Fetal Life Through Early Childhood." *Pediatrics.* 2016 Jun; 137(6): e20154661. doi: 10.1542/peds.2015-4661.

36.

Gevirtz R. "The Promise of Heart Rate Variability Biofeedback: Evidence-Based Applications." *Biofeedback.* 2013 Sept. 41(3):110-120.

37.
Criswell SR. "Cognitive Behavioral Therapy with Heart Rate Variability Biofeedback for Adults with Persistent Noncombat-Related Posttraumatic Stress Disorder." *The Permanente Journal.* 2018;22. pii: 17-207. doi: 10.7812/TPP/17-207.

38.
Thayer JF, et. al. "Heart rate variability, prefrontal neural function, and cognitive performance: the neurovisceral integration perspective on self-regulation, adaptation, and health." *Annals of Behavioral Medicine.* 2009 Apr;37(2):141-53.

39.
McCraty R. "Psychophysiological Coherence: A Proposed Link Among Appreciation, Cognitive Performance, and Health." *Proceedings of the American Psychological Association 109th Annual Convention, Symposium on Gratitude and Positive Emotionality as Links Between Social and Clinical Science*, San Francisco, CA, Aug. 2001. Retrieved January 28, 2019 at: https://www.heartmath.org/.

40.
McCraty R. "The Science of Heart Math." Video and overview of HeartMath science. Accessed February 11, 2019 at https://www.heartmath.com/science/?_ga=2.97602591.1021265871.1549543207-1147853743.1549543207.

41.
Tsulji H, et. al. "Reduced heart rate variability and mortality risk in an elderly cohort: The Framingham Heart Study." *Circulation.* 1994 Aug;90(2):878-83.

42.
Carnevali L, et. al. "Autonomic and Brain Morphological Predictors of Stress Resilience." *Frontiers in Neuroscience.* 2018; 12: 228. Published online 2018 Apr 6. doi: 10.3389/fnins.2018.00228

43.
Chamary JV. "The Ice Bucket Challenge Can Kill, Here's Why You're Doing it Wrong." *Forbes.* 2014 Aug 25. Retrieved January 28, 2019 at https://www.forbes.com/sites/jvchamary/2014/08/25/ice-bucket-challenge/#2d51335b32d5.

44.

Tipton M, Golden F. *Essentials of Sea Survival.* Champaign, IL; USA: Human Kinetics. 2002.

45.
Ibid.

46.
Shattock MJ, Tipton MJ. "'Autonomic Conflict': a different way to die during cold water immersion?" *The Journal of Physiology.* 2012 Jul 15;590(14):3219-30.

47.
Tipton M, Golden F. *Essentials of Sea Survival.* Champaign, IL; USA: Human Kinetics. 2002.

48.
Castellani JW, Young AJ. "Human physiological responses to cold exposure: Acute responses and acclimatization to prolonged exposure." *Autonomic Neuroscience.* 2016 Apr;196:63-74.

Chapter 7

1.
Pomatto LCD, Davies KJA. "The role of declining adaptive homeostasis in ageing." *Journal of Physiology.* 2017 Dec 15;595(24):7275-7309.

2.
Booth FW, Roberts CK, Laye MJ. "Lack of exercise is a major cause of chronic diseases." *Comprehensive Physiology.* 2012 Apr; 2(2):1143-1211.

3.
Wang A, et. al. "Opposing Effects of Fasting Metabolism on Tissue Tolerance in Bacterial and Viral Inflammation." *Cell.* 2016 Sep 8;166(6):1512-1525.e12. doi: 10.1016/j.cell.2016.07.026.

4.
Howden EJ, et. al. "Reversing the Cardiac Effects of Sedentary Aging in Middle Age-A Randomized Controlled Trial: Implications For Heart Failure Prevention." *Circulation.* 2018 Apr 10;137(15):1549-1560.

5.

Pomatto LCD, Davies KJA. “The role of declining adaptive homeostasis in ageing.” *Journal of Physiology*. 2017 Dec 15;595(24):7275-7309.

6.
Shallenberger F. “Prolozone: Regenerating Joints and Eliminating Pain.” *Journal of Prolotherapy*. 2011;3(2):630-638.

7.
Rich PR. “The molecular machinery of Keilin’s respiratory chain.” *Biochemical Society Transactions*. 2003 Dec: 31(Pt 6): 1095–1105.

8.
Neubauer R, Walker M. *Hyperbaric Oxygen Therapy: Using HBOT to increase circulation, repair damaged tissue, fight infection, save limbs, and relieve pain.* Garden City Park, New York: Avery Publishing Group, Inc.; 2001.

9.
Shallenberger F. “Prolozone: Regenerating Joints and Eliminating Pain.” *Journal of Prolotherapy*. 2011;3(2):630-638.

10.
Di Somma C, et. al. “Somatopause: state of the art.” *Minerva Endocrinologica*. 2011 Sep;36(3):243-55.

11.
Ambrose KR, Golightly YM. “Physical exercise as non-pharmacological treatment of chronic pain: Why and when.” *Best Practice & Research: Clinical Rheumatology*. 2015 Feb;29(1):120-30.

12.
Chow J, et. al. “Mitochondrial disease and endocrine dysfunction.” *Nature Reviews: Endocrinology*. 2017 Feb;13(2):92-104.

13.
Muscogiuri G, et. al. “Obesogenic endocrine disruptors and obesity: myths and truths.” *Archives of Toxicology*. 2017 Nov;91(11):3469-3475.

14.
Hill AJ. “The Psychology of Food Craving.” *The Proceedings of the Nutrition Society*. 2007 May;66(2):277-85.

15.

Longo VD, Panda S. "Fasting, circadian rhythms, and time restricted feeding in healthy lifespan." *Cell Metabolism.* 2016 Jun 14; 23(6):1048-1059.

16.
Booth FW, Roberts CK, Laye MJ. "Lack of exercise is a major cause of chronic diseases." *Comprehensive Physiology.* 2012 Apr; 2(2):1143-1211.

17.
Wideman L, et. al. "Growth hormone release during acute and chronic aerobic and resistance exercise: recent findings." *Sports Medicine (Auckland, NZ).* 2002;32(15):987-1004.

18.
Van Marken Lichtenbelt WD, et. al. "Cold-activated brown adipose tissue in healthy men." *New England Journal of Medicine.* 2009 Apr 9;360(15):1500-8.

19.
Stadje R, et. al. "The differential diagnosis of tiredness: a systematic review." *BMC Family Practice.* 2016 Oct 20;17(1):147.

20.
Shallenberger F. *Bursting with Energy: The Breakthrough Method to Renew Youthful Energy and Restore Health.* Laguna Beach, California: Basic Health Publications, Inc.; 2007.

21.
McCabe E. *Flood Your Body with Oxygen.* Miami Shores, Florida: Energy Publications; 2003.

22.
Shallenberger F. *Principles and Applications of Ozone Therapy: A practical guideline for physicians.* 1st edition. Carson City, Nevada: Author; 2011.

23.
Douglas WC. *Into the Light: The exciting story of the life-saving breakthrough therapy of the age.* Muskogee, Oklahoma: Artisan Publishers. 2003.

24.
Harch PG, McCullough V. *The Oxygen Revolution: Hyperbaric Oxygen Therapy.* Hobart, New York: Hatherleigh Press (Penguin, Random House); 2010.

25.
Peskin B. *The Hidden Story of Cancer.* Houston, Texas: Pinnacle Press; 2011.

26.
Winters N, Kelley JH. *The Metabolic Approach to Cancer: Integrating Deep Nutrition, the Ketogenic Diet, and Nontoxic Bio-Individualized Therapies.* White River Junction, Vermont; Chelsea Green; May 2017.

27.
Ibid.

28.
Zhou X, et. al. "Heart rate variability in the prediction of survival in patients with cancer: A systematic review and meta-analysis." *Journal of Psychosomatic Research.* 2016 Oct;89:20-5.

29.
Hojman P. "Exercise protects from cancer through regulation of immune function and inflammation." *Biochemical Society Transactions.* 2017 Aug 15;45(4):905-11.

30.
Adlan AM, et. al. "Cardiovascular autonomic regulation, inflammation and pain in rheumatoid arthritis." *Autonomic Neuroscience: Basic & Clinical.* 2017 Dec;208:137-145.

31.
Nimmo MA. "The effect of physical activity on mediators of inflammation." *Diabetes, Obesity & Metabolism.* 2013 Sep;15 Suppl 3:51-60.

32.
Strobel ES, et. al. "Tissue oxygen measurement and 31P magnetic resonance spectroscopy in patients with muscle tension and fibromyalgia." *Rheumatology International.* 1997;16(5):175-80.

33.
Shallenberger F. "Prolozone: Regenerating Joints and Eliminating Pain." *Journal of Prolotherapy.* 2011;3(2):630-638.

34.
Schwartz A. *Combined therapy of concentrated growth factors, CD34 cells, and ozone.* Ozone Training Course. Fiorella Clinic. Madrid, Spain; Mar 2018.

35.
Demling RH. "Nutrition, Anabolism, and the Wound Healing Process: An Overview." *ePlasty*. 2009; 9:e9. PMCID: PMC2642618. Published online 2009 Feb 3.

36.
MacGregor EA. "Migraine, menopause and hormone replacement therapy." *Post Reproductive Health*. 2018 Mar;24(1):11-18.

37.
Huhtaniemi IT. "Andropause: lessons from the European Male Ageing Study." *Annales d'Endocrinologie (Paris)*. 2014 May;75(2):128-31.
38.
Wright JV, Lenard L. *Stay Young & Sexy with Bio-Identical Hormone Replacement: The Science Explained*. Petaluma, California: Smart Publications; 2010.

39.
Shallenberger F. *Principles and Applications of Ozone Therapy: A practical guideline for physicians*. 1st edition. Carson City, Nevada: Author; 2011.

40.
Rogers SA. *Detoxify or Die*. Solvay, New York: Prestige Publishing; 2002.

41.
"Benefits of Exercise." MedlinePlus Monograph. U.S. National Library of Medicine, NIH. Last updated 2017 Aug 30. Accessed December 26, 2018 at: https://medlineplus.gov/benefitsofexercise.html

42.
Mira JC, et. al. "Sepsis Pathophysiology, Chronic Critical Illness, and Persistent Inflammation-Immunosuppression and Catabolism Syndrome." *Critical Care Medicine*. 2017 Feb;45(2):253-262.

43.
Klein DW, Lansing M, Harley J. *Microbiology (6th ed.)* New York: McGraw-Hill, 2006.

44.
Brom B. "Integrative medicine and leaky gut syndrome." *South African Family Practice*. 2010;52:314–316.

45.

Rehman K, et. al. "Prevalence of exposure of heavy metals and their impact on health consequences." *Journal of Cellular Biochemistry.* 2018 Jan;119(1):157-184.

46.
Shallenberger F. *Principles and Applications of Ozone Therapy: A practical guideline for physicians.* 1st edition. Carson City, Nevada: Author; 2011.

47.
"Infections in People with Cancer." Monograph collection at American Cancer Society website. Accessed online February 14, 2019 at: https://www.cancer.org/treatment/treatments-and-side-effects/physical-side-effects/infections/infections-in-people-with-cancer.html

48.
Rolston KVI. "Infections in Cancer Patients with Solid Tumors: A Review." *Infectious Diseases and Therapy.* 2017 Mar; 6(1): 69–83.

49.
Winters N, Kelley JH. *The Metabolic Approach to Cancer: Integrating Deep Nutrition, the Ketogenic Diet, and Nontoxic Bio-Individualized Therapies.* White River Junction, Vermont; Chelsea Green; May 2017.

50.
Shallenberger F. "Prolozone: Regenerating Joints and Eliminating Pain." *Journal of Prolotherapy.* 2011;3(2):630-638.

51.
Jeon HS, et. al. "Effects of pulsed electromagnetic field therapy on delayed-onset muscle soreness in biceps brachii." *Physical Therapy in Sport.* 2015 Feb;16(1):34-9.

52.
Yin Y, et. al. "The Effects of Pulsed Electromagnetic Field on the Proliferation and Osteogenic Differentiation of Human Adipose-Derived Stem Cells." *Medical Science Monitor.* 2018 May 18;24:3274-3282.

53.
Crinnion WJ "Sauna as a valuable clinical tool for cardiovascular, autoimmune, toxicant-induced and other chronic health problems." *Alternative Medicine Review.* 2011 Sep;16(3):215-25.

54.
Shallenberger F. *Principles and Applications of Ozone Therapy: A practical guideline for physicians.* 1st edition. Carson City, Nevada: Author; 2011.

55.
Bocci V, et. al. "Studies on the biological effects of ozone: 6. Production of transforming growth factor 1 by human blood after ozone treatment." *Journal of Biological Regulators and Homeostatic Agents.* 1994 Oct-Dec;8(4):108-12.

56.
Campbell P. *Ready, Set, Go! Synergy Fitness.* 2nd edition. Nashville, Tennessee: Pristine Publishers Inc.; 2002.

57.
McCabe E. *Flood Your Body with Oxygen.* Miami Shores, Florida: Energy Publications; 2003.

Made in the USA
Columbia, SC
13 May 2020

95875616R00195